# The Incredible Scream Machine

# The Incredible Scream Machine

## A History of the Roller Coaster

**Robert Cartmell**

Amusement Park Books, Inc.
Fairview Park, Ohio 44126
Bowling Green State University Popular Press
Bowling Green, Ohio 43403

All illustrations, unless otherwise credited, are from the Robert Cartmell Collection

(Front endpaper) Switchback Railway, Euclid Beach Park, Cleveland, Oh.
        Courtesy Amusement Park Books Inc.

(Back endpaper) *American Eagle*, Six Flags Great America, Gurnee, Ill.
        Courtesy Six Flags Great America

Copyright © 1987 by Amusement Park Books, Inc. and the Bowling Green
State University Popular Press

791.06

Library of Congress Catalogue Card No.: 87-70175

ISBN:  0-87972-341-6  Clothbound
       0-87972-342-1  Paperback

# DEDICATION

*The Incredible Scream Machine* is gratefully
dedicated to John Allen;
and with love to Ann, Lisa, and Bram.

# Contents

# Preface and Acknowledgements

It seems impossible. This is the first book on the history of roller coasters. Impossible! How can something that immense be ignored over so many years? How can the epitome of thrills, the ultimate terror ride, not be seen? Roller coasters are a part of us, after all. They're everywhere and not just at amusement parks. The term roller coaster contributes an important color to our vocabulary and has come to describe everything that vaguely has an up and down or violent motion:

**"Rock 'N' Roller Coaster.** The Music Biz on a Joyride." Headlines of the *Village Voice,* February 7, 1984.

**"The White House Roller Coaster."** ". . . The trick for getting to be president is to have the election the day you're at the top of the roller coaster." Andy Rooney, April 20, 1984, as carried in the *Knickerbocker News* and all other newspapers running Andy Rooney's column.

**"Fortunes Ride Coleco Roller Coaster."** Page 1 headlines of the March 30, 1984, *Knickerbocker News* (describing company layoffs).

**"Hurtling Ride on Film's Emotional Roller Coaster is a Downer."** Page A18 headline movie review of *Indiana Jones and The Temple of Doom* by Haynes Johnson in *The Washington Post,* June 17, 1984.

**"Addicts Ride Emotional Roller Coaster."** Page 1 headlines of the February 29, 1984, *Los Angeles Times* (describing cocaine addiction).

". . . There was a roller-coaster character to Dallas Opera's 1983 season." *Opera News.* March 3, 1984. Volume 48, No. 12. Page 42, paragraph 4 (a publications of Metropolitan Guild, Inc.).

They are seen in countless movies (fig. Pref.:1) from *Beast from 20,000 Fathoms* to the full-length motion picture, *Rollercoaster.* They're part of television shows from *Alfred Hitchcock Presents* and *The Partridge Family* to *The Twilight Zone;* and in countless ads including the classic of running a coaster train through a mound of shaving cream.

They're part of many songs and are a natural to describe the ups-and-downs of love—or life itself:

> I recall when I was young
> My poppa said, "Don't cry

> Life is full of ups and downs, like a roller
>   coaster ride
> There'll be times you'll get so scared
>   rollin' down those hills
> That you'll hold on tight with all your
>   might
> 'Cause you won't know what you feel"
> You go up, down, all around on a cycle
>   that's never ending
> You got this train when you were born
>   and the wheels just keep on spinning.
>
> Like a roller coaster
>   it keeps going faster, time going past
>   you
> Thrills coming at you
> Hey, hey, up down, all around like a
>   roller coaster....[1]
>
>> *Roller Coaster* by Mark James
>> (as recorded by Blood, Sweat,
>> & Tears).

A complete study would be required to list its many appearances in art. An example could be seen in October, 1979, at the O.K. Harris Gallery, New York City, when a roller coaster appeared as part of a completely *ceramic* amusement park over 12 feet long (fig. Pref.:2).

Even Albert Einstein used the roller coaster to demonstrate "energy conversions in a mechanical system" in his book, *Evolution of Physics.*[2]

They're everywhere you look—immense, colossal, thrilling—*but not seen.* The roller coaster is the supreme "neglected giant." It's almost as if the ride disappears from the mind outside of an amusement park, dazzling but invisible.

It might seem farfetched but the roller coaster could be compared to the idea of gravity during pre-Newton days. "Of course an apple falls down. What else could it do?" This cosmographical force, gravity, was not seen until it was pinpointed and measured. Similarly, the roller coaster as architecture, or as any form, has not been seen until recent years.

Now, finally, the ride is being pinpointed and measured and treated as the magnificent creation it really is. They are now seen as aesthetic objects.[3] Original roller coaster drawings, plans, and blueprints have become collector's items, often desperately pursued. Anything relating to the ride demands competitive and sharply rising prices.

(Pref: 1). The roller coaster in movies. *Oh What a Lovely War*. 1969. Courtesy Paramount Pictures.

(Pref: 2). A ceramic amusement park with roller coaster was the showpiece of Artist Raymon Elozua's exhibition at the OK Harris Gallery, New York, N.Y. 42″H x 50″W x 98″L, 1982. Courtesy OK Harris Gallery.

What brought about this respectability? In a small way, earlier books on carousels, such as Frederick Fried's *A Pictorial History of the Carousel,* and the formation of a carousel club in 1973 helped.[4] The aesthetic qualities of the carousel were deservedly noted, and it wasn't long before some started looking at other amusement park rides. The stamp of approval on roller coasters by the Smithsonian Institution and *The New York Times* (see Chapter XIII) helped immensely. But recognition through articles, letters, and word-of-mouth in the 1970's, that thousands of other diehard roller coaster buffs existed over the world, seemed to remove blinders from many eyes and is probably the main reason roller coasters are "seen" today.

Before this approval, plans, records, files — anything pertaining to roller coasters—were routinely destroyed or treated, at best, as peripheral. All the invaluable Traver Company files were destroyed c.1972. Philadelphia Toboggan and National Amusement Device junked many of their files. Worse yet, entire companies have been bulldozed under.

With this in mind, the prospect of writing a book on roller coasters seemed a bleak project in 1974, and it has taken nearly eleven years to put this volume together. Fortunately, there were many farsighted people (See "Acknowledgements") that helped make its completion possible. They carefully stored valuable photos, files, and artifacts and were generous enough to share them with me.

Three other avenues made *The Incredible Scream Machine* possible:

(1) *Interviews with designers.* John Allen of the Philadelphia Toboggan Company told me in 1973, "Interview the designers while they're still around. They won't be around much longer."[5] He was indeed prophetic. With the exception of Bill Cobb and Andrew Vettel, all of the designers interviewed in this book are gone, including John Allen. Their voices, fortunately, live for us on tape.

(2) *Postcards.* In too many cases all records and photographs of certain rides have disappeared without a trace except for *postcards.* Picture postcard collectors have rescued many categories of American life from oblivion, but none more important than their preservation and cataloguing of scenes at amusement parks. These cheap, often poorly reproduced illustrations are, in many cases, the only picture we have of certain coasters. But it's not just the front of the card that's important. The reverse, with its comments on the roller coaster, is often as valuable. Agatha Wales's famous comment, "...it was something dreadful. I never was so frightened in my life and if the dear Lord will forgive me this time, I will never do so again.," is from a 1914 postcard (fig. Pref.:6) depicting the Scenic Railway in Venice, California.

(Pref: 3). This coaster model was built by Roger D. Francis as part of occupational therapy in a state institution. He tired of basket weaving and turned instead to roller coasters and created this model entirely from imagination. Built of over 400 yards of hand-cut and glued balsa wood, the rail supports are cardboard with tracks of leather lacing. 14"H x 21"W x 78"L, 1974. Photograph by Robert H. Peters.

(3) *Patents*. To the coaster buff, the Patent Office in Washington, D.C., is a treasure-trove comparable to the Library of Alexandria. Patent records beautifully show the thinking and ideas of many designers, some completely forgotten. Often these records reveal the home town and working quarters of inventors. They also—fairly or not—establish "firsts" (first chain-lift, first lap-bar, etc.) and establish the credentials of authentic contributors to amusement parks.

The establishment of the roller coaster club, ACE, (see Chapter XIV) and its membership, has also helped immensely in recording the history of roller coasters. The magazine *Roller Coaster!* (previously titled *Coaster World*), is already a superb depository of coaster lore. Its members have classified coasters, recorded dates, and have revealed many unknown rides and designers.

Tenacity and good luck have also contributed to the completion of this book. Yet, with all these sources in mind, things are bound to run amuck. Dates, written or by word of mouth, are often contradictory, and many remembrances inaccurate. Amusement parks are notorious for exaggerations with claims of their coasters traveling 150 miles per hour, rides lasting 15 minutes, and always the persistent hoax of their ride being the highest in the world. Measurements, too, often are suspect: Was the highest hill measured from ground to track-tops or to the flag-pole or gazebo decorating the summit? I have tried to use double and triple references, including blueprints and patents, to verify such measurements and to confirm names and dates; yet there are bound to be frustrating errors.

It is naturally impossible to list every roller coaster, but it is hoped the important rides have all been mentioned. Many borderline coasters have been intentionally omitted such as dark rides, carnival portables, and Flumes.

One of my chief concerns is to recognize the pioneer inventors. They have given us so much magic through this wondrous—or devilish—machine. If these designers were not recognized during their lifetimes perhaps this book, belatedly, will at least help memorialize their names. They'll never be household words, but to all coaster buffs their names remain glorious.

My special debt of gratitude to John Allen whose time and great patience pointed me in the right directions; to Fred and Mary Fried for not only opening

their Archives but for their hospitality and friendship as well; to Ed Cowley for his constant encouragement and humor over many years. And to those people who gave most generously of their time and expertise: Charlie Jacques and his *Amusement Park Journal;* Jim Payer; American Coaster Enthusiasts, in particular B. Derek Shaw, Joe Heflin, Renee O'Connell (for finding the first roller coaster patent), Liucija and Allen Ambrosini, and Richard Munch; the International Association of Amusement Parks and Attractions, in particular Robert Blundred, Robert Ott, and Carl and Ann Hughes and their wonderful staff at Kennywood including Andy Vettel; Fred Pierce, Jr.; Barbara Charles; Russell Nye; International Amusement Devices; John Still of the New York State Museum; June Schetterer; William Cobb; and Park Ranger Ric Choley and his jeep for personally driving me over the layout of the *Mauch Chunk Switchback*.

Grateful acknowledgements are due Carol Lyons for her patient help with research; the skilled professional staff at Bowling Green State University and Amusement Park Books, Inc., particularly Lee Bush and Richard Hershey and their encouragement; and to Ann, Lisa, and Bram for their contributions of love, wit, and good spirit that enabled me to carry the work to completion.

Altamont, New York

## Timetable

Important Dates in the History of Roller Coasters

| | |
|---|---|
| 15th and 16th Centuries | First known constructed gravity rides for the public, Russian Mountains (later Flying Turns) built in St. Petersburg and surrounding areas. |
| Middle 18th Century | The first wheeled coaster, built for Russian royalty, St. Petersburg. |
| 1792 | Beginning of the Mauch Chunk railway, Mauch Chunk, Pa. |
| 1804 | Russian Mountains built in Ternes quarter of Paris. |
| 1817 | *Belleville Mountains*, France. The first roller coaster with cars locked to the tracks. |
| 1817 | *Aerial Walk*, Paris. The first racing coaster. |
| 1826 | M. Lebonjer installs first mechanical system (cables) to hoist cars up first hill. |
| 1827 | The Mauch Chunk railroad uses gravity to transport coal. |
| 1845 | Completion of the lifts and track system of the now *Mauch Chunk Switchback*. |

| | |
|---|---|
| 1846 | First Centrifugal Railway (Loop-the-Loop) opens at Frascati Gardens, Paris. |
| 1848 | Birth of La Marcus Adna Thompson. |
| 1867 | Opening of Charles T. Harvey's *West Side and Yonker's Railway,* New York City. |
| 1872 | First U.S. roller coaster patent is granted J.G. Taylor. |
| | Birth of John Miller. |
| 1873 | *Mauch Chunk Switchback* becomes exclusively a passenger pleasure ride. |
| 1884 | La Marcus Thompson builds first known roller coaster in the U.S. at Coney Island, Brooklyn, N.Y. |
| | Charles Alcoke ties track ends together to form continuous circle coaster. |
| 1885 | Philip Hinckle faces seats forward and uses a mechanical hoist for coaster cars. |
| 1886 | Opening of Coney Island, Cincinnati, Ohio. |
| 1887 | Opening of *Sliding Hill and Toboggan* in Haverhill, Massachusetts. |
| c.1891 | John Miller becomes La Marcus Thompson's chief engineer. |
| 1893 | Opening of the World's Columbian Exposition in Chicago. Opening of the *Snow and Ice Railway* and *Ferris Wheel.* |
| 1895 | Captain Paul Boyton opens Sea Lion Park and *Flip-Flap Coaster.* |
| | Opening of Euclid Beach, Cleveland, Ohio. |
| 1897 | George Tilyou opens Steeplechase Park at Coney Island, Brooklyn, N.Y. |
| 1901 | Opening of the *Loop-the-Loop* at Coney Island, Brooklyn, N.Y. |
| 1903 | Luna Park opens at Coney Island, Brooklyn, N.Y. |
| | The Wright Brother's first flight. |
| 1904 | Opening of Riverview Park, Chicago, Ill. |
| | Opening of the Philadelphia Toboggan Company, Germantown, Pa. |
| 1905 | Opening of Ingersoll's Luna Park, his first, in Pittsburgh, Pa. |
| 1907 | Opening of the first modern high-speed roller coaster, *Drop-the-Dip,* Coney Island, Brooklyn, N.Y. |
| | Birth of John Allen. |
| 1913 | Opening of Palisades Park, Fort Lee, N.J. |
| 1915 | Opening of Fred Pearce's *Trip-Thru-the-Clouds,* Riverview Park, Detroit, Mich. |
| 1919 | Death of La Marcus Thompson. |
| | Harry Traver opens the Traver Engineering Company in Beaver Falls, Pa. |
| 1924 | Opening of the Church/Traver *Bobs,* Riverview Park, Chicago, Ill. |
| c.1925 | Opening of the Dayton Fun House and Riding Device Manufacturing Company (later National Amusement Device Company), Dayton, Ohio. |
| | Anton Schwartzkopf opens factory in Munsterhausen, Germany. |
| 1927 | Opening of the *Cyclone,* Coney Island, Brooklyn, N.Y. |
| | Harry Traver's *Cyclones* are built at Crystal Beach, Canada, Palisades Park, Fort Lee, N.J., and as *Lightning,* at Revere Beach, Boston, Mass. |
| 1928 | Frederick Church's *Aero-Coaster* opens in Rye Beach, N.Y. |
| 1929 | Opening of Bartlett/Miller *Flying Turns* in Dayton, Ohio. |
| 1930 | Church/Traver *Cyclone Racer* opens in Long Beach, Calif. |
| 1938 | The last car runs on the *Mauch Chunk Switchback.* |
| 1941 | Death of John Miller. |
| 1946 | Opening of Arrow Development Company, Mountain View, Calif. |
| | Crystal Beach *Cyclone* destroyed. |
| 1952 | Opening of movie *Cinerama.* |
| 1955 | Opening of Disneyland, Anaheim, Calif. |
| 1957 | Destruction of the *Aero-Coaster,* Rye Beach, N.Y. |
| 1964 | *Mr. Twister* roller coaster opens at Elitch Gardens, Denver, Colo. Remodelled in 1965. |
| 1967 | Riverview Park, Chicago, is closed. |
| | Formation of Intamin Ag., Zurich, Switzerland. |
| 1968 | Destruction of *Cyclone Racer,* Long Beach, Calif. |
| | Andy Vettel designs *Thunderbolt* by remodelling existing *Pippin* coaster at Kennywood Park, Pittsburgh, Pa. |
| 1969 | Euclid Beach, Cleveland, Ohio, is closed. |
| 1970 | Coney Island, Cincinnati, Ohio, is closed. |
| 1972 | Opening of John Allen's *Racer,* at Kings Island, Cincinnati, Ohio, and the beginning of the Coaster Boom. |
| | Palisades Park, Fort Lee, N.J. is closed. |
| 1974 | Article "Quest for the Ultimate Roller Coaster" published in the Sunday, June 9, *N.Y. Times.* |
| 1975 | Opening of *Space Mountain,* Walt Disney World, near Orlando, Fla. |
| 1976 | Opening of *Texas Cyclone,* Astroworld, Houston, Texas. |
| 1978 | Formation of club, American Coaster Enthusiasts at Busch Gardens, Williamsburg, Va. |
| 1979 | Opening of *The Beast,* Kings Island, Cincinnati, Ohio. |
| | Death of John Allen. |
| 1983 | Opening of the *Riverside Cyclone* Riverside Park, Agawam, Mass. |

*(Pre: 5). A belt buckle designed to commemorate the opoening of the* American Eagle *roller coaster. Marriot's Great America, Gurnee, Illinois, 1981..*

(Pref: 4). A roller coaster towel by artist Loriot. From the Oktoberfest, Munich, Germany.

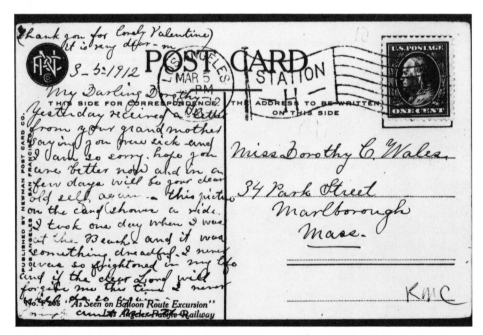

(Pref: 6). The original and often-quoted March 5, 1912 postcard from Agatha Wales.

# Introduction

In 1984 America celebrated the 100th anniversary of the first successful roller coaster device – La Marcus A. Thompson's switchback railway – erected at Coney Island. Although a century has gone by, the literature of the amusement park and its history is still in its infancy.

Today, however there is a rapidly-moving trend toward the recognition of the achievements of our native pioneer inventors, designers and builders of all amusement devices, especially of the roller coaster and the carousel.

We are just beginning to discover those pioneers who have contributed to their creation, and those artisans whose embellishments are now receiving recognition. This awareness has also resulted in the formation of organizations with the goal of enlightening the public to the need for preserving our rapidly vanishing heritage. Their publications are beginning to attract the notice of the more influential media. The publication of a major scholarly work accelerates this process and is to be heralded for filling the void.

To this date no important survey study of the history of the roller coaster has appeared. That archival material was available was well known. However, scholarly attention to the subject has now been given. Robert Cartmell's *The Incredible Scream Machine* dissects the complete subject, examining every phase from the use of the roller coaster by Albert Einstein to demonstrate his theory of physics, to John Allen's use of psychology in designing one.

Robert Cartmell is Assistant Professor in drawing and printmaking at the State University of New York at Albany. For America's Bicentennial in 1976 he initiated and organized an exhibit of the complete history of the roller coaster titled *Coast to Coast Coasters*. The exhibit, sponsored by the Smithsonian Institution, toured the United States for two years and was displayed in over seventy-five preselected sites, among them San Francisco, Kansas City, Memphis, New Orleans, Pittsburgh and other areas throughout the country. The subject appealed to the audiences and to the visual median which projected the exhibit through its national network. The exhibit consisted of sixty 30 x 40 inch panels containing 180 photographs, 36 of which were in full color. Through the exhibit, Mr. Cartmell reached an important sector of the American public and has made Americans conscious of this long-neglected, and exciting phase of our history.

To me, the coaster with its matchstick framework, as seen from afar, conjures up a prehistoric monster that at a moment's notice could rattle its bones and expel a roar that travels along its spinework, from tip to tail, to put the fear of the devil even in the stouthearted. Mr. Cartmell's quotes from riders make this one of the most illuminating and entertaining chapters, illustrating the love/hate/torture aspects of this gravity ride.

An insight into the coaster's earliest development in the United States can be gained from the correspondence between two of the ride's most noted designers and builders. In 1936 John A. Miller wrote a letter to James A. Griffiths requesting information. The following is abstracted from Mr. Griffiths's reply:

"Dear Mr. Miller:

"My Sister in Law at Lancaster, Pa. sent me your letter asking for information on the early erection of our Scenic and Pleasure Railways. All of my booklets and advertising matter on Amusement was burned up in a storage house fire.

"I sent to George S. Crane asking him to send me what he had. He wrote me that all of his old booklets had been lost, but he sent me a list of roads we built (from memory) But he overlooked quite a few.

"I built a scenic railway in New Orleans built on piling out into the lake. George S. Crane and John McKay Supt. of Construction. George S. Crane and myself are the only living ones who was interested in the Construction of the first Scenic Railway.

"It was built on my ground in Atlantic City, located on the Board Walk between New York & Tennessee Aves.

"Crane, McKay and myself took over the first car ever run over a Scenic Railway. It was financed by L.A. Thompson and myself. Thompson and myself built a serpentine Railway all under the same roof and our electric plant made quite an amusement those early days (1887). Hoping this stuff will be of some use to you I am truly - J.A. Griffiths,

4601 Chester Ave., Phila.''

The letter lists names and locates the rides built under the names of Griffiths & Thompson, also several built for T.M. Harton Co. of Pittsburgh, all of which will be found within the pages of this definitive volume.

The creative design and construction by these early pioneers influenced others. It is notable that the race to create more exciting rides carried over into the first decade of the twentieth century. From 1901 to 1904 six patents were filed with the United States Patent Office on some form of the centrifugal railway, and in 1912, William Bickford of Washington, Iowa, filed his patent for a double loop ''Loop-The-Loop/Pleasure Railway'', the forerunner of today's CORKSCREW, thrill ride.

With the publication of this book, the knowledge of American inventiveness, design and engineering skills should reach a world-wide readership. A most valuable document has been added to our history.

*Frederick Fried*

# The Ride

*A Thrilling Coaster Ride from Start to Finish*

— My grandmother told me years ago that on her honeymoon they had to go to Boston. They decided to take the elevated cars out to Revere Beach when it was a popular resort. After riding the roller coaster for the first time in her life, she said she was so petrified that they had to walk back to the city of Boston because the elevated cars reminded her of the roller coaster. That was 1900.

> Ken Smith. Letter to the author, March 10, 1977.

— I had long hair pinned up and I didn't have a hairpin left on my head. It was terrible!

> Hazel Dunigan. 1927.

— Clanking up the first hill is the most unnerving part of any ride because it allows you ample time to ponder your folly. This long interval, reserved for the plunges to follow, may be the best rebuttal to atheism ever devised.

> John Pastier. *Los Angeles Times.* September 1, 1974.

— Why do I ride them? Because it makes my blood hurt.

> Donna Johnson. Rye Beach, New York, 1976.

— With all the mechanized experiences of the 1970's, only the coaster offers that glorious instant of suspended animation before the great plunge, the excitement of being at the mercy of the force of gravity and yet safe, the joy of total freedom.

> Irene Clurman. *The Rocky Mountain News* (Denver), July 14, 1974.

— A good roller coaster is better than sex.

> Michael Quinn. Letters to the Editor. *Oui* magazine, January, 1978.

— *Family Weekly.* November 13, 1983. Letter to movie star Nancy Allen from U.S., Anderson, Indiana:

What's the most frightening film you've ever seen? What was the most frightening situation you've ever been in? NANCY ALLEN: When I was 10, I saw *Psycho* . . . it terrified me. To this day I have a transparent shower curtain. *Jaws* also frightened me. Before I saw it, I loved to swim. Now I'm nervous when I'm in the water. My most frightening experience was the first time I got on a roller coaster. I was 16. I thought I'd die on that roller coaster.

— On the whole, I'd rather have someone take a chain and beat me.

> Anonymous, when asked about their ride on the Coney Island *Cyclone,* 1977.

— There are things you needn't do in life and this is one of them.

> Anonymous, when asked about their ride on the *Thunderbolt,* Kennywood Park, Pittsburgh, 1973.

— Perhaps it's the fact that one can loose a loud and satisfying primal scream while riding a coaster that brings such a feeling of satisfaction.

> Vee K. Wertime. Letter to the author, 1974.

— In the 1920's, Washington, D.C.'s amusement park was Glen Echo, operated—as many of the parks were in those days—by the streetcar company into whose coffers the fares rolled.

The roller coaster there was a goodly ride. One evening in the years 1926-1929 (I can't be more specific) a car was off on its journey. In the front seat was a young couple. During the ride, he decided to show off by standing up.

I believe his head struck an overhanging beam, though momentum may have thrown him out. In any case, he plunged to rocks below and was instantly killed. Sad. But wait —

The other seats—and I think they were five in number—had been filled. Say, five other couples. They saw the whole affair, of course, because it was right in front of them. So the car continued its course, and finally slowed down at the station. The young lady whose escort had just been killed stepped out. And —

*All* the other (ten?) passengers stayed on for another ride!

> Donald M. Brown. Letter to the author, June 13, 1974.

— Part of the appeal is the imagined danger. That's why many passengers start screaming before the coaster even takes off.

> John Allen (designer) when interviewed by the author, 1973.

— The first hill of the *Cyclone* is the best glimpse of death since E.S.P. and the ouiji board.

> Melanie Todd. Letter to the author, July 4, 1982.

— One night we went to the park and rode the damndest roller coaster this side of Hades. There have been many *Cyclones* in amusement parks but I think this *outcycloned* any other in the whole East or country, maybe. This was one hell of a swinger, man. It was really a tornado, which is bigger than a cyclone. It looked rough and it was rough. It banked like nothing ever seen before or since; it dropped down maybe 60 feet or more and rushed up the other side like the world had come apart; it tore around curves like a possessed thing at God knows how much per, and you hung sideways as it did that like a pretzel (it was that twisted) while your hands kept clinging for life to the bar in front of you and your head almost came off at the turns. You got out feeling like you'd had more than a couple or maybe been in some *Twilight Zone* before that place was ever created by Rod Serling . . . .

> William E. Monaghan. Letter to the author, June 9, 1974, describing the 1927 *Cyclone* at Palisades Park, New Jersey.

— Other people may like their summer houses and yachts, but my idea of heaven would be to have the *Texas Cyclone* in my backyard.

> Bob Strickland. Letter to the Editor. *Oui* magazine, January, 1978.

— Growing up in Brooklyn, I could walk to Coney by myself in the winter months when it was cold and lonely. I'd climb onto the tracks of the L.A. Thompson, a smaller coaster, and walk the length of the track, climbing slowly up and down the wooden hills and around the turns.

In the summer I'd ride the *Tornado* and the *Bobsled,* savoring the feeling of falling, that dropping sensation in the pit of your stomach, the screams of the riders as the wind blows in your face, the abrupt turns and sudden spurts of speed.

. . . The roller coaster, like entertaining, is an escape from the ordinary.

For a short while the performer and the audience are thrown into a fantasy world. A world of laughter and rain.

> Neil Sedaka. *Laughter in the Rain.* New York: G.P. Putnam's Sons, 1982, p. 82.

— All patrons are possessed with an odd suicidal instinct and the wisest operator devises means to prevent them from doing away with themselves. We just have to figure the customer as an accident looking for a place to happen.

> Silvio Pinto (owner, Coney Island *Cyclone)* when interviewed by the author, 1973.

— You're God's lowliest creature with gravitation gone back on you. ...That *Cyclone* doesn't play fair. It's not content to drag you up an incline, toss you down the other side. It drags you up an incline, tosses you down the other side, turns you over this way, turns you over that way, and before you can remember what comes after "Thy Kingdom Come," shoots you to the stars again.

> Robert Garland. *The New York Telegram.* June 14, 1928, describing the 1927 *Cyclone* at Palisades Park, New Jersey.

— At Conneaut Lake in western Pennsylvania, the coaster entered a dark tunnel midway through the ride. Nightmarish screams could be heard for miles as the cars echoed through the dark recesses. The screams continued until the train reached the unloading platform. Passengers flew off the cars, stumbling, arms flying, gasping for breath. The front car had hit a skunk.

> *Smithsonian* magazine. August, 1977.

— Sure you can make them higher, you can make them longer, but I really don't think you could improve the quality of fear.

> Bill Cobb (designer) speaking about his *Texas Cyclone* roller coaster, 1976.

— Carl Jeske operated the *Bobs* for twenty-two years. In his office were boxes of sunglasses, piles of wallets and even false teeth that had been found on the ground around the *Bobs*. On the platform of the ride, Jeske kept a large purple satin-covered board, which held over seven thousand earrings that the *Bobs* had wrenched loose from ears. None of the earrings were pairs. If you could match one, it was yours. Jeske once turned down twelve thousand dollars for the earring board.

> John R. Powers. *The Chicagoan*. July, 1974.

— It was something dreadful. I never was so frightened in my life and if the dear Lord will forgive me this time, I will never do so again.

> Agatha Wales, 1914, describing her ride on the *Scenic Railway*, Venice, California.

(Ride: 1). *Quiet Roller Coaster*. Pencil drawing by Robert Cartmell. 12¾" x 16½", 1982.

(Ride: 2). *Texas Cyclone*. Astroworld, Houston, Texas.

(Ride: 3). *Grand Thrillerr.* Salisbury Beach, Mass., (n.d.). Courtesy B. Derek Shaw.

(Ride: 4). Roller coaster. Old Orchard, Maine, (n.d.). Courtesy B. Derek Shaw.

(Ride: 5). *Texas Cyclone*. Astroworld, Houston, Texas. Courtesy Astroworld.

(Ride: 6). Roller coaster. Pacific Ocean Park, Long Beach, Calif. Courtesy New York Public Library.

(Ride: 7). *Comet*. Crystal Beach, Ontario, Canada.

(Ride: 8). *Giant Coaster*. Lagoon Park, Salt Lake City. Courtesy Jim Payer.

(Ride: 10). First drop, *Comet*. Crystal Beach, Ontario, Canada.

(Ride: 9). First drop, *Racer*. Kings Island, Kings Mill, Ohio. Courtesy Kings Island.

(Ride: 11). *Giant Coaster* (using *Comet* cars). Paragon Park, Nantasket Beach, Mass. Courtesy Paragon Park.

(Ride: 12). *Rebel Yell*. Kings Dominion, Doswell, Virginia. Courtesy Kings Dominion.

(Ride: 13). *First Hill.* Pencil drawing by Robert Cartmell. 12¾″ x 16½″, 1982.

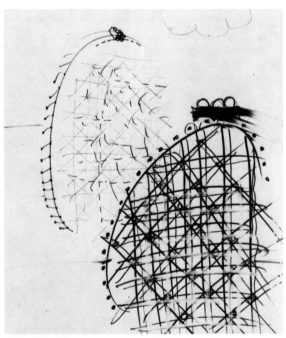

(Ride: 14). *Second Hill.* Pencil drawing by Robert Cartmell. 16½″ x 12¾″. 1982.

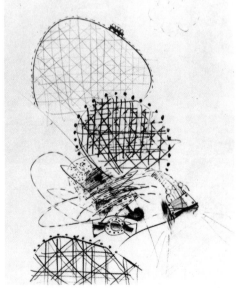

(Ride: 15). *Into the Third Curve.* Pencil drawing by Robert Cartmell. 16½″ x 12¾″. 1982.

(Ride: 16). *Cyclone*. Coney Island, Brooklyn, N.Y. Courtesy *New York Times*.

(Ride: 17). *Mr. Twister*. Elitch Gardens, Denver, Colo. Infrared photograph by Robert Cartmell.

(Ride: 18). *Mr. Twister*. Elitch Gardens, Denver, Colo. Infrared photograph by Robert Cartmell.

(Ride: 19). *Cyclone*. Coney Island, Brooklyn, New York. Courtesy *New York Times*.

(Ride: 20). Unloading platform, *Rebel Yell*. Kings Dominion, Doswell, Virginia.

# Chapter I
## Early European Roller Coasters

Finding the first European roller coaster is easy compared to reasoning why man felt the compulsion in the first place to turn pleasurable relaxation on a slide into brutal *Bobs, Thunderbolts,* and *Cyclones;* why man over the centuries turned the innocent ramp into nightmarish drops twisting through spirals and tunnels, parading riders through every gravitational wrench the body can endure.*

Early 19th century roller coasters were called Russian Mountains, a particularly curious name when you consider Russia is not known for mountains and is notoriously flat. The country does have several high elevations, such as 24,590' Stalin Peak, but is best known for its steppes and deserts. An inquisitive mind with this clue alone could easily trace roller coasters back to their source, but this is not altogether necessary. Several publications, notably *Récreations et Passe-temps* by Henry d'Allemagne (1905), have done creditable jobs and discuss the history of Russian Mountains in some detail. *Récreations et Passe-temps* must also be cited for its superb

reproductions — several used in this book — and color engravings of early amusement park rides.

Of course, slides and ramps can probably be traced back to cavemen or even amoebas, but such roller coaster ancestry, as with many history books on other subjects, can be carried to futile and boring extremes. Most ramp information is lost in antiquity although evidence of such pastimes can be found in Byzantine fairs, Greek marathons, and even slides of the Wishram Indians in Washington state. This book is more concerned with finding the first ride that somehow compares with modern roller coasters and from all descriptions, Russian Mountains, more than hold their own.

These devices can be traced back to 15th and 16th century, Ice Slides found among winter amusements in Russian villages and towns, particularly St. Petersburg (fig. I:1). They were usually built near

*Attempts to answer this most difficult of roller coaster questions can be found in Appendix I.

(I:1) The Russian Mountains. Outskirts of St. Petersburg, 17th century. The prototype for all roller coasters, they had drops as severe as today's most frightening rides. Courtesy Frederick Fried Archives.

rivers, often to dizzying heights, of wood anchored by logs and tree trunks. They were immensely popular. Two plateaus were built accessible by stairs with long slides parallel to one another. The sleds after speeding down one hill would reach the stair-base of the other. The hills followed the pattern of roller coasters with an initial abrupt drop gradually leveling to reduce speed. Sand was often necessary at the end of each ramp to slow hurtling sleds.

The earliest sleds were chipped from ice blocks with straw stuffed in chiseled hollows for the seat and a rope tied to a hole, the rider's only attachment to the sled. Daily watering kept the slides ice-mirrored. Boys and girls developed great skills maneuvering the descents.

Eventually ice slides became popular with royalty and the crude ramps became more sophisticated and splendidly ornate. The nickname Flying Mountains became commonplace. The Ice Slides even became tourist attractions. Here is a description during the Court of Anna Ioannovna:

> ...a new diversion we have had at court this winter. There is a machine made of boards, that goes from the upper story down to the yard; it is broad enough for a coach, with a little ledge on each side. This had water flung upon it, which soon froze, and then more was flung, till it was covered with ice of a considerable thickness. The ladies and gentlemen of the court sit on sledges, and they are set going at the top, and fly down to the bottom; for the motion is so swift, that nothing but flying is a proper term. Sometimes, if these sledges meet with any resistance, the person in them tumbles head over heels; that, I suppose, is the joke..... I was terrified out of my wits for fear of being obliged to go down this shocking place, for I had not only the dread of breaking my neck, but of being exposed to indecency too frightful to think on without horror.[1]

The slides built during festivals in Moscow and St. Petersburg were marvelous constructions and stretched several city blocks. Chinese pagodas often topped the mountains while finest craftsmen decorated stairs and sleds. Newly planted fir trees enclosed the slides. The hills now accommodated up to thirty sleds and now required, for a fee, skilled guides to aid new riders. R. Ker Porter in *Travelling Sketches in Russia and Sweden* (1813) notes:

> A sort of sledge, without projections of any kind, but in shape and flatness like a butcher's tray most fantastically ornamented with carving and colors is placed on the summit of the hill. The native sits himself upon it, very far back, legs extending in front perfectly straight. The person to be conveyed places himself in front in similar attitude, and both remaining steady, pass down the frozen torrent. The native guides with his hands, and so cleverly that they steer around groups of upset persons. Many go down alone, and others on skates, who fly forward in a perfectly upright position. ...The sensation excited in the person who

descends in the sledge is at first extremely painful, but after a few times, passing through the cutting air, it is exquisitely pleasurable. This seems strange, but it is so; as you shoot along a sort of ethereal intoxication takes hold of the senses which is absolutely delightful.[2]

How do the Ice Slides compare to contemporary roller coasters? Some hills were up to seventy feet tall! More amazing, some of the slopes were angled at 50 degrees. The famous *Texas Cyclone* in Houston, considered by many to be the finest standing roller coaster, has a first drop of 53 degrees. Yet the Ice Slides had few accidents, although daredevils often illegally took the drops on their stomachs or chests without sleds.

The rides became so popular that torches eventually bordered the entire run so that the slides could be used at night. Slides were even built indoors, often of waxed mahogany. The last Tsarevich, Alexis, and his sisters used pillows for sleds. A cruder version is described in *Letters from the Continent describing the manners and Customs of Germany, Poland, Russia and Switzerland in the years 1790-92,* London, 1812:

> ...the Ambassador had ice hills built in his room, for the amusement of his company; understand that it was built with boards, and rendered slippery by means of soap and water. We all climbed to the top, then sat in little sledges, and slided down with great velocity.[3]

It is not known when wheels were finally added to these sleds. The French usually receive credit for the invention. The prevalent story goes that an enterprising Frenchman took the ice slides to Paris, added wheels to stretch the riding season into summer, and created the first roller coaster.

The story is not true! A wheeled roller coaster, referred to as a Switchback, existed as early as 1784 in Russia, 100 years before La Marcus Thompson's pioneering work in America. The ride was part of an unbelievable fairy tale pleasure palace called Katalnaya Gorka in the Gardens of Orienbaum, St. Petersburg. Figure I:2 speaks for itself. The ride had summer carriages placed in grooved tracks which ran over undulating hills. The carriages were then returned to the top by means of rope drawn by a windlass.

Russia must be given credit for not only the ice slide system but wheeled roller coasters as well.

It is documented, however, that after several clumsy tries between 1804 and 1817, two roller coasters, *Les Montagnes Russes a Belleville* and *Promenades Aeriennes,* opened in 1817 of such significance that Paris hereafter is considered the birthplace of the modern roller coaster.

### French Russian Mountains

...The speed with which these cars descended the inclined plane caused a violent displacement of air and a lively sensation of freshness...
...This amusement was most complimentary to the health of the persistent riders and that it was moreover the most certain manner of combating the diseases of the nerves and of dissipating all low spirits.[4]

According to the authoritative *Récreations et Passe-temps,* a crude wheeled roller coaster opened as early as 1804 in the Ternes quarter of Paris. It was called *Les Montagnes Russes (Russian Mountains)* and apparently was both frightening and quite dangerous. It lacked any safety devices and passengers grabbed the sides to stay in the cars. Newspaper reports claim wheels fell off and cars often did not stop at the base of the hill.

The 1804 Russian Mountains also provided a psychological oddity. The first recorded instance of injuries to passengers, rather than decreasing the popularity of the ride, actually increased the attendance.

...where the experience of fright experienced by many people at the moment when the chariot was launched from the top of the mountain caused some serious accidents which even added to the passion of Parisians for this dangerous pastime which placed in this manner a mark of honor in displaying their courage and self-control.[5]

It was not just accidents that led to the ride's quick demise. The climb by stairs to the summit was a serious drawback both to popularity and revenue. Repeat rides became fatiguing and intolerable.

*Les Montagnes Russes a Belleville (Belleville Mountain),* thirteen years later, was almost as crude but more closely followed the Ice Slides of St. Petersburg (fig. I:3,4). It had two parallel runs which at least placed riders nearer the stairs when they finished the second incline. There was one significant and far-reaching improvement, cars were locked to the tracks by wheel axles projecting into grooves carved into the inner walls of the tracks (fig. I:5).

Dizziness and fainting still occurred, however, and severe accidents were not uncommon.

During that same year, 1817, a great ride called *Promenades Aeriennes, (Aerial Walks),* opened at Beaujon Gardens in Paris (fig I:6,7,8). The ride consisted of two separate but continuous tracks. Cars leaving at the same time would run down curving ramps before circling at the bottom right or left to points near the summit. Attendants would then push the cars, often filled with passengers, back to the top. This permitted the first example of "re-rides" and great lengths of tickets were often purchased.

It contained many features that are standard of today's roller coasters. Speeds were estimated at 40 miles per hour. Cars were locked to the tracks on

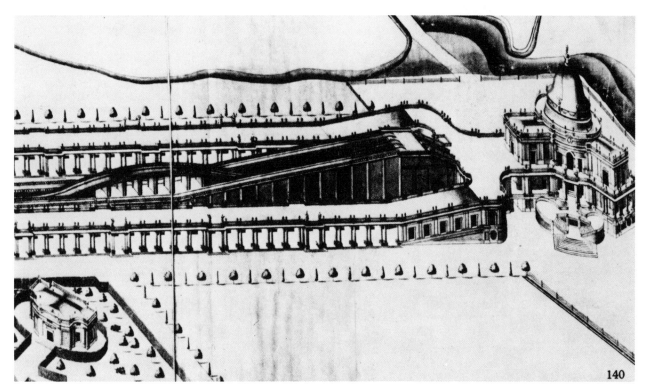

140

(I:2). The first wheeled roller coaster? Gardens of Orienbaum, St. Petersburg, c. 1784. Courtesy G.P. Putnam's Sons.

LE JEU DES MONTAGNES RUSSES
D'APRÈS UN ABÉCÉDAIRE ILLUSTRÉ DU COMMENCEMENT
DU XIXᵉ SIÈCLE.

rock steady wheels. A primitive cable system, invented by M. Lebonjer in 1826, was later added to hoist cars to the top. This pioneering ride can also be seen as a forerunner of the Racing Coaster. Racing was not the intention of the *Aerial Walks,* but before long "waging booths" appeared, and betting occured on which car came out of the loops first.

Competitors immediately appeared. *Montagnes Russes* dites de Santé, Folie du Jour Déssinée d'après Nature, Barrière du Roule, (fig. I:9) promised:

> ...You are incredibly happy, the crowds are inconceivable. It is four o'clock and already in less than an hour your lady friends and you have been tossed and jostled together at 25 centimes a bump. Your lady friends are satisfied with this healthy and modern exercise (I know several women who use the mountains as a gourmet eats ovsters chez Balaine)...[6] (Taken from the text in fig. I: 10).

There were Egyptian Mountains and Swiss Mountains and every other type of mountain, but it was the offbeat gravity rides of this era that left their mark on future amusement devices.

The *Niagara Falls* of Ruggiery Gardens (fig. I:11,12) was the precursor of the Shoot-the-Chutes. The Gardens boasted a sign at the entrance stating: "The police would not have permitted this amusement if it could jeopardize the lives of its citizens." Parisians entered a car gaudily painted like a Venetian gondola. The car was then lifted on the end of a giant teeter-totter. At its highest point, the car was released where it sped with great fury into a river 60 feet below. The ride was patented April 9, 1817, by

(I:3,4,5).
*The Russian Mountains of Belleville.* Paris, 1817. One of the earliest Parisian roller coasters, it is the first to lock cars to the tracks. A fifteen-foot stature of Mercury, symbol of lightning speed, adorns its roof.

LES MONTAGNES DE BELLEVILLE
D'APRÈS UNE GRAVURE EN COULEUR DESSINÉE PAR GARNEREY, 1817.

(I:6,7,8). *Aerial Walks.* Beaujon Gardens, Paris, 1817. This beautiful ride was park landscaped and had a miniature house at its top. The *Aerial Walks* used the first cable-life in 1826 and eventually became the first racing coaster.

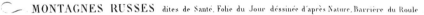

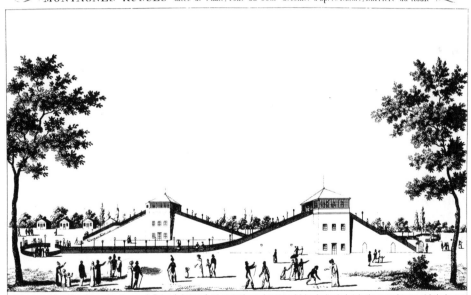

(I:9,10). *Montagnes Russes* dites de Santé, Folie du Jour désinée dápres Nature Barrière du Roule. The *Aerial Walks* most famous competitor, it featured side by side twin rides. The name Barrière du Roule (approximately "Rolling Turnpike") is the closest Europeans came to the title "roller coaster." I:9 Courtesy Russell Hehr, I:10 Courtesy Robert Blundred.

(I:11,12). *Niagara Falls.* Ruggiery Gardens, c. 1817. A teeter-totter mechanism lifted passengers to the roof. Their boat-car then descended with great fury to the river 60 feet below.

(I:12). *Niagara Falls.*

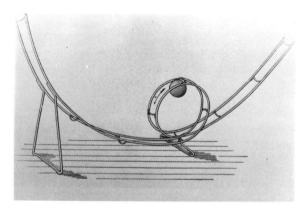

(I:13). Loop-the-Loop toy. France, early 19th Century.

Beurg and Ruggiery.

It seems inevitable during this period that someone would add a vertical somersaulting loop to the tracks, and the invention appeared in France in 1848. One of the favorite toys at this time in England and France was a Loop-the-Loop device that used centrifugal force to hold a ball on tracks (fig. I:13). Like many other inventions, Galileo turning telescopic toys into astronomical instruments, for instance, this ball/loop mechanism was a forerunner of the Centrifugal Railway at Frascati Gardens.

The inventor of this looping ride was one Clavieres, an engineer at the Paris Hippodrome, who claimed he had the idea as early as 1833 but needed

13 years to perfect it.

A smaller version of the Centrifugal Railway with a questionably tiny loop of 6½ feet was briefly tried in England before appearing in France. A superior Parisian ride opened at Frascati Gardens in 1846 (fig. I:14). This version had its starting point 30 feet above the ground. A single car ran down a sloping 100 foot track where, at the hill's end, it somersaulted through a 13 foot-high spiral/circle. The car came to a stop by rolling up another hill to the unloading platform.

Sandbags and monkeys were used to test the ride. A description of the first human passenger appears in the August, 1846, *Journal du Havre:*

Enioyment in Paris. An easy somerset--Paris. France.COLLECTION

(I:14). Centrifugal Railway. Frascati Gardens, Paris, 1846. The first Loop-the-Loop had an incredibly small circle of thirteen feet. A collection was made for its first rider. Courtesy Frederick Fried Archives.

Today has been tested for the first time in France, in the Frascati Garden, the only existing *Chemin du Centrifuge* we have in France. ...The terrific speed at which the cars enter the loop (more than one hundred and fifty miles per hour) was especially noted. One should understand, of course, that at a certain moment the car is completely upside down and is maintained on the rails only by centrifugal force. The cars have been filled with eggs, flowers, glasses of water...and a workman, even has ridden as a passenger. Starting from the highest point, he reached, in eight seconds, the extremity of two hundred and forty-eight feet. On landing, he appeared very satisfied with his journey. While going down he could see everything around him, but when within the loop he was unable to see anything. Going upgrade, he had clapped his hands as he ascended. He had no trouble breathing and during the loop proper experienced such a delicious feeling that he wanted to try again. A collection made for him after each run amounted to one hundred and twenty francs, the first time, and sixty francs the second.[7]

The claim of cars traveling 150 mph through a 13 foot loop must be one of the earliest examples of amusement park hyperbole extant.

Rides opened in Havre, Bordeaux, and Lyons, but the ride was not popular and quickly disappeared. There was an attempt to revive the Centrifugal Railway in 1865 when it was reconstructed in the Circus Napoleon. A car derailed the first trip and police immediately prohibited further trials.

The ride was not popular and quickly disappeared.

It also became the butt of jokes in the press as shown in the six derisive cartoons appearing on the next few pages (fig. I:15 through 20) from the *L'Illustration, Journal Universel.*

After this explosion of amusement devices, things seem to have hit a deadly calm in Europe and few rides surfaced of any consequence. Roller coasters went out of fashion. Parks disappeared and the only innovative rides or the remains of any rides at all appeared in carnivals and traveling shows (fig. I:21). Customers came to prefer rides as sedate as the popular *Mechanical Electric Race Course* (fig. I:22).

A notable exception was La Marcus Thomson's Russian Mountains of 1888 at the Boulevard des Capucines (fig. I:23). The ride was located in the center of Paris between two houses, seated ten passengers, ran 80 meters, was beautifully illuminated by electric lights, and was completely roofed.

But it was built by an American company. The tall cliff hanging coasters that later appeared in early 20th century England and Germany were built by American companies (fig. I:24-26). Eventually it reached the point where roller coasters invented in Europe were considered just to be another form of

Comment on devrait placer les voyageurs afin qu'ils n'aient pas la tête
en bas pendant le voyage.

(Un convoi jeté hors de la voie par la rupture du cercle.)

(I:15,16,17,18,19,20). Caricatures by Cham. Translations from 1846 *L Illustration Journal Universel* read as follows: (15). How one seats the passengers so they will not be upside-down during the ride; (16). The inconvenience of a passenger in a loop too small; (17). A surprise for the passengers on the upper deck of the train; (18). A train jumps the track breaking the circle; (19). A roadsman exercises his duties on the Centrifugal Railroad; (20). What workmanship, the train travels in slow motion, the passengers arrive at the station before the train. (Translation by Lisa Cartmell.) Courtesy Frederick Fried Archives.

(Inconvénient de voyager dans un cercle d'un trop petit diamètre.)

(Un cantonnier dans l'exercice de ses fonctions sur le chemin de fer centrifuge.)

Sapristi! moi qui croyais avoir pris ma place sur l'impériale de la voiture.

(De quelle façon, le convoi venant à ralentir sa marche, les voyageurs arrivent
à la station avant le train.)

(I:22). *Mechanical Electric Race Course.* Nice, France, 1889. After the hectic Russian Mountains era, patrons turned to more sedate rides. The *Mechanical Race Course* was one of the earliest to use electricity—and a musical band. Invented by M. Salle, it ran at 14 feet per second. Courtesy New York Public Library.

American violence.

The name Russian Mountains still exists. Probably the best known is *La Montana Rusa* in Chapultepec Park, Mexico City (see Chapter XI). A few Russian Mountains survive in Europe, the most beautiful being *Montaña Rusa* at the Casino de la Rabassada, Barcelona (fig. I:27-29).

Only a handful of Ice Slides or roller coasters can be found in Russia. Russian Mountains are now better known through a wind-up toy of the same name exported from that country. The toy has more to do with ski lifts than roller coasters. (fig. I:30).

Confusion of names reached the Tower of Babel status when a Russian track team visited Kings Dominion amusement park in Virginia. When they boarded the *Rebel Yell* roller coaster they repeatedly chanted the name now used for roller coasters in Russia, "American Mountains!"

(I:21). Portable roller coaster. Lyons, France, 1930s. One of the last survivors from the original French Russian Mountains design.

(I:23). The La Marcus Thompson Switchback travels to Paris using the French name, *Montagnes Russes*. 1888. The ride was completely indoors.

(I:24). *Figure 8* (portable). Oktoberfest, Munich, Germany, 1909.

(I:25). *Figure 8 Railway*. Southport, England, 1909. Courtesy B. Derek Shaw.

(I:26). *Canadian Toboggan*. Franco-British Exhibition, London, England, 1908. Courtesy B. Derek Shaw.

(I:27, 28, 29). One of the few remaining coasters in the world with the name "Russian Mountains." *Montana Rusas*, Barcelona, Spain. Courtesy John Still.

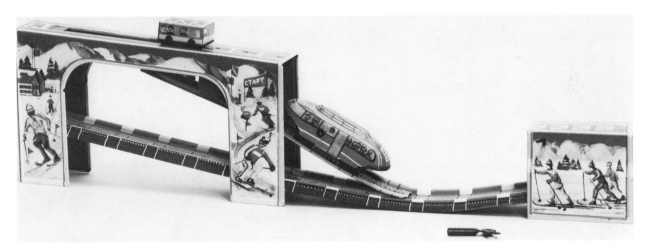

(I:30). Wind-up toy, *Russian Mountains*. Manufactured in Russia, 1960s.

# *Chapter II*
## America's First Roller Coaster

Everyone has a theory on the first gravity ride in the U.S. and the arguments are endless. Each section of the country claims or *insists* that the idea of the roller coaster started there. Four of my favorites are listed below with major emphasis on the *Mauch Chunk Switchback*. With its screaming passengers, raucous and death-defying ride, the roller coaster seems inseparable from crowded urban traffic; yet these candidates for America's first roller coaster thrived in peaceful settings.

### Far North: Logs Ridden by Lumberjacks

A 1980 *Believe-it-or-Not* cartoons two millionaires daring a reporter to ride their log water chute in the Sierra Nevada Mountains, California. The article says they went 100 miles per hour down the 23 mile run. The date was 1875 making it one of the earliest, and certainly the longest and fastest flume ride ever built. A recently discovered engraving shows 14 suited gentlemen with top hats shooting perilous rapids on a log raft. The engraving bears the caption, "Prince of Wales Descending a Timber Slide in Ottawa in 1860 (fig. II:1).

(II:1). *Prince of Wales Descending a Timber Slide in Ottawa in 1860.* Engraving. Courtesy New York Public Library, Prints and Photographs Division.

### Northeast: Ramps With Ice Blocks (fig. II:2).

A rope frozen to a block of ice was the only attachment riders had to the blocks as they guided them down treacherous, mile-long wooden ramps. At the base, these ice projectiles would either skid across frozen surfaces or plunge into bone-cold water.

### South: Riding Bales of Cotton

Chutes that shuttled cotton to boats during the day (fig. II:3) were extended into the river at evening. Riding the bales like a bronco-pony, reins in hand, the brave-at-heart would steer their cotton to a teeth shattering splash.

The flaw in each of the above is they do not have tracks and wheels. After the 1817 Parisian rides, such ingredients must be considered part of a roller coaster definition. With that in mind, America's first roller coaster grew up with the railroad system. It was built in mountains of eastern Pennsylvania so spectacular that the site was called "Switzerland of America."

(II:2). Ice slide. Damanscotta River, Maine. Courtesy Richard Hershey.

(II:3). Cotton chute on the Alabama River. Courtesy New York Public Library, Prints and Photographs Division.

### The Mauch Chunk Switchback Railway

The real pioneers of the railroad system experimented in the coal country of Pennsylvania around Mauch Chunk. Their efforts were regarded as folly. With the canal building period well underway in Pennsylvania in the 1820's, enthusiasts for the railway as a means of transportation, commercial or public, were disdainfully ignored. Railroads were financed only for coal fields or terrain where canals were impractical.

It was under such clouds of skepticism that America's first roller coaster laid its tracks. In 1792, the Lehigh Coal Company raised $48.40 to build an access road from the Summit Hill mines to the Lehigh River at Mauch Chunk, Pennsylvania. At that time coal was broken in open pits and was transported by wagon to smithies or river arks. Realizing the importance and abundance of anthracite coal in eastern Pennsylvania, Erskine Hazard, Josiah White, and George F. A. Hauto arrived in Mauch Chunk in 1818 to establish a mining company. Their first order was to smooth the old road for more efficient transportation of coal. The new road proved a stop-gap measure. By 1827, construction had begun on canals for slackwater navigation and Hazard, White, and Hauto's business was booming. A more profitable means of transportation to the river was needed.

Josiah White hit on a brilliant roller coaster type plan. He used gravity a penny-cheap, inexhaustible, source of power to transport his coal. With the slope from Summit Hill to Mauch Chunk at 96 feet to the mile, the trains needed only a slight nudge to speed down the mountain. White called his marvelous creation the *Gravity Road* and in 1827 installed wooden rails topped with iron, laid on ties held in place by stones that often rolled down the mountainside. Loaded cars were connected in trains of six to fourteen cars and followed the old mountain road. A single heroic figure known as a runner sat at the rear gripping an upright brake lever and edged 50,000 pounds down the precipitous mountain.

The trip to the bottom lasted thirty minutes but the return ordeal required three hours. Mules were used to haul the empty cars to the Summit Hill mines. After reaching the top, the animals would foot down the mountain to wait for more empty cars. This treadmill circuit made the mules increasingly weary and balky. Josiah White was not blind to this and ordered a train built for the animals. After 1828, the mules rode to Mauch Chunk with the loaded wagons in their own special cars. It is reported once the mules learned to enjoy the trip, they could never be persuaded to walk down again. The mules were fed at the same time, making stalls, according to old-timers, the first dining cars.

The train was a social success as well. Ann Royal, "The Intrepid Traveler," described an 1829 visit to Mauch Chunk in her book *Travels in America*. She wrote that coal wagons were run in the morning while afternoons were reserved for a growing number of gawking tourists. These passengers were the first on what was to become the most popular ride in America. The complete run cost 50 cents.

Coal was running low over the U.S. in 1844. The demand was high and the single track from the Summit Hill mines was proving a bottleneck. To meet competition, Josiah White built a backtrack. Construction commenced in spring of 1844 and was completed by fall of 1845. The backtrack eliminated mules and greatly speeded transportation. Cars could now make continuous circuits with empties travelling to Summit Hill over the backtrack and loaded cars to Mauch Chunk over the original *Gravity Road*.

This ingenious feat was accomplished by the addition of two parallel tracks from Mauch Chunk to the top of Mt. Pisgah. It was a dizzying climb with cars rising 664 vertical feet on 2322 foot long tracks. Two huge stationary steam engines, each generating 120 horsepower and issuing clouds of billowing smoke that could be seen for miles (fig. II:4), were installed at the top of Mt. Pisgah. They powered drums 28 feet in diameter that reeled cars up the plane by 7½'' Swedish iron-band cables.

A small flat, four-wheeled car called a booster, barney, or safety car was housed beneath the tracks at the foot of the mountain. When drums were set in motion, bands pulled one booster to the top while lowering another. The booster rose out of its pit and pushed cars up the steep incline to the summit. (fig. II:5).

Another important feature was the use of safety ratchets on the booster. This mechanism prevented cars rolling backward and eventually became part and sound of every roller coaster in the world. (See Appendix I)

After the climb to the top of Mt. Pisgah, trains were formed, brakes released, and cars rolled by gravity along the backtrack to the foot of Mt. Jefferson six miles away. Cars were again raised by engine.

The loaded trains then coasted from the summit of Mt. Jefferson along the original 1827 route to Mauch Chunk. The complete circuit ran 18 miles — 17 of it downhill (fig. II:6,7).

The *Mauch Chunk Switchback,* as it came to be known, was an engineering marvel. Experts said "It was quiet as a whisper." Thomas Alva Edison many years later, when asked to convert the switchback to electricity, refused on grounds that the "engineering was already perfect."

Almost overnight, the *Mauch Chunk Switchback* became obsolete. On February 1, 1872, Hauto Tunnel was completed through nearby North Mountain and it offered more efficient transportation than the Summit Hill run. It was a blessing in disguise. Farsighted members of Mauch Chunk, realizing the tourist potential of the Switchback, wisely changed cargo from coal to people. By 1873, the Switchback served 35,000 tourists annually (fig. II:8).

In 1874, the Central Railway of New Jersey purchased the Switchback but left its operation in the hands of Mauch Chunk. Special trains from New York and New Jersey were now run to the "Switzerland of America," as the area came to be known, and tourists arrived in droves. The Switchback was a phenomenal success. Arriving at the depot, passengers transferred to cars which ran by gravity to the foot of Mt. Pisgah. Cars departed every six minutes, the time it took to reach the top of the mountain on a heavily booked day. Patrons then transferred to excursion cars (fig. II:9-12). The summer car, the season ran from May 30 to the first heavy snow, was a flat car with rounded roof. The winter train resembled a boxcar with two long benches and potbelly stove. Each seated 70 passengers.

The cost of the trip was now one dollar and a round-trip took one hour and twenty minutes. The 18 mile excursion began on the precarious Mt. Pisgah plane. *Appleton's Illustrated Hand Book of American Summer Resorts* (1877) wrote of the climb:

> ...The plane appears, when standing at its foot, to reach almost perpendicularly up into the air; and when at last the ascent begins, one feels as if he were drawn up into the clouds, and naturally commences to speculate with what terrible swiftness the car would shoot down the plane if it should get loose. ...One discovers that his imagination takes a strange pleasure in depicting the terrible whirl through space and the horrible splintering upon the rocks, should it please Fate to give the pleasure-trip a tragical turn. As the car ascends, the prospect enlarges....[1]

(II:4). Mauch Chunk, Pa. and Mount Pisgah. c. 1845. The smoke from two huge stationary steam engines that powered cars to the top of Mt. Pisgah could be seen for miles.

(II:5). *Mauch Chunk Switchback Railway.* The barney or booster car pushed cars up the 664 feet (vertical) of Mt. Pisgah along 2322 feet of track. Courtesy Library of Congress.

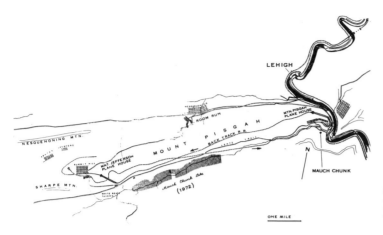

(II:6). Overhead map of the *Mauch Chunk Switchback Railway*. Map drawn by Ric Choley, Mauch Chunk Lake Park, Jim Thrope, Pa.

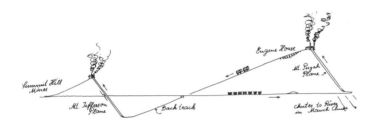

(II:7). Profile map of the *Mauch Chunk Switchback Railway*. Map drawn by Ric Choley, Mauch Chunk Lake Park, Jim Thorpe, Pa.

(II:8). Poster for the *Mauch Chunk Switchback Railway*. Courtesy Chris Paul.

(II:9). The second of two crossing bridges, at the Mount Jefferson Plane. Courtesy Jim Thorpe Chamber of Commerce.

(II:10). Work crew on the *Mauch Chunk Switchback Railway*. Courtesy Jim Thorpe Chamber of Commerce.

(II: 11). The perilous descent from Mount Jefferson. Courtesy Jim Thorpe Chamber of Commerce.

One tourist described the lift, "If our readers will place their feet on the mantlepiece and imagine that the house is climbing over the house next door, they will have a slight idea of the position we assumed."[2]

At the top of Mt. Pisgah, also known as High Point, the car stopped for three minutes. High Point offered a spectacular view of the Blue Ridge Mountains, the Lehigh River, Lehigh Water Gap, and when the haze lifted, Schooley's Mountains nearly 70 miles away in New Jersey.

With all aboard, trains sped down the backtrack's slow grade under canopies of trees through the village of Hacklebernie to the base of Mt. Jefferson (fig. II:11). A booster reeled cars to the top and Summit Hill station. Passengers were now free to leisurely roam the mountain or relax on a hillside. Bags of sulphur diamonds were sold. Sightseers could watch the "Amazing Burning Mines" in flames since 1832. Spring Tunnel cooled tired walkers and offered icicles all year long. The Eagle Hotel and Switchback Restaurant had food and refreshments. Bands struck up the *Switch-Back March*, a two-step by John Mollard.

After the tours, passengers reboarded to begin the unbelievable plunge to Mauch Chunk. Tourists believing the final trip to be a repetition of the earlier scenic climb arrived at the unloading platform in a state of shock. Here is a description from the *Valley Gazette*, Lansford, Pa.:

....THE CAR SPUN ALONG AT FRIGHTENING SPEED. On the curve a man's straw hat flew into the air like a kite. Women dug their nails into the wooden seats to keep from being whisked out of the car. The train shot under a trestle.
A little boy lost the button on his shirt. His mother's grip on him was like a vise. He wondered why she looked so pale. The ladies were struggling to keep their skirts down over their knees, but the driver showed no mercy. Faster they went until birches, pines, hemlocks, rocks, stumps, earth and sky all blurred into one. Plunging down hill they could hardly remain seated. Rounding corners, everyone was flying to the opposite side in a squeezing heap. The elderly man whose straw hat had vanished began to wonder why he came. His will wasn't in order and the valley looked like it was 100 miles straight down. The small boy was beginning to enjoy the ride, but his mother felt she might faint.
On and on the Switchback car plummeted, barely hanging onto the mountain's ledge. It leaped toward the valley and around another curve. Farms, cows, horses, fields all piled into each other as the vehicle rushed under a trestle, past 5

Mile Tree. At the dirt road (Lentz Trail) they entered the home stretch. The driver spun the brake wheel as far as it would go as the train lunged downward. Coming around the wide curve at incredible speed, passengers were certain they'd be embedded in the hard wooden seats and just when everyone thought they could stand no more, the car slid to a stop at Hacklebernie station.[3]

By charter in 1912, the system's name was officially changed to *The Mauch Chunk Switchback Railway.*

Abruptly in 1929 the Central Railroad of New Jersey cancelled all excursions to Mauch Chunk and sold the Switchback. The loss of tourists combined with the Great Depression and competition from automobiles marked the end of the Switchback. The ride was abandoned in 1937. On October 28, 1938, the last car ran the tracks before all was sold as scrap metal for $18,100.00.

The Switchback has not completely disappeared. Tracks can still be found near Mauch Chunk. On July 3, 1976, the *Mauch Chunk Switchback Railway* was declared an historical monument, and its trails are now open to hikers. A foot race is held annually to climb its terrain.

The Switchback was not only America's first track roller coaster, it was, according to some historians, America's first railroad. While this can be disputed (the "Granite Railway" of 1826 in Quincy, Mass., is usually considered the first), there is little argument that it was the first railroad of any importance in the United States.

The Switchback was the first railroad in the U.S. to be surveyed and, more important, the rails imported from England in 1827 were the first used in this country.

The Switchback's safety record was phenomenal with only two recorded accidents.

Its influence on roller coasters is inestimable. The Switchback's many innovations, such as the safety ratchet, remain part of today's roller coasters. The Switchback is the highest (1,126 feet) and longest (18 miles) coaster ever built. There has never been a ride that offered quite its range of thrills. Further, it was America's first Scenic Railway, an example not overlooked by La Marcus Thompson when he built his Scenic Railway in Atlantic City in 1887.

(II:12). Passengers enjoying a panoramic view during a stop at the Summit Hill station. Courtesy Jim Thorpe Chamber of Commerce.

# Chapter III
## La Marcus A. Thompson

It took the inventiveness, determination, and business skills of La Marcus A. Thompson to finally erect a true roller coaster in an American amusement park. He succeeded to such a degree that he became known as "Father of the Gravity Ride" or in several articles and books and a lost plaque at Coney Island, "Father of Gravity."

This is not to say Thompson invented the roller coaster. He most certainly did not as preceeding chapters demonstrate. He was not even the first within the United States. Earlier patents exist including J. G. Taylor's #128,674 of July 2, 1872, and R. Knudsen's #198,888 of January 1, 1978, (fig. III:4) both, which for reasons unknown, were never built, and P. Hinkle's #307,942 of November 11, 1884.

Thompson's #310,966 patent (fig. III:5) is dated later than the others, January 20, 1885. Thompson receives credit for the ride because he was the first to *build* a roller coaster. He built the Switchback Railway in 1884 at Coney Island, one year before his patent.

He deserves his due. If the roller coaster was a religion, then Thompson was the zealot-missionary spreading the message over the world. Amusement parks were mankind's saving grace. L. A. Thompson, along with John A. Miller, must be regarded as a most important figure in the history of roller coasters.

La Marcus Adna Thompson (fig. III:1, 3), the eighth of ten children, was born in Jersey, Licking County, Ohio, on March 8, 1848. By the age of 12, he had designed and built numerous mechanical toys, had invented a butter churn for his mother and an ox-cart for his father, constructed cross-bows, wagons, and an ingenious miniature saw-mill with log carriers, gauge and buzz-saw. At 17, he was already a master carpenter having built many farms in the area, handling the framing and construction work without assistance.

He attended Hillsdale College in Michigan and completed his schooling in 1866. After moderately successful ventures in the wagon and carriage business, Thompson settled into a marketing partnership. During that time he experimented in many other fields and his inventive genius began to reassert itself. In 1875 he devised a new product called seamless hosiery. After the production of a few samples by hand-run machines, he traveled to Chicago and displayed the product to leading wholesale jobbers including Field, Leiter, and Company (later Marshall Field and Company). They immediately placed a $10,000 order. While this was encouraging, it meant no immediate financial returns. Thompson did not have a factory let alone equipment to fill such an order. He and his partner sold their marketing business, founded the famous Eagle Knitting Company, and opened their first factory in 1877 in a small loft in Elkhart, Indiana. The business boomed. By 1882, the company had built and owned a complete mill, employed over 300, and annually netted over $250,000 in various grades of hosiery, leggings, scarfs, and mittens distributed over the United States.

The business took its toll on Thompson. His health suffered severely, and he was near a nervous breakdown. His doctors ordered a complete rest. Thompson was forced to sell his interest in the mill and recuperated in Arizona. He despised such inactive life and shortly returned to Elkhart where he devoted his time to inventions. His talents finally concentrated on devising a form of amusement that would entertain grownups as well as children while being adaptable to amusement parks and seaside resorts. With the example of the *Mauch Chunk Switchback Railway* before him, he developed his own immensely popular Switchback Railway (fig. III:6,7).

Thompson's invention opened in 1884 on West Tenth Avenue, Coney Island, Brooklyn, and was an immediate money-maker. It was crude, ran about six miles an hour, and was little more than a scenic tour of the beach. But the response was electrifying. Lines formed early in the morning and waiting time ran over three hours. Admission was 5 cents and Thompson found he was continually in the black grossing an average of $600 a day. Inquiries about purchasing the apparatus were received from all over the world and Thompson was quickly on his way to a financial empire.

(III:1). La Marcus Adna Thompson (1848-1919). "Father of the Gravity Ride." Courtesy Frederick Fried Archives.

(III:2). Souvenir tag for L.A. Thompson's Scenic Railway. Courtesy Staples and Charles Ltd.

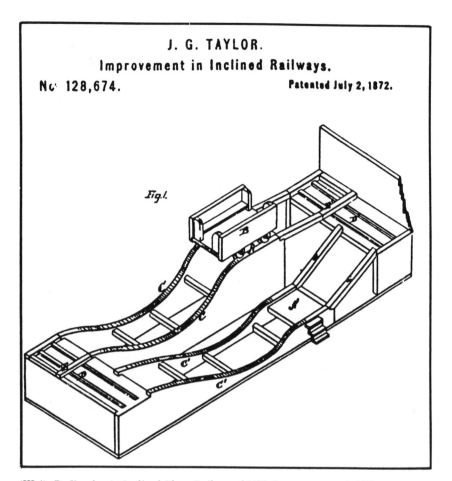

## J. G. TAYLOR.
### Improvement in Inclined Railways.
No. 128,674.                    Patented July 2, 1872.

*Fig.1.*

(III:4). R. Knudsen's *Inclined-Plane Railway* of 1878. Its patent preceded Thompson *Switchback* but for reasons unknown, it was never built.

(III:3). La Marcus Thompson (front seat, right) enjoying a roller coaster ride. (Coaster and date not specified). Courtesy Frederick Fried Archives.

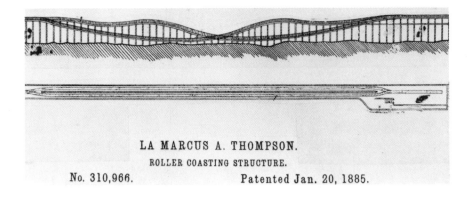

LA MARCUS A. THOMPSON.

ROLLER COASTING STRUCTURE.

No. 310,966.                    Patented Jan. 20, 1885.

(II:5). Left. La Marcus Thompson's patent for his influential Switchback Railway. The ride was built in 1884 although the patent dates 1885.

(III:6).  Engraving of the La Marcus Thompson Switchback Railway depicting its opening day on June 13, 1884. Admission was 5¢ and Thompson grossed an average of $600. a day.

(III:7). Detail of a remarkable model of Thompson's Switchback Railway built in 1984 by Gerald Keck to celebrate the roller coaster's 100th Anniversary. It was displayed at the 1984 ACE meeting, Crystal Beach, Ontario, Canada.

(III:8) Switchback Railway. Euclid Beach Park, Cleveland, Ohio. The Humphrey's Company was an early champion of Thompson. They improved their *Switchback* by adding an escalator (before 1904) and built a Scenic Railway in 1907. Courtesy Amusement Park Books, Inc.

(III:9). Charles Alcoke's roller coaster of 1884. Alcoke tied the track ends together and made the ride of a continuous oval. Courtesy New York Public Library.

Compared to the sophisticated *Mauch Chunk Switchback,* Thompson's ride was embarrassingly simple in operation. It consisted of tracks undulating over a wooden structure six hundred feet long. A small train started on a fifty foot peak at one end of the beach and ran the grade by gravity until the momentum died. Passengers then left the train and attendants pushed the cars over a switch to a higher level. The passengers then returned and rode to the original starting point. They departed and attendants repeated the procedure.

Thompson's Coney Island monopoly lasted only a few months. Eighteen eighty-four marked the opening of another roller coaster. Charles Alcoke of Hamilton, Ohio, tied the track ends together and ran his gravity ride on a continuous oval. The Alcoke ride was later described in an 1886 *Frank Leslie's Weekly:*

> The Coney Island roller coaster is a contrivance designed to give passengers, for the insignificant expenditure of five cents, all the sensation of being carried away by a cyclone, without attendant sacrifice of life and limb. The roller coaster makes a complete circuit in a few minutes. The elliptical track is laid on a system of precipitous descents and gently billowy risings. Half a dozen can ride at once, seated sidewise upon a long bench.[1]

The speeds actually remained slow, the tracks mildly undulant, and the bench seats faced to the side for sight-seeing reasons (fig. III:9).

Alcoke's ride eroded Thompson's profits, but it was 1885 that drove him to near bankruptcy. Phililp Hinkle of San Francisco opened a new roller coaster at Coney Island. His device was a great advance on the Thompson and Alcoke machines. It was elliptical; it had a hoist to pull cars to the top of a precipitous hill. The higher hill meant faster speeds and the seats faced forward to capture the sight of perilous drops and curves. It was the first true roller coaster to offer only thrills instead of a tour of the countryside.

Other designs were on rival drawing boards and Thompson knew his business was dwindling. He wisely decided to revamp his Switchback Railway but strongly defended sight-seeing as a feature of his roller coasters.

Two years later, in 1887, the *Sliding-Hill and Toboggan* opened in Haverhill, Massachusetts (Chapter V), the first roller coaster built to trace the pattern of a figure-eight. Many Figure Eights followed including the *Gravity and Cable Pleasure Railway* patented in 1897 by Thompson's later partner, James A. Griffiths. It effectively combined Thompson's Switchback Railway with, midway through the ride, spiraling figure-eights in a darkened tower (Patent #577,549). Griffiths, however, was completely upstaged six years earlier by Hermann Bormann's horribly convoluted *Sinuous Pleasure Railway* of 1891 (Patent #450,660). Bormann writes in his patent description:

> ...My invention consists of a pleasure-railway compromising a substantially S-shaped course located at or near the ground, a second substantially S-shaped course located above and inversely disposed with relation to the first course, and two inclined semi-circular courses connected, respectively, with opposite extremeties of the S-shaped courses.[2]

Thompson was a visionary. He realized the full potential of the roller coaster and quickly put his ideas into practice. From 1884 to 1887, Thompson was granted thirty patents, all leading to the improvement of the gravity ride. Shortly after the opening of Hinkle's coaster, Thompson began the planning of his most famous invention, the Scenic Railway. In developing the ride he collaborated with another designer, James A. Griffiths of Philadelphia, and hired as his chief engineer, John Miller, a figure to later dominate roller coaster design. It was a revolutionary ride combining new mechanics with the finest ideas then in practice, the adoption of the returning track; construction of an articulated train; a device under the lead car that automatically gripped a moving cable on contact combined with a sensitive trigger release; and steam power and cables to lift cars up inclines. But it was not mechanical features that passengers would later remember. Thompson, surrounded his tracks with elaborate artificial scenery. Not content with cheap cardboard landscapes, the Scenic Railway used beautiful grottos in blue and purple with blinking colored lights. At strategic points cars tripped switches and flood lamps illuminating tableaus or Biblical scenes (fig. III:10).

The Scenic Railway opened in 1887 on the Boardwalk in Atlantic City between New York and Tennessee Avenues and was a jubilant success (fig. III:10). The ride quickly became the most popular and famous amusement device in the world. Thompson formed the L.A. Thompson Scenic Railway Company the following season with offices on Broadway in New York City. Scenic Railways spread over the world, each an improvement on its predecessor. He hired the finest stage designers to blueprint his rides, hired top-notch engineers to create breathtaking special effects, and created a

(III:11). La Marcus Thompson's first Scenic Railway. 1887. The ride was partly indoors with scenic effects. The outdoor section made little effort to hide clotheslines and other "unscenic" features. Courtesy Frederick Fried Archives.

(III:10). The indoor sections of Thompson's Scenic Railway included cars tripping lights to illuminate tableaus, panoramas, and Biblical scenes. Courtesy Frederick Fried Archives.

world of illusions, thrills, and escape that looked forward to another empire of make believe, the magic of cinema.

Indeed, Thompson regarded his work as Utopian. Enthralled by the happiness his rides brought to millions, he wrote:

> Many of the evils of society, much of the vice and crime which we deplore come from the degrading nature of amusements entered into. To inveigh against them avails little, but to substitute something better, something clean and wholesome and persuade men to choose it, is worthy of all endeavor
>
> …sunshine that glows bright in the afterthought and scatters the darkness of the tenement for the price of a nickel or dime.[3]

Royalty competed to attend Thompson's rides. His 1910 catalogue lists the following passengers:

The Prince of Wales
The Princess Victoria of Wales
The Princess Maude of Wales
The Princess Louise of Wales
The Princess Victoria of Prussia
The Princess of Saxe-Meiningen
The Queen of Hawaii
The Queen of Denmark
The King of Saxony
The King of Greece
The Crown Prince of Austria
The Crown Prince of Sweden
The Grand Duke Michael of Russia
Prince Albert Victor
Prince George of Wales
Prince George of Greece
The Duke of Sparta
The Hereditary Prince of Saxe-Meiningen
Prince Louis of Baden
The Prince of Siam[4]

The 1910 catalogue also notes 2,800,000 men, women, and children rode his cars during the 1908 Franco-British Exposition, and in 1909 over 8,000,000 patronized his rides in the United States.

Thompson's first Scenic Railway appears drab when compared with his later efforts. The Atlantic City ride did not disguise clothlines or land-fills (fig. III:11). Thompson's later cosmetics blotted out such imperfections. Egyptian panoramas with three-dimensional pyramids and sphinxes, disasters with moving parts, Biblical scenes, devils and *Dragon's Gorge* (fig. III:12) were soon part of the Thompson trademark.

His masterpiece was built in Venice, California, in 1910 (fig. III:13-15). Huge artificial mountains of

plaster, burlap, and wire were assembled like an elaborate movie set while tracks extended over an ocean pier. Cars on pretzel tracks tunneled the mountain heights from peak to valley. The inky darkness was loaded with Thompson's most spectacular effects. Passengers at one point blinked their eyes at the mirage of a complete Egyptian temple. The Venice Scenic Railway was the granddaddy of all dark rides with a lineage that includes Disneyland's *Matterhorn* and Walt Disney World's *Haunted Mansion* and *Space Mountain*.

By 1901, Thompson was working out of newly purchased headquarters at what is now Rockaway's Playland, Rockaway Beach, New York. The site was called the L.A. Thompson Amusement Park (fig. III:16). It remained under that name until 1928 when the park was sold.

Thompson's partner in the planning and construction of the first Scenic Railway, James A. Griffiths, (fig. III:17) pooled his talent with designer George C. Crane and formed the Griffiths and Crane Scenic and Gravity Railway Company. The Griffiths and Thompson companies became immediate rivals in a market where Scenic Railways were in great demand. While some minor lawsuits erupted between the two, both companies thrived with little hostility. Although Thompson dominated the field, Griffiths and Crane made great contributions to roller coasters. The rides they built over the U.S. and Canada were many and are considered among the most beautiful ever built (fig. III:18,19). The elaborate carvings of Griffiths are particularly remembered. Like a master ship carver, he adorned the fronts of his trains with elaborate gargoyles, animals, and scrolls (fig. III:20). Museums today seek his carvings to add to their collections of valuable carousel carvings.

Of great historic interest is a letter found in the Frederick Fried Archives from James A. Griffiths to John Miller:

> Dear Mr. Miller:
>
> My Sister in Law at Lancaster, Pa. sent me your letter asking for information on the early erection of our Scenic and Pleasure Railways. All of my booklets and advertising matter on Amusements was burned up in a storage house fire.
>
> I sent to George S. Crane asking him to send me what he had. He wrote me that all of his old booklets had been lost, but he sent me a list of roads we built (from memory) but he overlooked quite a few.
>
> I built a scenic railway in New Orleans built on piling out into the lake, George S. Crane and John McKay Supt. of Construction. George S. Crane and myself are the only living ones who was interested in the Construction of the first Scenic Railway.
>
> It was built on my ground in Atlantic City, located on the

Dragon's Gorge.
Luna Park,
Coney Island, N.Y.

(III:12). *Dragon's Gorge.* Luna Park, Coney Island, Brooklyn, N.Y.  c. 1906. Thompson's most famous use of the Scenic Railway was the *Dragon Gorge.* They were built with little variation in amusement parks over the world.

Board Walk between New York and Tennessee Aves.
    Crane, McKay and myself took over the first car ever run over a Scenic Railway. It was financed by L. A. Thompson and myself. ...Thompson and myself built a Serpentine Railway with Scenic Pavilion and Serpentine Railway and Merry-Go-Round all under the same roof and our own electric light plant made quite an amusement for those early days (1887)....
    Hoping this stuff will be of some use to you. I am yours Truly — J. A. Griffiths, 4601 Chester Ave., Phila.

### The Griffiths's letter includes the following lists:

Scenic Railways—L. A. Thompson patented
    Atlantic City, Uptown (1st ever built)
    Atlantic City, Downtown
    Neshaminy Falls, Pa.
    Chicago, Ill.
    Cleveland, Ohio

Scenic Railways—J. A. Griffiths design and Patented
    White City, Phila.
    Omaha Exposition
    Chesapeake Beach, Md.
Scenic Railways—Patented by George S. Crane
    Brandywine Springs, Wilmington, Del.
    Ocean View, Norfolk, Va.
Roller Coasters constructed for T. M. Harton Co., Pittsburgh
    Newark, N.J.
    Union Hall, N.J.
    Schenectady, New York
    Toledo, Ohio
    Rochester, New York
    Palisades Park, N.J.
    York, Pa.

(III:13,14,15). Scenic Railway. Venice, Calif., 1910. The Venice ride was Thompson's masterpiece. It led to Disneyland's *Matterhorn* and Disney World's *Haunted Mansion* and *Space Mountain*. Courtesy Frederick Fried Archives.

(III:15). Scenic Railway.

(III:17). (Left to right) W.M. Griffiths, H.B. Griffiths, J.A. Griffiths. J.A. Griffiths became Thompson's chief rival in the manufacture of Switchbacks, Scenic Railways, and other devices. Courtesy Frederick Fried Archives.

(III:16). The L.A. Thompson Amusement Park. Rockaway Beach, N.Y. Thompson opened his own park in 1901. It later became Rockaway's Playland (1928). Courtesy Library of Congress.

Hoboken, N.J.
Classon Point, N.Y.
Montreal, Canada
Bayonne, N.J.
Easton, Pa.
Kinderhook Lake, N.Y.
Serpentine Railways—Patented by L. A. Thompson
(firm name—Griffiths & Thompson) built 1889 to
1893
 Kelly's Hall-8th & Christian St., Phila.
 Gloucester, N.J.
 Atlantic City, N.J.
 Chicago, Ill.
 South Beach, Staten Island, N.J.
Switchback Railways—Patented by L. A. Thompson
 Indianapolis, Ind.
 Omaha, Neb.
 Creve-Cour, Mo.
 Elmira, N.Y.
 Hamilton, Ohio
 Binghamton, N.Y.
 Richmond, Va.
 Mt. Gretna, Pa.
Gravity Railways—designed by George S. Crane,
Patented by J. A. Griffiths
 Pittsburgh, Pa. (Exposition)
 Holyoke, Mass.
 Knoxville, Tenn.
 Lynchburg, Va.
 Bass Point, Nahant, Mass.
 McKeesport, Pa.
 Reading, Pa.
 Lebanon, Pa.
Mystic Chutes
 Rochester, N.Y.
 Union Hill, N.J.
 Pittsburgh (North Side)
 Baltimore, Md.
Egyptian Labyrinth
 Brandywine Springs, Wilmington, Del.
Amusement Park operation—Griffiths & Crane,
lessees and mgrs.
 Courtland Beach, Omaha, Neb.
 Luna Park, Schenectady, N.Y.
 Moxahala Park, Easton, Pa.
 University Park, Easton, Pa.
 Wheeling Park, Wheeling, W. Va.[5]

GRIFFITHS & CRANE'S CYCLONE COASTER

(III:18, 19). Switchback Railways and roller coasters from the Griffiths and Crane catalogue. (Names and sites not specified), c. 1904. Their roller coasters are still considered among the most beautiful ever built. Courtesy Frederick Fried Archives.

 Thompson, for many years, was in poor health. He retired in 1915, and Frank W. Darling took over all enterprises that year. Although illness drained Thompson physically, he continued inventing and produced an automatic car coupler which the Pullman firm purchased for $50,000 and a number of other patents in his favorite hobby, astronomy. La

(III:20). The carvings on Griffith's roller coaster cars are collected by museums to join their valuable carousel works. Courtesy Frederick Fried Archives.

Marcus Adna Thompson died May 8, 1919.

The Thompson Company under Frank Darling continued to produce roller coasters including the famous *Tornado* (fig. III:21) built in 1926 at Coney Island. A favorite Coney Island tale is that Thompson could be seen working in the *Tornado's* tower at night. At least two books claim Thompson had offices on its top floors and that he planned many rides there. The tower must have been truly haunted — the ride with its dark catacombs did have an uneasy, ghostly feeling to it — since Thompson died 7 years before its construction.

Thompson's influence remains to this day. He was a powerful man and an international celebrity. John Allen, the great roller coaster designer of the 1960's and 70's said:

> I remember being at Luna Park as a kid with my father. They had a big Scenic Railway and the cars went into a big dragon's mouth but you would never see them come out. That impressed me when I was a kid. I thought that was great. It was one of L.A. Thompson's last Scenic Railways. He was a fantastic designer! He got me into this business with that dragon.[6]

(III: 21). *Bobs* (later *Tornado*). Coney Island, Brooklyn. Built by the Thompson Company under Frank Darling, stories claim Thompson could be seen working in its tower although he died seven years before its 1926 completion. Courtesy Charles J. Jacques, Jr./*Amusement Park Journal*.

# Chapter IV
## Light, Speed, and Entertainment: Early American Parks

Amusement parks and roller coasters are so closely related that it's almost impossible to separate the two. When the park is destroyed so goes the roller coaster. Other rides are more fortunate and often can be transported to different parks. The carousel, for instance, can be reassembled at other sites or, to the horror of the conservationist, individual animals can be cannibalized as antiques for museums and private collectors.

The roller coaster does not have this luxury although successful moves have been made. Andy Brown, John Miller's chief engineer, tells of transporting a roller coaster from Moxahala Park in Zanesville, Ohio, to LeSourdsville Lake 130 miles away and of a board by board move from Chicago to Battle Creek, Michigan. The Coney Island *Cyclone* was almost trucked to Astroworld in the mid-1970's before a sane decision was made to construct a close twin in Houston. Such moves are prohibitively ex-

pensive and almost always foolhardy. Besides, roller coasters are a symbol. When an amusement park is folding, the first ride to be bulldozed is that which represents and glorifies the park, the roller coaster. The King is gone; the park is truly finished.

It would seem then that the most profitable way to trace the progress of roller coasters in the United States would be the exploration of early parks, and this is the case after the Coney Island boom. Before the 1893 World's Columbian Exposition, however, rides were often isolated with minor concessions developing around them. Often lone slides were the only ride. A convincing argument can be made that slides in one form or another, when combined with picnic grounds, were America's first amusement parks.

And what slides they were! Early engravings show American Ice Slides that rival their Russian counterparts (fig.IV:1,2). It is amazing how closely they

(IV: 1). *Tobogganing in New York City.* Engraving by W.P. Snyder for *Harper's Weekly.* December 25, 1886.

55

resemble one another even down to the torches bordering the runs. Figure IV:3 shows an 1885 toboggan drop in Saratoga Springs, New York, that rivals the *Loch Ness Monster* in Williamsburg, Virginia.

Innumerable Water Slides existed in the early 18th century and followed a history of their own (fig. IV:4-6). Shoot-the-Chutes soon became part of every amusement park and a trademark of the hundreds of Luna Parks, White Cities, and Electric Parks built in the 1920's (fig.IV:7). They have remained a necessary ingredient in most parks culminating in the ideal July-August hot weather ride, today known as Log Flumes, and those labyrinth Water Slides for swimmers such as the *Waterworks* in Fort Lauderdale, Florida. (fig.IV:8).

Dry slides, without ice or water, often reached dizzying heights in the 19th century and more closely follow the history of roller coasters. Not satisfied with straight runs and by adding twists and bruising turns (fig.IV:9-11), dry slides progressed to the point where a car or some enclosure was needed simply to protect patrons from the imaginations of designers. The long slide remains with us today, of course, often in prefabricated forms at carnivals and traveling shows (fig.IV:12). More inventive, the *Alpine Slide* manufactured by Inventex in Vermont, follows the contours of real mountains and uses small wheeled sleds. (fig.IV:13).

(IV:3) *Tobogganing at Saratoga.* Engraving by W.P. Snyder for *Harper's Weekly.* February 7, 1885.

(IV: 2). *The Toboggan Spill.* Engraving from a photograph by William Notman for *Harper's Weekly.* February 16, 1889.

(IV:4). *The Baths at Monterey, California.* Engraving by W.P. Snyder for *Harper's Weekly.* January 29, 1887.

(IV: 6). *Toboggan Rides.* Jefferson Beach, Detroit, 1927. Courtesy Fred W. Pearce.

(IV:5). *Marine Toboggan Slide.* (n.d.) Courtesy Library of Congress.

(IV: 7). Electric Park. Kansas City, Mo. Shoot-the-Chutes became trademarks of Electric Parks, White Cities, and Luna Parks over the world.

(IV: 8). The *Waterworks* in Fort Lauderdale, Fla., shows contemporary use of Water Slides with 400 feet of twists and turns. Courtesy New York Public Library.

(IV: 9). *Helter Skelter*. Chicago, Ill., c. 1900. Poster
from the Library of Congress collection.

(IV: 10). *Razzle Dazzle*. Probably the Franco-British Exposition, London, England, 1908. Courtesy Frederick Fried Archives.

(IV:12).  Contemporary slide. Geauga Lake Park, Aurora, Ohio.

(IV: 11).  *Helter Skelter*. Luna Park, Brooklyn,  N.Y. 1903.  **Courtesy Library of Congress.**

(IV: 13).  *Alpine Slide*. Bromley, Peru, Vermont, 1976. These contoured to the mountain side slides can be found coast to coast, Canada, and Germany. Courtesy Inventex Corporation.

(IV: 14) Miniature train ride. Louisiana Purchase Exposition, 1904. The ride as parody and mirror of transportation. Courtesy Library of Congress.

Another link in the parallel development of parks and roller coasters is commercial transportation, particularly trains and streetcars. The Mauch Chunk railroad and La Marcus Thompson's Switchback of 1884 evolved out of the burgeoning railway system. Yet the definition goes beyond this. Scholar and Pulitzer-Prize winner Russel Nye when listing "Ten Ways of Looking at Amusement Parks" at the Coastermania conference in Sandusky, Ohio, in 1978 noted in his park definition, "Amusement rides are often *parodies* and extensions of outside technology including railroads, trolleys, autos, steam engines, rockets, and bridge building. Rides can be seen as mirrors and parodies of transportation."[1]

Nowhere can this parody be better seen than in the roller coaster's early relative, the miniature train that appeared with regularity in the 19th century at fairs and expositions (fig.IV:14). It was with these innocent toys that experiments with tracks and train cars began. Park owners, like earlier slide owners, not

satisfied with staid flat tracks, started adding bumps and when possible, sharper and sharper curves.

When it was technically impossible to thrill customers by clever track use, the trains were often paraded through dark enclosures (fig.IV:15). Pitch black tunnels became increasing popular culminating in the "tunnel craze" of the 1920's. The *Dragon Coaster,* still standing at Rye Beach, New York, is a remnant and fine example of that craze. Midway through the ride, cars run the full tunnel length of the dragon's body.

Often the train itself became the frightening object. If the ride didn't provide sufficient thrills, why not turn the cars into dragons? (fig.IV:16).

This parody of transportation was strongly encouraged by the park owners since they were often streetcar companies. It was marvelously self-serving. Streetcar companies would place parks at the end of the run as an inducement to ride their line (fig.IV:17). A trolley ride in the cool of the evening

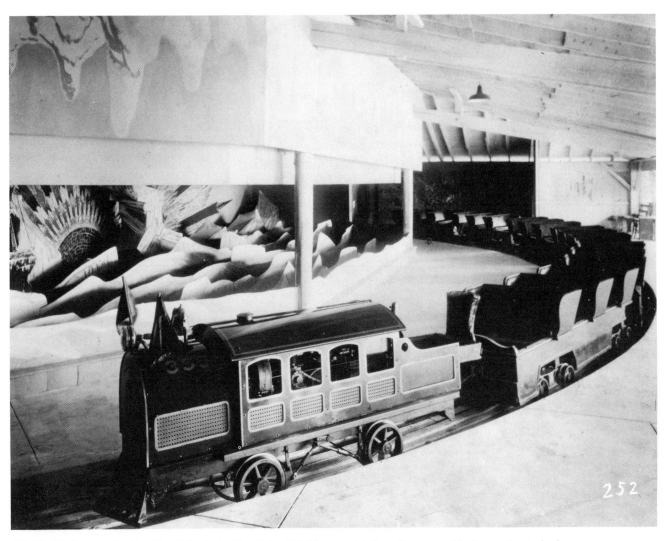

(IV: 15). Miniature train ride. Glen Echo Park, Glen Echo, Md. The use of dark enclosures on rides became increasingly popular through the 1920s.

(IV: 16). Interior of the driver's cabin in the *Sea Serpent*. 1900. Courtesy New York Public Library.

(IV: 17). Streetcar to the *Big Dipper*. Playland, San Francisco, Calif. Streetcar companies would place parks at the end of a run as an inducement to ride their lines. Courtesy Jim Payer.

soon became part of America's summers. It was a gentle era where getting to the park was almost as much fun as the rides themselves (fig.IV:18).

### Chicago's Columbian Exposition, 1893

Chicago in 1993 will celebrate the 100th anniversary of that landmark extravaganza The World's Columbian Exposition, by constructing what many Chicagoans have already claimed, will be its equal or better. If this is the case it will be sheer joy for amusement park and roller coaster buffs. The 1893 Midway for the Columbian Exposition, after all, was the first of its kind and model for future amusement parks, particularly Coney Island. It introduced many innovative rides including the Ferris Wheel, lent the name White City to amusement parks over the world, and was one of the most influential fairs ever built.

This is ironic for it was the intention of the founders of the Columbian Exposition to create a new cultural renaissance. Built to celebrate the four-hundredth anniversary of the discovery of America, the Exposition's architects hoped to form a White City, a neoclassic dream, to uplift the character and taste of America. It was to be an ideal city of marble displaying the loftier achievements of American society, pointing the way to civic virtue and worthy aesthetic and ethical goals. True, the marble was counterfeit, but the intentions were noble, at least according to a select committee of officials, artists, and architects.

The Midway where "amusements were trumpeted" was an embarrasment to the founders. This carnival complex was pushed to a corner of the grounds where it would not compete with cultural strivings. It was grudgingly displayed across the railway that split the park, possibly where the term "the other side of the tracks" originated. Although thoroughly American in character, it was given the French title *Midway Plaisance (Midway of Pleasure)*.

Pleasure is not what the founders had in mind, but the Midway became a perfect outlet. Its "Barnumesque" crudeness and vitality seemed to be what culturally exhausted patrons wanted. It was an immense success. Some of the Midway's attractions included the sixty shops of the "Streets of Cairo," a Moorish palace, a Chinese village, North African belly dancers in the Algerian and Egyptian theatres, a preview of motion pictures, Jim Corbett demonstrating how he defeated John L. Sullivan, a captive balloon ride and "Little Egypt" performing the "hootchy-kootchy."

The fair is well remembered for its rides. When boats docked at Casino Pier on Lake Michigan, passengers were met by a *Movable Sidewalk* (fig. IV: 19, 20) that carried them the length of the pier. The ride was quite slow but a worthy introduction to the Exposition. One of the first sights at the end of the

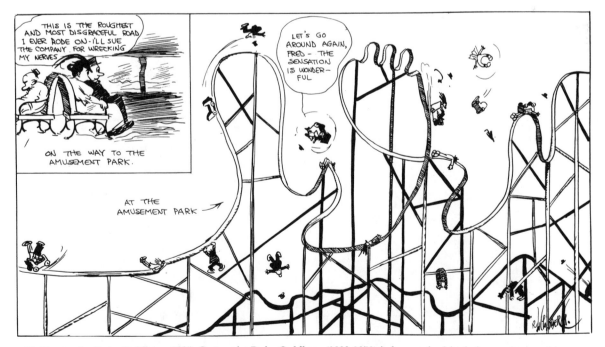

(IV: 18) Cartoon by Rube Goldberg. 1925. Cartoonist Rube Goldberg (1883-1970) is famous for his chain reaction machines that, after long periods of complicated performance, accomplish very little. The name *Rube Goldberg* appears in many dictionaries as a term for nonsensical machinery.

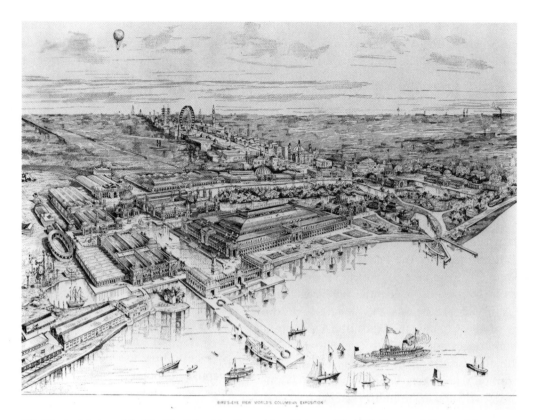

(IV: 19).  Aerial view of the World's Columbian Exposition. Chicago, Ill., 1893. Courtesy Library of Congress.

(IV: 20).  *Movable Sidewalk*. World's Columbian Exposition. Chicago, Ill., 1893. Courtesy Chicago Historical Society.

*Movable Sidewalk* was the Ferris Wheel towering above all across the park (fig. IV: 21). It was perhaps the world's first big ride. The Ferris Wheel resembled a giant bicycle wheel with a diameter of 250 feet, a total height of 264 feet, and a weight of 2,807,498 pounds. Each of the 36 cars accommodated 60 passengers.

The giant wheel by engineer George Washington Gale Ferris served the same promotional purposes as Eiffel's tower at the Universal Exposition, at Paris, in 1889.

Almost lost in the shadow of the Ferris Wheel was Thomas Rankin's *Snow and Ice Railway* (fig. IV: 22). The ride was described as follows:

October 19th 1892, a contract was entered into with John C. De La Vergne and Thomas L. Rankin to set apart to them a tract of land 60 x 400 feet in dimension upon the southernly portion of the Midway Plaisance near Lexington Avenue for the purpose of constructing a snow and ice railway and the necessary machinery for making artificially the snow and ice necessary to operate the same. As completed this railway was built upon a loop having one point of high elevation, the surface of the run-way being covered with artificial ice. There were two trains of four bob sleds each, capable of seating six people in each sled. These trains were drawn by a cable to the high point and then liberated and allowed to slide down the inclines. They afforded much pleasure to the patrons and became quite popular.[2]

(IV: 21) Ferris Wheel. World's Columbian Exposition. Chicago, Ill., 1893. Courtesy Library of Congress.

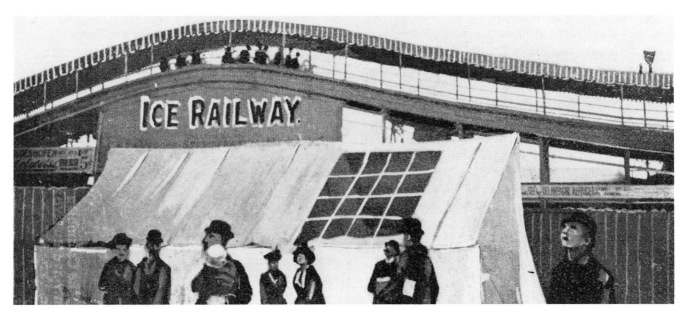

(IV: 22). *Snow and Ice Railway.* World's Columbian Exposition. Chicago, Ill., 1893. Courtesy Chicago Historical Society.

The idea of this ice roller coaster was not lost on Norman Barlett when he developed his famous *Flying Turns* in Dayton, Ohio, nearly three decades later.

At the close of the Fair the *Snow and Ice Railway* was moved to Coney Island in Brooklyn, but direct sunlight and insufficient refrigeration quickly closed the ride. It was not the first idea to be duplicated from Chicago at Coney Island. It would seem that if certain entrepreneurs had their way, the complete Midway Plaisance would have been moved to Brooklyn. Fortunately, other farsighted showmen had their own ideas.

### Coney Island

Coney Island, Brooklyn, from the early 1880's into the 1920's was the great testing ground for roller coasters. One Coney Island old-timer referred to the coasters during this era as, "Weeds that popped up as fast as we tore them down." It's impossible to give a detailed description, that would require an encyclopedia, but Coney Island and its roller coasters are a constant in this book and some background is immediately necessary on this dazzling string of parks that made Surf Avenue famous.

One of the starting points was 1884 when pioneer La Marcus Thompson installed the Switchback discussed in Chapter III. Another starting point was 1893 when George Tilyou, the founder of Steeplechase Park and probably the most influential figure in the history of Coney Island, visited the Columbian Exposition during his honeymoon. He immediately realized the potential of the Midway and even offered to buy the Ferris Wheel. When he was told it had been purchased for use at the St. Louis World's Fair (1904), he ordered a much smaller version for Coney Island and in true amusement park fashion, put up a sign claiming, "On This Site Will be Erected the World's Largest Ferris Wheel."

Besides the Ferris Wheel, Tilyou had an Aerial Ride, imported an *Intramural Bicycle Railway,* and built a *Double Dip Chutes*. He haphazardly scattered the rides the length of Coney Island.

Captain Paul Boyton, the first frogman and celebrated swimmer of the English Channel, opened an enclosed Sea Lion Park in 1895. Often called America's first amusement park, it had 40 trained seals and several water rides, including the *Shoot-the-Chutes* (fig.IV:23,24) that later became the center of Luna Park. Situated on Sea Lion Park's lagoon was the *Flip-Flap Coaster,* the Loop-the-Loop's first

relative to appear in nearly thirty years (see Chapter VI).

It was not the *Flip-Flap Coaster* that intrigued George Tilyou, however. Tilyou seized upon Boyton's idea of an enclosed park with admission charged at the gate, and immediately started looking for a sure-fire revenue producing ride. He watched with interest the huge crowds at the nearby horse tracks and when he stumbled on a British mechanical race course, an invention by J.W. Cawdry, he knew he had found his ride. After some tinkering, he installed an undulant, curving racetrack over which metal horses ran on wheels sped by gravity (fig. IV:25-27). With the addition of a huge fun warehouse and more spectacular rides, the complex became known as Steeplechase Park and the real beginning of the Coney Island boom. The park opened in 1897.

A visit to the 1901 Pan-American Exposition in Buffalo brought Tilyou his next sensation. *Trip to the Moon* was the fair's money card and one of the first Illusion Rides. Patrons entered a high ceilinged room and boarded an airship housing 30 passengers. Lights were dimmed and the ship was manually rocked and swayed to stimulate a trip to the moon. A spectacular light show took place outside the portholes with scenes of flying over the Fair and Niagara Falls complete with an electrical storm. The landing included a tour of the moon with souvenir chunks of cheese given out by moon midgets. The ride was very convincing, and some passengers actually fainted.

Tilyou brought the ride and its inventor Frederic Thompson with partner Skip Dundy to Steeplechase only to see them leave a year later (1903) to develop their own competitive park nearby. Thompson and Dundy purchased Boyton's Sea Lion Park and established one of the most amazing amusement centers ever built, Luna Park (fig.IV:28-30). It was a magical Oriental-Moroccan-Renaissance plaster extravaganza of spires and minarets and, with the addition of 500,000 light bulbs, Luna's candy colored buildings became an iridescent fairyland at night. "Ah God," said one hypnotized visitor, "what might the Prophet have written in Revelations, if only he had first beheld a spectacle like this!"

Immediately competitors appeared. Luna Park was so spectacular that real-estate tycoon William Reynolds spent $3½ million to build Dreamland park directly across Surf Avenue in 1904. Everything was to be on a grander scale (fig.IV:31). Wedding-

(IV: 23). Sea Lion Park. Brooklyn, N.Y., 1895. Often called America's first amusement park, it was created by Captain Paul Boyton. The park housed both the *Flip Flap Coaster* and a Shoot-the-Chutes that later became the center of Luna Park. Courtesy James A. Kelley Historical Studies Institute.

(IV:24). Sea Lion Park, Brooklyn, N.Y. 1895. Poster from the Library of Congress.

(IV: 25). Steeplechase Park. Brooklyn, N.Y. 1897. George Tilyou's Park featured an undulant, curving racetrack over which metal horses ran on wheels sped by gravity. Artist: Leo McKay. Courtesy Museum of the City of New York.

(IV: 26). Steeplechase Park. Brooklyn N.Y. 1923. Courtesy James A. Kelley Historical Studies Institute.

(IV: 27). Steeplechase Park. Brooklyn, N.Y. 1942. Courtesy Brooklyn Library.

(IV: 28). *Luna Park*. Oil on canvas, 24"x36", 1972. Folk artist Vestie Davis (1903-1978) was a chronicler of Luna Park and other Brooklyn scenes. His paintings of Coney Island's *Cyclone* (see fig. IX:13) are among the finest roller coasters. Davis' work hangs in museums throughout the country and is collected world wide. Courtesy Hundred Acres Gallery, New York. Photographer: Eric Politzer.

(IV: 29, 30). Luna Park. Brooklyn, N.Y. 1903. Thompson and Dundy's Magical Oriental-Morrocan-Renaissance Extravaganza was one of the most spectacular amusement centers ever built. Both photographs are from Detroit Publishing Co. glass negatives in the Library of Congress collection.

cake white Dreamland doubled Luna's lights by brightening the skies with one-million light bulbs. One hundred thousand were used to accent the 375 foot tower which was freely translated from the tower at the Pan-American Exposition in Buffalo and the Giralda in Seville (fig.IV:32).

In 1900 a good-sized Sunday crowd at Coney Island was 100,000; by 1914 a hot Sunday pulled in one million. July 3, 1947, saw a record 2.5 million.

The "hot dog" first appeared at Coney Island. Charles Dickens claims it was the only place he liked in America. Houdini learned his trade here. Maxim Gorki wrote, "...Fabulous beyond conceiving, ineffably beautiful..."[3] George Burns, Irving Berlin, and many others first appeared at the Beer Gardens here. Coney Island was the entertainment mecca of the world.

(IV: 31, 32). Dreamland, Brooklyn, N.Y. 1904. William Reynolds used one million light bulbs at his park. The tower was modeled from the Giralda in Seville, Spain, and the tower at the Pan-American Exposition, Buffalo, N.Y. Both photographs are from Detroit Publishing Co. glass negatives in the Library of Congress collection.

# *Chapter V*
# The Haverhill Three

Coaster buffs will argue into the late hours over the origin of the term "roller coaster." The label was never applied to early European rides. The most popular explanation comes from historian William F. Mangels who believes the term is derived from gravity rides of the early 1880's that used a conveyor system with large rollers beneath the belt. John Allen, the great coaster designer of the Philadelphia Toboggan Company, believes the term comes from the Hyatt Roller Bearing Company, an early manufacturer of roller coasters. There is much evidence, however, that the phrase originated in an unlikely spot in northern New England, the birthplace of John Greenleaf Whittier, Haverhill, Massachusetts.

A ride was built in this quiet, religious community that competes with the most fanciful efforts of Coney Island. The device called a *Sliding-Hill and*

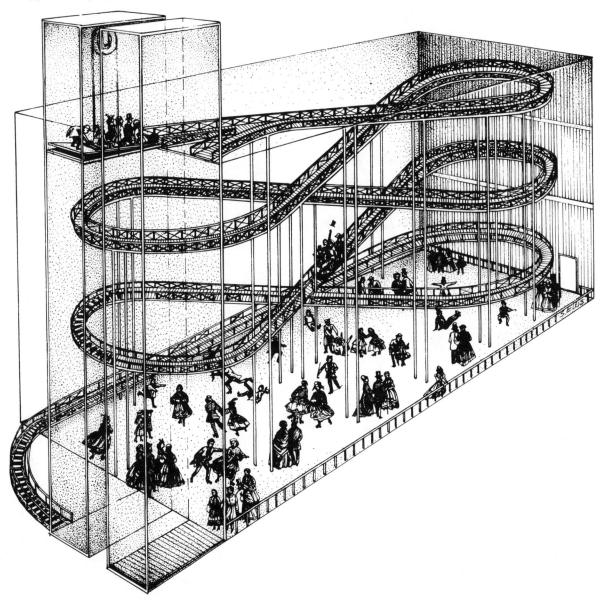

(V: 1) *Sliding-Hill and Toboggan.* Haverhill, Mass., 1887-1890. Artist Sharon Ellis, by studying patents and other descriptions, has depicted the *Sliding-Hill and Toboggan* in line, pen and ink. This perspective drawing is the only known picture of the Haverhill ride. It is argued that, because cars truly coasted on hundreds of rollers, the *Sliding-Hill and Toboggan* is the source of the term "roller coaster." Tracks spiraled in figure eight fashion above an ice-skating rink. (For graphic reasons the Hoosac Tunnel has been omitted.)

*Toboggan* (fig.VII:2) was built around the inner walls of a skating rink on the third floor of a brick building. The 1500 foot tracks ran around the walls from ceiling to floor criss-crossing the rink in a spiraling figure eight formation. The opening was a gala event. The *Haverhill Daily Bulletin* of September 12, 1887, gives the following description:

> The Haverhill Roller Toboggan Chute was formally opened to the public on Wednesday evening and was a grand treat to an immense crowd. As soon as the doors of the Globe Rink were opened, the people, including many visitors from out of town, streamed in and looked upon one of the greatest inventions of the times and one that has every promise of becoming the most popular amusement of its day. The rink was brilliantly illuminated and handsomely decorated and everything about the place was attractive. A band of music discoursed enlivening strains and the spectators were wrapped up in enthusiasm. It was a sight seldom seen here. There were large groups in every part of the rink and everybody was in the height of enjoyment. The floor surface was covered with skaters who glided to and fro while the toboggan chute was sought by everybody. The cars were kept in constant motion and interest was intense. A big crowd surrounded the starting elevators and all were excited over the event of the ride.... The elevators alternated, one carrying up a load and the other returning for one at the same time. Arriving at the head, the car with its occupants is slid onto the tracks and glides swiftly into the first bend which has been named 'Niagara Falls.'
>
> ...It was with considerable fear and trembling that three *Daily Bulletin* reporters stepped onto a toboggan which rested on the wooden roadbed and were rolled by the inventor, Mr. Floyd and his assistant, onto the platform of an elevator which was lifted to the roof of the building. The moment the elevator platform strikes the top, the cars begin their perilous journey. On the Niagara Falls drop the newspaper men claimed that they were for once deprived of speech or motion and when a moment after the car darted into a tunnel named Hoosac Tunnel, the top of which seemed about level with the breast of the riders, their discomfiture was completed, and it was a thoroughly frightened set of men who finally rolled up to the very spot from whence they started having gone through three times around the rink in just one minute from the time of starting. The ride although fearful was so exciting that it had to be tried again and so much were the reporters delighted with their sensations that they could hardly get sliding enough and during a short hour they must have made the descent at least ten times and if their experience proves anything the roller toboggan will be the prize of the winter.
>
> Admission     15ᶜ
> Skate checks 10ᶜ
> Skate owners   5ᶜ
> Sliding checks 5ᶜ or 6 for 25ᶜ[1]

Pictures do not seem to exist of the *Roller Toboggan*. Artist Sharon Ellis, working from newspaper reports and the original patent (#374,736, Dec. 13, 1887), has put together a remarkable pen and ink drawing especially commissioned for the book (fig.V:1).

Stephen E. Jackman and Byron B. Floyd were the patentees of the *Roller Toboggan* (fig.V:1). Both claimed not only the coinage of the phrase "roller coaster" but the invention of the coaster itself, overlooking the early European rides and the American patents of J.G. Taylor (1872), Richard Knudsen (1876), Alexander (1882), Hinkle, Alcoke, and L.A. Thompson. On the other hand, Jackman and Floyd had grounds for their claim. Their ride more accurately fit the term "roller coaster" than previous gravity rides. Hundreds of wheels were located on their tracks and the cars tobogganed the entire run. The passengers truly coasted on rollers.

On January 16, 1888, Jackman and Floyd joined inventor Ezra F. Merrill of Stratford, New Hampshire, to form the Haverhill Toboggan Company, a group that was later called the Haverhill Three. The ride and Globe Skating Rink barely lasted three years but was such a success that similar devices were installed in Minneapolis, St. Paul, Oshkosh, Milwaukee, Cincinnati, Pawtucket (R.I.), Brooklyn, Philadelphia, Salem, and Salisbury Beach (Mass.). On July 13, 1888, the most spectacular ride was installed at the Princess Rink in Cincinnati at the cost of $31,000 on a site where bicycles set speed records and the famous Cardiff/Sullivan fight was staged. It was one of the first buildings to have its own engines and dynamos to power the rink's thousands of electric lights.

All the toboggans were immensely popular but rivalries developed among the Haverhill Three, and on December 7, 1888, S.E. Jackman sold his share of the toboggan company and purchased interest in a coal business. Jackman later built many roller coasters over the world (fig.V:2) and realized a fortune from his inventions before retiring to St. Petersburg, Florida.

A number of accidents occurred on the Haverhill ride and its popularity seriously declined. A headline story in the *Haverhill Daily Bulletin* of December 26, 1888, reads:

> A roller toboggan in motion is a bad thing to fool in. Many accidents have been recorded heretofore but yesterday occurred one which bid fare to prove a serious one. A young man, while being carried swiftly around the rink, when just opposite the skate room door, attempted to stand up in the car and step from one seat to the other. The car was going with such force that he was flung headlong from the seat and was hurled violently into the skate room, where he landed on the floor. Had the skate room door been closed, instant death might have occurred. A young man standing in the door narrowly escaped injury by being hit by the flying youth.[2]

On September 10, 1889, B.B. Floyd sued E.F. Merrill claiming that much money was made from the business but "he scarcely got a cent." Floyd later received $80,000 from the case.

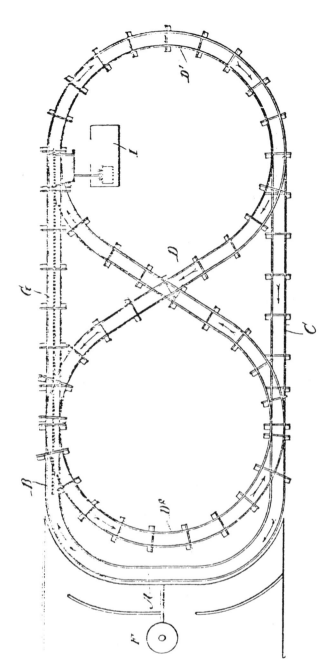

(V: 2). 1903. *Pleasure Railway* patent of Stephen E. Jackman. The patent represents one of many in the career of Jackman who retired to Florida a millionaire.

B.B. Floyd, outside of a few important patents, will probably be remembered for a ride that was never built. The *Rompo Frolique* poster (fig. V:3) was discovered in the Chicago Historical Society collection. The name *Rompo Frolique* has been used for several minor rides but not a trace of this clanking apparatus has been found. Close study reveals the erratic but brilliant imagination of B.B. Floyd, pictured in the rop left corner of the poster (fig. V:4), and why the *Rompo Frolique* best symbolizes that

improbable era at the end of the 19th century.

The Globe Skating Rink was demolished on February 21, 1890, and a seven story factory called the Winchell Building was erected on its site. The building still stands on Locust Street in Haverhill.

By the end of the century, the Patent Office was swamped with bizarre and wondrous devices from many inventors. The opening decades of the new century supplied some of the finest rides ever built.

(V: 3). B.B. Floyd's *Rompo Frolique*. Lithograph by Breuker and Kessler Co., Philadelphia, (n.d.). This fanciful creation of Byron B. Floyd was, regretably, never built. Courtesy Chicago Historical Society.

(V: 4). Portrait of Byron B. Floyd from the *Rompo Frolique* poster. Courtesy Chicago Historical Society.

# Chapter VI
## 1900-1920:
## Defying Gravity—Trial and Error

It was the age of experimentation, the beginning of a new century, and it lasted until World War I. The skies were dotted with innovative gliders and kites. The Wright brothers in 1903 quietly launched the Age of Flight. Painting was rocked to its foundations by Picasso, Braque, and Cubism. All was seen through new eyes and nothing was taken for granted.

Albert Einstein developed his General Theory of Relativity in 1915, crumbling our ways of looking at the Universe. Einstein was fascinated by elevators and roller coasters and the idea of being transported from one place to another. He even used the roller coaster as an example of "energy conversions in a mechanical system" in his *Evolution of Physics* (1961).[1]

Adventure and instability were keys to the new century, and the roller coaster was swept along in this age of experimentation. Perhaps "Age of Trial and Error" is the proper term judging by the deluge of amusement park inventions that filled the Patent Office (fig.VI:1,2). Many patents were sound and far-reaching, but as many ideas were simply treacherous. It is a blessing some never left the drawing boards or, when built, were closed by lawsuits. Every deviation with tracks was attempted and the eventual safety codes or inspections by insurance companies became beneficial restraints.

Speed, boldness, and recklessness were part of the era, and designers, by necessity, had to update their rides to mirror the times. Roller coasters and Scenic Railways at the beginning of the century were extremely slow. Some never exceeded 6 miles per hour. The best illustration of the speed of these early rides was given by W. Earl Austen when interviewed at Conneaut Lake, Pennsylvania, in 1973:

> ...We had brakemen on the rides, yeah, and I was one of them. There were only a couple of places you could stop on the ride though. One was up the hills. It wouldn't do any good going down. The other was around sharp curves....You had to get off every once in awhile. I ran the thing until I would actually find myself falling asleep. Dozens of times I've eaten sandwiches on them. They'd hand us coffee or something on the way up.[2]

The speeds were so slow that the Patent Office classified roller coasters "Pleasure Railways," a perfectly adequate term for a ride as in figure VI:3.

(VI: 1). A hand propelled unicycle. 1902. This engraving well exemplifies the bizarre rides entering the Patent Office at the turn of the century. Courtesy Frederick Fried Archives.

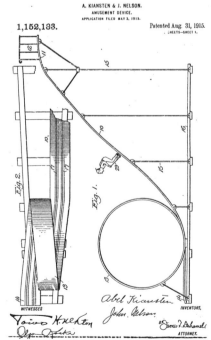

(VI:2). Amusement Device patent by Abel Kiansten and John Nelson. 1915. It is not known if this roller skate "loop-the-loop" was ever built. The patent states the inventors were "...subjects of the Czar of Russia and residents of New York."

(VI: 3). *Pleasure Railway at Hoboken.* Hoboken, New Jersey, 1835. Lithograph.
Courtesy Library of Congress.

By 1910 the term became amusing. By the 1920's it was ludicrous. The Patent Office still classifies roller coasters "Pleasure Railways," a term that remains bewildering to coaster inventors and researchers alike.

To survive roller coasters obviously needed to increase their speeds to compete with new inventions, such as the automobile, that were becoming more and more available to the public. But, as designers soon observed, safety and the restrictions such standards imposed, had to be considered. These obstacles proved to be a plus. Limitations always lead to great inventions and this proved true with roller coasters. John Miller, by considering safety, opened the door to more thrills and speed and transformed the industry through his remarkable patents. (see Chapter VIII)

Besides speed, more thrills were needed, and showmen stalked many outside ideas. The roller coaster would seem to be a self-contained thrill-machine not needing outside inspiration. It became that in the 1920's; that is, it was not necessary to look to other ideas when the roller coaster was finally deemed the supreme thrill ride.

Before that time, inventors freely borrowed from any source that would produce a better ride. The circus is one case in point. Engineer Andy Brown was first to underline this during a 1973 interview. The circus was the proving ground for acrobatic stunts and often used bizarre equipment to perform flips, somersaults, dives, soaring flights, jumps, cannon shots, and high wire acts (fig. VI:4-7). The stunts were often heralded in full-page newspaper ads across the country and to patrons these truly dangerous exploits appeared to be the ultimate in thrills and foolhardiness.

When it was decided the roller coaster was not a scenic tour, park owners wanted in heavy doses the aura of the circus daredevil. Anything from the big top was now fair game.

The combination of roller coaster and circus stunts was a profitable one leading to hundreds of patents into the 1920's. Patrons were thrilled. "Show the customer that he can be a circus acrobat without getting hurt," said Andy Brown, "and they'll line up for hours at the ticket booth dollars in hand."[3]

The top of the daredevil list at the beginning of the century belonged to flight. The beauty of pretending to be a bird — this was the supreme act of risk taking, and the roller coaster offered every opportunity to perform this wondrous act.

Since we crept from dark caves, perhaps the most consistent dream over the centuries has been that of flying. Many nights have been glorified with the thought of effortlessly gliding through soft breezes above all, and the dream has been a favorite subject of psychoanalysts with their various sexual interpretations. What an opportunity for roller coasters!

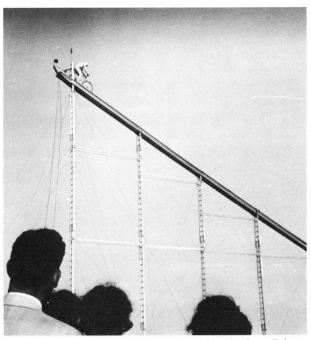

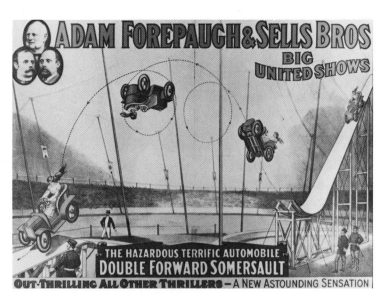

(VI: 6). *Double Forward Automobile Somersault.* Adam Forepaugh and Sells Brothers circus poster. (n.d.), Courtesy New York State Museum, Albany, N.Y.

(VI: 4).Daredevil plunges into water on bicycle. State Fair, Donaldsville, La., (n.d.). Courtesy Library of Congress.

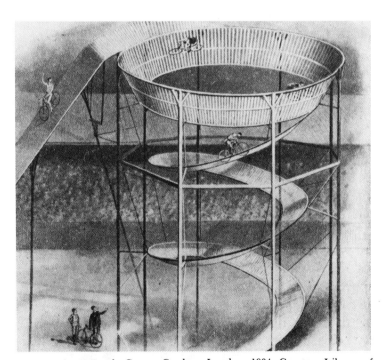

(VI: 7). *Circle of Death.* Covent Gardens, London, 1904. Courtesy Library of Congress.

(VI: 5). *The Mysterious Sphere.* Strobridge Litho Co. circus poster, 1898. The Barnum and Bailey circus program notes, "*The Mysterious Sphere*—ascending and descending the novel spiral incline without visible means, when at the apex discharging a pistol and waving 'old glory,' and when reaching the platform bursting asunder, thus disclosing the secret of the hidden and mysterious motive power, Leon La Roche." Courtesy Margaret Woodbury Strong Museum.

Indeed, flying is one of the reasons persistently given when passengers are asked why they ride a coaster.

Flight was at the height of popularity from 1900 to 1920. Kites and gliders were being tested world wide. Alexander Graham Bell was experimenting with box kites the size of garages. The Wright Brothers successfully flew their *Flyer* December 17, 1903, although they were not universally believed until 1908.

Amusement parks too were caught in the flight craze. Airplane swings and other aerial devices were among the most popular rides (fig. VI:8) culminating in Frederick Church's 1928 *Airplane Coaster* at Rye Beach, New York, which is still considered by many, the finest roller coaster ever built.

One of the most fortunate events in my life was living near Orville Wright in Oakwood, Ohio. Although very young, I was able to occasionally visit him and was delighted that he and third brother, Lorin, designed toys. We talked about roller coasters and Orville was very interested in them, although they had little bearing on their flights, with the exception of the monorail track that launched the early planes. A more detailed account of these visits is included in Appendix IV.

Charles Lindbergh was always a favorite for roller coaster quotes since he actually worked at an amusement park early in his career. One of the favorite tales is that he was riding the Coney Island *Cyclone* before his famous Transatlantic flight. It's a good story but sadly not ture. Lindbergh crossed the Atlantic May 20, 1927. The Coney Island *Cyclone* opened June 26, 1927.

One of the all-time roller coaster quotes is Lindbergh's "A ride on the *Cyclone* is a greater thrill than flying an airplane at top speed." Whether he actually made this often quoted statement is not known, but there is evidence he enjoyed many rides on the *Cyclone.*

Harry Traver (Chapter X) was an early and avid fan of gyroplanes and flight itself. Perhaps this interest was the seed of the vicious *Cyclones* he built in the 1920's.

Circus and flight are but two sources designers used to improve roller coasters. Not everything was this calculated, however, for it was an age of masterly improvisation. John Allen, Andy Brown, and Aurel Vaszin all commented on how quickly roller coasters were built and designed. Andy Brown mentioned, perhaps tongue-in-cheek, of finishing a ride in one week before heading for the next town and another roller coaster. The record for construction has to belong to the Fred Pearce Company. One half of the Excelsior Park *Cyclone,* Minnesota, was demolished by a windstorm with tracks spilled sideways on the road. It was wrecked at 4:30 p.m., August 1, and was operating by 9:45 p.m., August 4th.

(VI: 8). *Gyroplane.* Luna Park, Brooklyn, N.Y., 1917. Courtesy Library of Congress.

Another repeating thought in the Allen, Brown, Vaszin interviews was the lack of any scientific approach in building roller coasters during this time. All stressed that designers worked from experience, not parabolas or measurements of g.-forces. They said cars with sandbags were sent out when the coaster was finished. If it didn't come back they'd make a hill higher or change a curve. The attitude was improvisation rather than blueprinted accuracy.

### Illusion

Since it was impossible for customers to actually fly at parks without danger, every trick of the trade was used to duplicate flight, aerial acts, bicycle jumps, and other stunts. Rides more and more came to rely on a word from the popular magic acts of the time, illusion.

Alfred Pitzer's *Haunted Swing* (fig.VI:9) of 1909 is typical of the illusion that parks were now seeking. A large swing was hung from a bar extending across a room near the ceiling. Passengers felt the swing gently rocking back and forth, increasing in fury until the ride completely somersaulted. Actually the swing barely moved. It was the room with furniture glued to the floor that was being rocked and turned upside-down. It worked. Passengers grabbed anything and everyone in sight to keep from falling.

Illusion, or deception, made everything possible at amusement parks and this applies with strength to roller coasters. Designers made the ride seem faster, scarier, and higher by planning the climb up the first hill to be intentionally slow. The car was allowed to dangle at the top to let passengers realize the height and think of the supposed terrors ahead. Then the open cars bulleted through a forest of trestles to provide the illusion of traveling 100 miles per hour. When momentum decreased, passengers were thrown in a curve to hide the loss of speed.

"You don't need a degree in engineering to design roller coasters," said John Allen, "you need a degree in psychology—plus courage. A roller coaster is as theatrically contrived as a Broadway play."[4] Frederick Thompson called it "Manufacturing the carnival experience," and it was that calculated. Illusion combined with new technology opened a showcase of unbelievable ideas. Parks from 1900-1920 transformed the commonplace into the extraordinary and became laboratories of the sometimes ridiculous.

Parodies of transportation continued. Although the bicycle craze was dying out by the beginning of

(VI: 9). Alfred Pitzer's *Haunted Swing*. 1909. At the turn of the century, illusion became a necessary part of rides. With the *Haunted Swing,* the room revolved while passengers remained stationary.

the century, more and more cycles were being used in circus stunts. Attempts were made to use bicycles at parks (fig.VI:10,11). A few succeeded, but they were not popular because riders had to generate the power. One example was a foot-propelled contraption called the *Hotchkiss Bicycle Railroad* located in Smithville, New Jersey. It was a grooved monorail where cycles were hung. Four passengers pedaled the 10 minute trip from the outskirts of Mount Holly to the center of Smithville. It was a favorite Sunday excursion for young couples but closed in 1898.

Edwin Prescott, the builder of Coney Island's 1904 *Loop-the-Loop,* patented a ghastly loop-the-loop for bicycles (Oct. 28, 1902, #712,407). It is not known if the ride was built.

It was also the era of the automobile and everyone wanted to drive. In 1906 A.G. Neville used imitation automobiles on a roller coaster at Coney Island.

A.G. Reynolds installed an *Auto Maze* at the same park in 1912. Through an ingenious chain system passengers were guided along tracks where cars crisscrossed barely avoiding collisions. To heighten apprehension and add to the rider's bewilderment, mirrors housed the entire course. The ride closed when crucial mechanisms failed and real smash-ups took place.

(VI: 10).  James Bancroft's *Flying Velocipede*. Patent, 1882.

(VI: 11).  *Racing Wheels*. Specifics not given, 1890s. Courtesy Frederick Fried Archives.

Collisions soon became intentional as exemplified by Bumper or Dodgem Cars. Probably the masterpiece of the collision type roller coaster was W.J. Mangels's *Tickler* (fig. VI:12). It amounted to a giant pinball machine with swivel-wheeled circular cars as balls. After being hauled by chain to the top of an inclined platform, the cars rolled downward, bashing against and spinning around posts. In many versions, cars collided. Some of the biggest crowds stood outside its unloading platform to watch entangled, disheveled, and sometimes angry customers.

Other devices were content to follow tracks while the cars spun in different directions either mechanically or by the whims of gravity and centrifugal force (fig. VI:13-15). One of the strangest was the *Hooper-Reverser* in Salt Lake City (fig. VI:16,17). It was a straightforward, legitimate roller coaster until the rear wheels swiveled out and around on tracks of their own. Passengers then rode sections backward until the next spin-about. Riders were never sure which way they would face during the run since there were several turning points.

The innocent slides of the 19th century continued but gradually turned into the most sinous drops inventors, probably influenced by the circus, could devise (fig. VI:18-21). The *Mystic Screw* (fig. VI:22) lifted passengers inside a huge rotating screw 18 feet in diameter. They spiraled to the top in the dark only to have their cars deposited on what seemed to be another ride 100 feet above the ground. Passengers then followed a swift journey to the bottom on one of three sets of tracks. The 75-foot screw was authentic in detail including even a slot for a giant screwdriver at the top.

### Third Railers

Perhaps the most devastating ride parodied the mechanism of subways. Many consider Third Railers the most frightening roller coasters ever built and there is good reason for this. In addition to unprecedented hills and curves, Third Railers claim the worst safety record of any ride in history.

The track system resembled a subway with power from a central third rail (fig. VI:23). Misfortune started here. One foot on the power rail with the other grounding an outside track totaled the electric chair. If the power switch was not closed, track walking for structural flaws on a Third Railer could be a deadly experience. Several grim newspaper reports proved just that.

Imagine driving a roller coaster. Any wish would

(VI: 12). *The Tickler.* 1906. William F. Mangels's ride was a giant pinball machine with cars colliding posts and, often, other cars. From the reprint of the *William Mangels Carousell Works* catalogue. Courtesy Vestal Press.

(VI: 13). *Virginia Reel.* Revere Beach, Mass., c. 1915.

(VI: 14). *Cyclone Bowls.* Site not specified, c. 1922. A mechanical arm-beam pushed passengers along and up one spiral where it was sped into another bowl and cars descended on a "...precipitious whirlpool of delirious motion."

(VI: 15). *Scenic Spiral Wheel.* Luna Park, Brooklyn, N.Y., 1917. Courtesy Frederick Fried Archives.

(VI:16,17). *Hooper Reverser.* Saltair Park, Salt Lake City, Utah, 1923-? Its cars not only quickly sped along tracks but revolved blindly on turntables at uncomfortable moments. fig. VI:17 reveals the ingenious track mechanism that made such reversals possible. Courtesy Frederick Fried Archives.

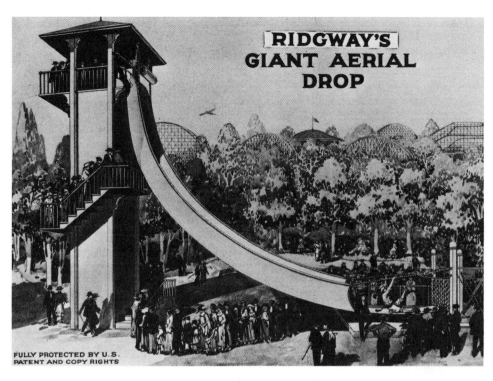

(VI: 18). *Ridgway's Giant Aerial Drop.* 1923. Passengers from a perch 35 feet high slid almost vertically before leveling out and a crash into spring braced rubber and leather cushions. The Ridgway catalogue calls it safe as a feather bed and notes two in operation at The Pit, Boston, Mass.

(VI: 19). Jack and Jill. Site not specified, 1922. Passengers were mechanically dumped from their cars at the top onto a slide and a swift descent home.

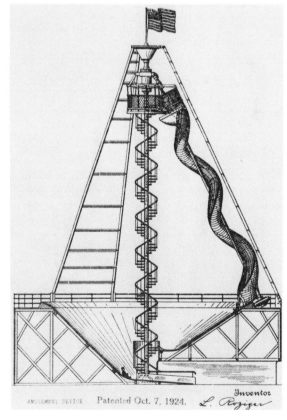

(VI: 20). L. Roziger Amusement Slide Patent. 1924.

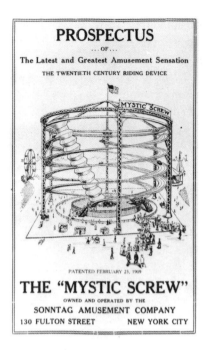

(VI: 22). The Mystic Screw. 1909. Passengers traveled to the top inside a screw then descended on spiraling tracks. Courtesy Frederick Fried Archives.

(VI: 21). *High Boy* slide, Ocean Park, Calif., 1920's. Courtesy Los Angeles Public Library and Jim Payer.

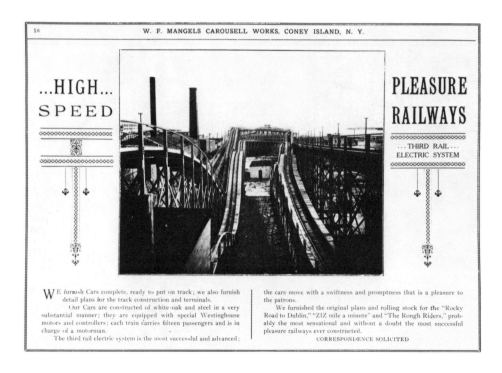

(VI: 23). The W.F. Mangels's catalogue lists the *Rocky Road to Dublin, ZIZ Mile Minute,* and *The Rough Riders* (all Coney Island, Brooklyn, N.Y.) as Third Railers. From the reprint of the *William Mangels Carousell Works* catalogue. Courtesy Vestal Press.

be granted. You could make it slow or deadly fast. If you wished a back curve at full speed, it was in your hands—as was the fate of other passengers. This was the principle of the Third Railer. A motorman piloted the coaster from the front seat with speed controlled by a central lever. When moved to the left, the cars rolled forward; when to the right, the cars rolled backward. The lever was also the braking system. If cars needed brakes around a hair-pin curve, the lever was moved several notches to the right (reverse). If cars were going backward, several notches to the left slowed the ride.

The most notorious Third Railer was at Fort George amusement park above the Harlem River in New York City (fig. VI:24). Cars started at the top and ran maneuvers down the cliffs with plunges to the valley floor. Figure-eights and zig-zags were thrown in and electric motors provided the traction to regain the starting point.

According to the late Commander E.J. Quinby, some of the motormen were maniacs. Where instructed to coast over certain hills and curves, they often used full power. Passengers were scared witless. Some actually plummeted to the valley below

causing massive lawsuits.

A 1911 fire closed the park before bankruptcy. The Third Railer with its protected position along the cliffs was not harmed. It was dismantled and reassembled at Palisades Park in Fort Lee, New Jersey. This time the ride towered above the cliffs giving patrons an incomparable view of the Hudson and a shuddering glimpse of the valley below. Mishaps continued, including a near collision with a dirigible that landed in desperation on the top tracks to keep from sailing into the river.

A rookie motorman accidentally threw cars into reverse atop the steepest hill of *Rocky Road to Dublin*, Coney Island. A senior motorman, through great skill and courage, calmed screaming passengers, rocked the cars back and forth between hills, and barely avoided disaster. Motormen drew straws to see who would make the first run on a Third Railer. E.J. Quinby called it "Russian Roulette."

- - - - -

The endurance of riders was being tested. Never before had nerves been so rattled for a fee; never had

829     HARLEM RIVER AND FORT GEORGE, NEW YORK.

(VI: 24). The Third Railer at Fort George, New York, N.Y., c. 1906. The ride ran up and down precipitous cliff sides. Courtesy B. Derek Shaw.

passengers been so dumped and scrambled. It was curtain-raising time for the ultimate illusion to reappear, *defying gravity,* and it came in the form of the *Flip-Flap.* Little had been done with somersaulting loops since 1848, and it was probably the circus again that prompted the idea.

Controversy shrouds who was responsible for the success of this invention particularly when dates of patents are followed. Lina Beecher invented, or reinvented, a looping machine in 1888 and tested the device in Toledo, Ohio. In 1895 he installed the results at Boyton's Sea Lion Park in Brooklyn under the name *Flip-Flap* (fig. VI:25). The cars seated 2

passengers and ran from a hill through a vertical loop at its base.

The ride had a flaw. It snapped passenger's necks. The *Flip-Flap's* 25 foot loop was too small to use a true circle. Seventy years later, parks were able to build 90 foot loops and run true circles, but in 1889 such technology was not available. Interest quickly dwindled and the *Flip-Flap* was dismantled before Luna Park took over the site in 1903. Interest in a somersaulting coaster remained high, however.

The *Loop-the-Loop,* erected by Edwin Prescott, opened in 1901 on West Tenth Avenue, Coney Island (fig. VI:26). It used the ellipse, thereby eliminating

(VI: 25). *Flip Flap.* Boyton's Sea Lion Park, Brooklyn, N.Y., 1889. It was the first centrifugal railway since the 1846 version in Paris. Courtesy Brooklyn Library.

(VI: 26). *Loop the Loop.* Coney Island, Brooklyn, N.Y., 1901. Edwin Prescott's ride used an ellipse rather than a circle to somersault riders. It produced a more comfortable ride but could not carry enough passengers to be profitable. Photograph from a Detroit Publishing Co. glass negative in the Library of Congress collection.

any strain on passenger's necks and bones. The ellipse was a breakthrough, but who was responsible? Credit is usually given to Edward A. Green's July 9, 1901, patent (#678,243). Yet Edwin Prescot's patent (#667,455), also using the ellipse, is dated February 5, 1901, five months before Green's. Green goes into more detail and provides precise diagrams and formulas. Inventor and historian W. F. Mangels says Prescott used Green's patent for his 1901 Coney Island ride.[5] But who knows? It remains a haunting question: Who really invented the ride that so dominates parks today and so often appears on TV commercials?

There were no harnesses like today's rides, yet the *Loop-the-Loop* claimed an amazing safety record. The cars had rubber wheels, carried four passengers, and used only centrifugal force to remain on the tracks, nothing else! Many advertisements claimed a glass of water on the *Loop-the-Loop's* seat made the trip without spilling a drop. It was one of the first rides to charge admission just to watch.

But it too had a flaw. Only four passengers per five minutes rode the Loop-the-Loop. Without consistent revenue, the former toast of Coney Island barely survived into World War I. Other rides opened in Buffalo, Chicago, Columbus, and Atlantic City but met the same fate.

There are many Loop-the-Loop patents besides Prescott and Green, including W.H. Bickford (Oct. 1, 1912, #1,040,125), an 1898 Prescott (#609,164) based on the circle, and a 1904 patent by *Flip-Flap's* Lina Beecher using the ellipse.

One ride that surfaced during this era was the Racing Coaster. Two trains on separate tracks raced side by side, usually splitting at a back curve and rejoining seconds later for a sprint to the unloading platform. Another type used a continuous circuit with cars crossing from inner track to outer track midway through the ride. The 1817 *Promenades Aeriennes,* Paris, (Chapter I) is considered the location of the first Racing Coaster, while J.A. Griffiths introduced the ride in the United States as the *Racing Dips* in 1895.

Unlike the Loop-the-Loop, the Racing Coaster was a great revenue producer. The formula was simple. Racers carried twice as many passengers as conventional coasters and, therefore, made twice the money. The principle remains true today; the Racing Coaster is a Board of Trustees favorite ride.

One of the most beautiful Racing Coasters was

produced by the Zarro Amusement Device Co. Ltd. (fig. VI:27) with machines, among others, at White City and Riverview in Chicago and Cincinnati's Coney Island.

By now artists and those with a discerning eye were finding roller coasters to be notable architecture. It is difficult to view John H. Brown's *Backety-Back Scenic Railroad,* Crystal Beach, Ontario, (fig. VI:28,29) as anything but extraordinarily beautiful. Roller coasters and amusement parks were now appearing in paintings and sculpture. Two examples are Joseph Stella's futuristic *Battle of Lights, Mardi Gras, Coney Island* (1913) with its multiple roller coaster arabesques and central Luna Tower (fig. VI:30); and Vladimir Tatlin's "coaster look alike" architecture, *Project for the Monument to the Third International* (1919-1920) (fig. VI:31). This Constructivist work was not intended by Tatlin as an amusement piece, but the proximity of Gorki Park,

THE ZARRO AMUSEMENT DEVICE CO. LTD.

RIDING DEVICES.

Coasters, Racing Coasters, Figure Eight's and Scenic Railways are attractions that can hold the public for hours at a time and are among the most popular of all park amusements. Business done by coasters each season in different parks run into five figures: At Riverview, Chicago, $85,000; at White City, Chicago, $80,000; at Holleywood, Baltimore, $45,000; at White City, Denver, $60,000; at Chester Park, Cincinnati, $40,000; at Coney Island, Cincinnati, $40,000; and so on without number. The merits of attractions of this kind have been demonstrated during the past seasons and the results will warrant the original outlay.

We build coasters on any scale, large or small, according to space that can be given same and the amount you desire to invest.

SYMPOSIUM.

"The structure of a coaster adds beauty to a park and arouses curiosity among its patrons." "Its popularity, its power of attracting the public to the park, and worth as a profitable investment are facts that cannot be controverted." "As a money maker it has no equal."

CAPACITY.

We equip coasters and scenic railways with the proper number of trains and cars to conform to the size and structure required and capacity is only limited by the ability of the ticket seller.

(VI: 27). Page from the Zarro Amusement Device Co. Ltd. catalogue depicting their elegant *Racing Coaster.* Courtesy Staples and Charles Ltd.

THE JOHN H. BROWN PATENT BACKETY-BACK RAILWAY.

AN INTERIOR VIEW OF THE MAMMOTH PAVILION ON BROWN'S BACKETY-BACK RAILWAY. THE CAR ABOVE IS JUST ENTERING THE PAVILION AT THE COMPLETION OF THE RIDE, AND TWO CARS ARE LOADED BELOW READY FOR THE START.

THE JOHN H. BROWN. PATENT BACKETY-BACK SCENIC RAILWAY

31

(VI: 30).   Joseph Stella, *Battle of Lights, Mardi Gras, Coney Island.* Oil on canvas, 75″x84″, 1913. Courtesy Yale University Art Gallery, Gift of Sociéte Anonyme.

(VI: 31).  Vladimir Tatlin, *Project for the Monument to the Third International.* Original model for tower, destroyed 1920; reconstructed by Arne Holm, Ulf Linde, Esil Nandorf, Per Olof Ultvedt, and Henrik Ostberg, 1967-68. Wood and metal with motor, 15′5″ high. Courtesy Moderna Museet, Stockholm, Sweden.

Moscow, to Tatlin's studio is telling. The final construction was meant to be 300 feet higher than the Eiffel Tower.

Toy manufacturers were now basing their models on amusement parks producing delightful carousels, Ferris Wheels, and even Scenic Railways. J. Chein and Company, Burlington, New Jersey, established a classic wind-up toy called #275 Roller Coaster based on a Figure-Eight (fig. VI:32).

Often toys were the influence. A toy led to the 1846 Loop-the-Loop (Chapter I), for instance, and Etienne Prost's 1925 *Roundabout* patent was obviously based on a common top (fig. VI:33). Perhaps the mechanical toys La Marcus Thompson designed and built as a child led to his 1884 Coney Island Switchback and later Scenic Railways.

A toy led to one of the most influential roller coasters ever built. In 1907 a ride opened at Jones Walk and the Bowery, Coney Island, that set new standards for ferocity. Old-timers still call it the best roller coaster ever built at Coney Island. Only 60 feet high, it was named *Drop-the-Dip,* later *Rough Riders,* and was designed and built by Christopher Feucht (fig. VI:34-36).

The story goes that Feucht built his *Drop-the-Dip* from a model he saw in his dentist's office. It was a roller coaster with all parts exaggerated, particularly the drops. The dentist, Dr. Welcome Mosley, believing the model to be an innocent toy, overdid everything and built the monstrous machine to scale detail. Feucht saw the lethal model to be the next step in thrill rides. A carpenter by heart, Feucht asked Dr. Mosely to be his partner and set about erecting the *Drop-the-Dip* at Coney Island. It opened June 6, 1907.

For one month it enjoyed great popularity before burning to the ground. Starting over again, but feeling he had been too conservative the first time around, Feucht added new and more fiendish features. The ride provoked miles of type in the newspapers with editors outdoing one another in descriptions of terror. They produced long lines at

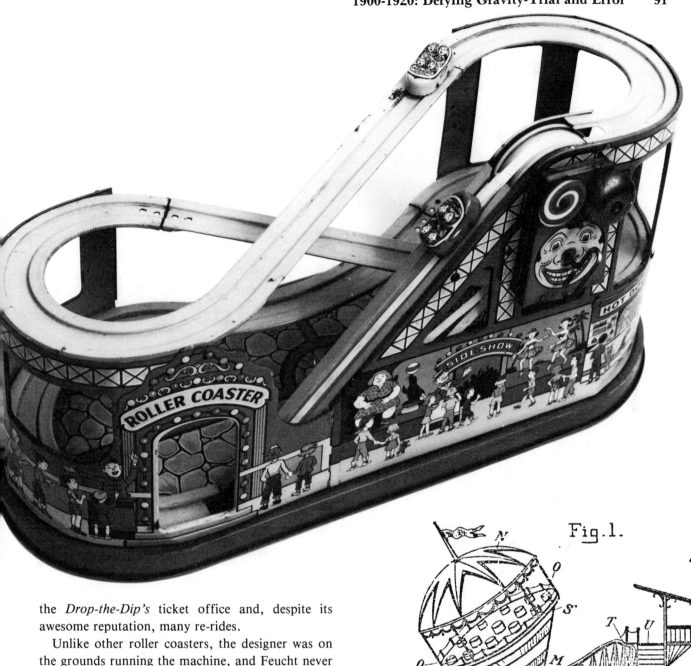

the *Drop-the-Dip's* ticket office and, despite its awesome reputation, many re-rides.

Unlike other roller coasters, the designer was on the grounds running the machine, and Feucht never stopped improving, adding and subtracting, tilting a curve, straightening a hill, tinkering and remodeling, and making the ride scarier. But Feucht was not a complete sadist. He invented the lap bar that keeps passengers from flying out of cars.

In 1910 Feucht actually moved the *Drop-the-Dip* across a street in 24 hours to avoid a raise in rent.

It was all trial and error and Chris Feucht best exemplifies the period. The *Drop-the-Dip* was the result, the first of the modern high-speed roller coasters.

(VI: 33). E. Prost's *Roundabout Affecting the Shape of a Giant Top.* Patent, 1925.

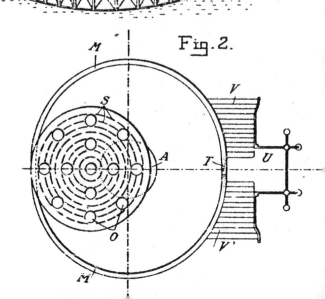

(VI: 34, 35, 36). *Drop-the-Dip*. Coney Island, Brooklyn, N.Y., 1907. Chris Feucht's  ferocious ride is considered the first high speed roller coaster. Courtesy James A. Kelley Historical Studies Institute.

# Chapter VII
## Roller Coasters Over the World:
## Luna Parks and White Cities

World's Fairs stopped producing innovative rides after the Buffalo Pan-American Exposition in 1901. This is not to say that rides were no longer part of the giant expositions. They were in strength: La Marcus Thompson built a Scenic Railway at the St. Louis World's Fair (1904) and the Traver Engineering Company built roller coasters at Chicago's 1933 Century of Progress Exposition, the 1937 Paris Exposition, and the 1939 New York World's Fair.

Nonetheless, the important inventions, the pioneering rides, were not being created at the expositions. Instead, they were springing from the many amusement parks now appearing all over the United States. There were several reasons for this: Ride owners wanted a steady and permanent clientele; inventors needed permanent sites for their creations; and park architects wanted grounds where they could plan present and future rides and events. With a roller coaster, for instance, they could ac-tually custom-fit the ride to the existing hills and landscape.

The expositions, realizing customers had amusement rides outside the gates in every town and village, simply turned their thoughts to other forms of entertainment.

Why the abundance of amusement parks from the beginning of the century to the Depression? The success of Coney Island is one obvious reason. It offered a visible example of the popularity of amusement parks, and its influence was world-wide. But that was not the main reason.

The amusement park boom must not be credited just to Coney Island, sociological forces, the new spirit of adventure, or the usual reasons scholars give for any shift in society. The credit for the spread of amusement parks over the world must be given to one man alone, a name almost forgotten by historians, Frederick Ingersoll (fig. VII:1).

(VII: 1). Frederick Ingersoll and Family. Frederick Ingersoll (center) is the man most responsible for the spread of amusement parks over the world. Courtesy Frederick Fried Archives.

Ingersoll's importance was known at the time. John Miller, at the height of his career in 1929 when Ingersoll died, said in tribute, "We all owe the success of the amusement park to Fred Ingersoll."[1] Lloyd Jeffries in the same eulogy, observed, "Ingersoll was the tree from which the amusement limbs branched forth, as many of the leading park men of today came from that tree in one way or another."[2]

Ingersoll was equally influential in the design of roller coasters. His first ride, a *Racer* of figure eight design, appeared at Pittsburgh's Kennywood Park in 1902. It was the first of 277 he designed or built during the next quarter-century (fig. VII:2).

But it was the park he built near his 307 Fourth Avenue workshop in Pittsburgh that made Ingersoll famous and started the flood of amusement parks throughout the United States. Named after the park in Coney Island, Ingersoll opened his own Luna Park

in 1905 (fig. VII:3). He followed Thompson and Dundy's format with a central Shoot-the-Chutes surrounded by rides, acts, and concessionaires. The beautiful 1905 catalogue includes this description of the park:

> The purpose of this great exposition park is to amuse and entertain and he who enters its gates leaves dull care behind. Exuberant life and action is to be seen on every hand, and when one finds himself amid the bewildering beauty and splendor of his surroundings he forgets the prosaic world in his indulgence of the ecstatic delights of a veritable dreamland. The picturesque architectural designs, including the Byzantine, Moorish, Japanese, Gothic, French Rennaissance and Corinthian, are sources of pleasure to the contemplative mind, while the numberless features tending to delight old as well as young make Luna Park a recreative spot that has no equal.[3]

A number of park men made their start at Pittsburgh's Luna, notably Joseph McKee who went on to build over 300 roller coasters and was a prominent figure at Palisades Park, New Jersey.

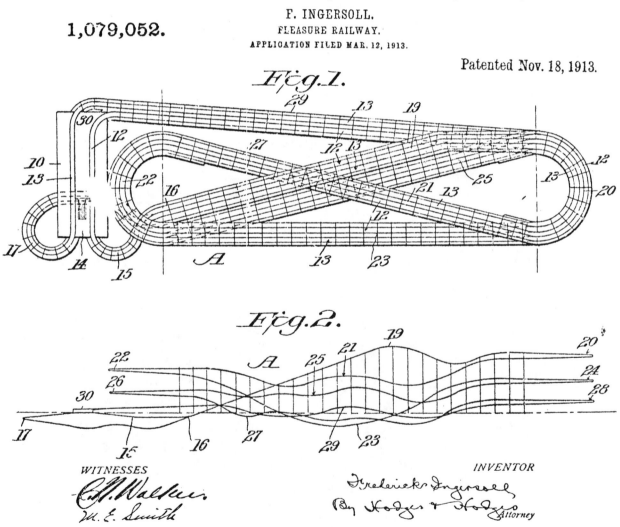

F. INGERSOLL.
PLEASURE RAILWAY.
APPLICATION FILED MAR. 12, 1913.

1,079,052.

Patented Nov. 18, 1913.

Fig. 1.

Fig. 2.

WITNESSES

INVENTOR

(VII: 2). Frederick Ingersoll's *Pleasure Railway*. Patent, 1913.

(VII: 3). Luna Park, Pittsburgh, Pa. 1905. The first Luna Park outside Coney Island, Brooklyn, N.Y. Photograph from a Detroit Publishing Co. glass negative in the Library of Congress collection.

Ingersoll opened a Luna Park in Cleveland the same year (fig. VII:4). Both parks were so popular that within ten years Luna Parks appeared in every part of the world (fig. VII:5-7). Not all of them were Ingersoll's. For awhile he used the name "Ingersoll's Luna Park" to ward off imitations. He finally gave in to the unstoppable; Luna Park was now part of the American vocabulary.

How many Luna Parks were there? Lost Lunas keep surfacing and a correct total will probably never be reached but a partial list would include Paris, Rome, Bombay (India), Honolulu, Buenos Aires, Phillipines, Madrid, Lisbon (Portugal), and Mexico City. In a sense, Lunas were prefabricated and every park, each ride and building, looked alike from Pittsburgh to Seattle. Roller coasters were part of the package and, by association, they spread as fast as

Lunas. Ingersoll through his system of parks made roller coasters available to millions and did as much as anyone to popularize the ride.

An early Ingersoll coaster is described in the 1905 catalogue:

> THE COASTER. There will be no end of diversions for the children and every opportunity for them to revel in fun. The Figure Eight Coaster is sure to give them a world of delight. It is one of the largest in the country, and its construction was the result of the most skillful mechanical ingenuity. Perfect safety is one of its striking features and as the large and commodious cars dash along at a high rate of speed the passengers experience the pleasantest exhilaration.[4]

Luna was not the only repeating park. Attempts were made to duplicate Coney Island's Steeplechase and a few succeeded (fig. VII:8,9). White Cities and Electric Parks covered the United States in much

(VII: 4). Ingersoll's Luna Park. Cleveland, Ohio. Courtesy
Staples and Charles Ltd.

(VII: 5). Luna Park. Seattle, Wash. Courtesy B. Derek Shaw.

(VII: 6). Luna Park. Sydney, Australia.

(VII: 7).  Luna Park. Terassen am Halensee, Germany. Courtesy John Still.

(VII: 8).  *Steeplechase* ride. Forest Park, Chicago, Ill.

(VII: 9).  Steeplechase Island.  Bridgeport, Conn.

greater numbers, however (fig. VII:10-13). In most cases they too followed the Luna Park format with a central Shoot-the-Chutes. The most famous White City (fig. VII:14) appeared shortly after the close of its namesake at the 1893 Columbian Exposition. In fact it was located not far from the exposition grounds at Sixty-third Street and South Park Way (Martin Luther King, Jr. Drive). It used architectural designs borrowed from the 1893 fair and is still considered one of the most beautiful of amusement parks. It even had an illustrated monthly. The August, 1905, *White City Magazine* tells of its *Toboggan* roller coaster:

> ...The participant in this sport takes a seat in a comfortable cushioned vehicle and sturdy attendants roll it down the track to a point where it is seized by a wire rope and is elevated up a steep incline, where the rapid and mirth-provoking journey begins. Upon reaching the top the cars seem imbued with life and dart down a gentle declivity as though fitted with powerful wings.
> Darting around unexpected curves, up slopes and down into valleys, the car is whirled at a rapid rate of speed upon a journey lasting almost two minutes. It finally returns to the original point of departure, where the merry passengers disembark and make way for others, who eagerly fill their places.
> All afternoon and evening crowds happily make their way to the Toboggan, and it is universally voted to be one of the jolliest forms of entertainment at WHITE CITY.[5]

White City later built a splendid *Racing Coaster* (c.

1909). Both the *Toboggan* and *Racing Coaster* were built by the Ingersoll Construction Company!

It is conservatively estimated that this century saw the appearance of 2000 parks before the Great Depression. If three-fourths of the parks had roller coasters, and few parks did not, then at least 1500 coasters stood in the United States alone.

(VII: 10).  White City Park.  Louisville,  Ky. Courtesy B. Derek Shaw.

(VII: 11). White City, Syracuse, N.Y. Courtesy Richard Hershey.

II: 12). White City. Binghamton, N.Y. Courtesy B. Derek Shaw.

(VII: 13). White City. Bellingham, Wash. Courtesy B. Derek Shaw.

(VII: 14). Aerial view of White City. Chicago, Ill. Courtesy Chicago Historical Society.

(VII: 15). Roller coaster at Coffeyville, Ks. 1907. Courtesy Library of Congress.

Again this estimate is conservative and does not take into account parks and roller coasters never registered. A roller coaster like that in Coffeyville, Kansas, (fig. VII:15) looks so precarious that only a high fanatic would attempt the ride. It appeared to be of tape and matchsticks. If a Kansas tornado hit the middle of such a structure, it's unlikely a recognizable trace would be found.

The late Roy Eddy, during an interview at his bait and tackle store in upstate New York revealed that he ran the roller coaster at Sacandaga Park. The park was nicknamed the ''Coney Island of the Adiron-dacks'' and was immensely popular (fig. VII:16). New York state decided to build a dam in 1930, and now the Coney Island of the Adirondacks is many feet under the Great Sacandaga Reservoir.

It's futile to guess how many roller coasters have disappeared without a clue beneath lakes, sky-scrapers, shopping malls, and garbage dumps. Perhaps future puzzled archaeologists will find them, but it's unlikely.

Here then is a pictorial treat for roller coaster buffs, a true roller coaster orgy — over forty rides that have disappeared over the United States, but that have not necessarily been forgotten.

Roller Coaster at Sacandaga, N. Y.

(VII: 16).  Sacandaga Park. Sacandaga, N.Y. Courtesy Roy Eddy.

(VII: 17). *Skyclone Coaster.* Central Park, Allentown, Pa. Courtesy B. Derek Shaw.

(VII: 18). *Dazy Dazer and Lovers Tub Rides.* Schifferdecker Electric Park, Joplin, Mo. Courtesy John Still.

(VII: 19). Twin City Amusement Park. Wonderland, Minneapolis/St. Paul, Minn. Courtesy John Still.

(VII: 20). *Dips.* Exposition Park, San Antonio, Texas. Courtesy John Still.

(VII: 21). *Whirlwind Dipper.* Santa Monica Pleasure Pier, Santa Monica, Calif. Courtesy Los Angeles Public Library.

(VII: 22). Electric Park. Kinderhook, N.Y. Courtesy John Still.

(VII: 23). *Figure 8.* Clement's Park, Putney, Vermont.

(VII: 24). *Figure Eight.* Island Park, Easton, Pa.

(VII: 25). *Mammoth Velvet Coaster.* The Zoo, Springfield, Ill. Courtesy B. Derek Shaw.

(VII: 26). Casino. Toledo, Ohio. Courtesy B. Derek Shaw.

(VII: 27). *Wild Cat Coaster.* Rocky Point, R.I. Courtesy John Still.

(VII: 28). The Chutes and roller coaster. Rocky Springs Park, Chester, W.Va.

(VII: 29). Glen Haven Park. Rochester, N.Y. Courtesy John Still.

(VII: 30). White City. New Haven, Ct. Courtesy B. Derek Shaw.

(VII: 31). Silver Beach Amusement Park. St. Joseph/Benton Harbor, Mich. Courtesy B. Derek Shaw.

(VII: 32). Steeplechase roller coaster. Steeplechase Park, Brooklyn, N.Y. Courtesy James A. Kelley Historical Studies Institute.

(VII: 33). Delmar Garden. Oklahoma City. Ok. Courtesy B. Derek Shaw.

(VII: 34). *Racing Coaster* Willow Grove Park, Philadelphia, Pa. Courtesy B. Derek Shaw.

(VII: 35). *Whirl-Pool Dips.* Tolchester Beach, Md. Courtesy B. Derek Shaw.

(VII: 36). Krug Park. Omaha, Nebr. Courtesy B. Derek Shaw.

(VII: 38).  Woodland Park. Ashtabula, Oh.

(VII: 37).  Hague Park. Vandercook's Lake, Jackson, Mich. Courtesy B. Derek Shaw.

2527  Figure Eight, Celoron Park, Chautauqua Lake, N. Y.

(VII: 39). *Figure Eight.* Celoron Park, Chautauqua Lake, N.Y. Courtesy B. Derek Shaw.

(VII: 40). Croop's Glen Park. Hunlock Creek, Pa. Courtesy Jimmy Croop and B. Derek Shaw.

(VII: 41).  Wonderland. Revere Beach,  Mass.

(VII: 42).  Electric Park. Galveston,  Tex.  Courtesy Russel Nye.

(VII: 43).  *Figure Eight*. Olcott Beach, Olcott, N.Y. Courtesy B. Derek Shaw.

(VII: 44).  Pleasure Pier. Port Arthur, Tex. Courtesy B. Derek Shaw.

(VII: 45).  Roller coaster. Michigan City, Ind.  Courtesy B. Derek Shaw.

(VII: 46).  *Figure Eight.* Silver Lake, Akron, Oh.

(VII: 47). Trout Park. Elgin, Ill. Courtesy B. Derek Shaw.

(VII: 48). Riverside Park. Sioux City, Iowa  Courtesy John Still.

(VII: 49). Monticello Amusement Park. Monticello, N.Y. Courtesy B. Derek Shaw.

(VII: 50). Wonderland Park. Wichita, Kans. Courtesy B. Derek Shaw.

(VII: 51). *Roller Boller Coaster*. Savin Rock, Conn. Courtesy B. Derek Shaw.

(VII: 52). Roller coaster. Council Crest, Washington. Courtesy John Still.

(VII: 53). Camden Park. Huntington, W. Va. Courtesy B. Derek Shaw.

(VII:54). Scenic Railway. West End, New Orleans, La. Courtesy
New York Public Library.

(VII: 55).  *The Bullet*. Portsmouth, Rhode Island. Courtesy B. Derek Shaw.

(VII: 56).  *Racing Whippet*. Westview Park, Pittsburgh, Pa.

(VII:57). *Wildcat*, Idora Park, Youngstown, Oh. Courtesy Richard Hershey.

# Chapter VIII
# John A. Miller

John Miller (fig. VIII:2) was the Thomas Edison of roller coasters or, to keep within the confines of the industry, what Frederick Ingersoll was to amusement parks, Miller was to roller coasters. It would be correct to say John Miller was the father of the modern high-speed roller coaster and the man most responsible for the myth of roller coasters being invented in the United States. He opened the way to the "mega-coaster" and the breaking of the 100 foot high barrier.

Miller owned many of the important patents — over 100 — and in a sense had a stranglehold on the industry. If park owners wanted a roller coaster, they eventually had to deal with John Miller.

Much of this chapter is based on a two day (June 14, 15, 1973) taped interview with the late Andy Brown in South Zanesville, Ohio. "Bridgeport Brownie" was Miller's chief engineer and troubleshooter. Brown had hoped to write a book on the great designer and had virtually every Miller drawing, blueprint, and patent filed in his large workshop. Andy Brown died in 1976, and we regretably are denied this indispensable publication.

Brown immediately noted during the 1973 interview that Miller seemed to own the roller coaster:

> ...Everyone was designing but Miller had all the patents. His designs were always more thrilling than others because the safety devices he invented allowed them to be more severe. He scared the hell out of people. He made his rides high right away. Most of the coasters then were 40 and 50 feet high. Miller right after the war had them 60, 70, 80 feet high. People thought he was going beyond what the body could stand. Yeah, he had the rollie coaster tied up with his patents and a lot of people resented it. Probably more jealousy than anything.[1]

Figure VIII:3 shows a few of the John Miller patents. An example of Miller's ingenuity is the safety ratchet. Miller was working on this invention as early as 1908 as shown in the original drawing (fig. VIII:4) for Patent #979,984 of December 27, 1910. This simple device prevents cars rolling backward while being hauled to the top of a coaster hill and is the cause of that clanking chain sound so associated with roller coasters.

His Patent #1038174 of September 10, 1912, locked coaster cars to the tracks with underfriction wheels. The drawing "Why a Coaster Doesn't Leave the Tracks" in Appendix I is based line for line on Miller's Patent #1319888, October 28, 1919. There was little reason to alter Miller's original drawing since, over the past seven decades, few notable improvements have been made on this remarkable invention.

The underfriction wheel patents were probably Miller's most important contribution. They led the way to the dizzying heights, vicious curves, and other lethal gravity-defying feats of the modern roller coaster. The 1923 Miller & Baker catalogue explains:

> The amusement-seeking public of the present day desire more than a ride when patronizing the modern amusement park. They want speed, sensationally deep and thrilling dips and plenty of them, and Mr. Miller has solved the problem of catering to these most exacting desires in his new type of construction and cars.
>
> This new type known as the MILLER Under Friction and Under Friction Locking Device is so designed and constructed as to permit of here-to-fore unheard of speed and apparently impossible steep, deep dips, with absolute safety, eliminating, as it does, the possibility of the cars leaping from the tracks, as would have been the case with the old type of construction and cars.
>
> The new construction of cars is so designed as to permit of sharp, vertical and horizontal curves and extremely steep ascents and descents, rendering the thrills and sensations so much sought after by the present day amusement seeker, with the element of risk of accident removed, thus creating business far in excess of any previous years or precedent.
>
> Another paramount feature of Mr. Miller's new designs, that immediately appeals to the Owner and Operator as well as to the public, is what is known as the Aero-Plane and Spiral Dips, which permits of steep ascents and descents on the sharp curves as well as on the straightaway, thereby making it practical to erect the new type of Deep Dipper on a much smaller area than was possible with the old type of construction.
>
> More caution is required in designing the new type of construction in order to keep within the limit of centrifugal gravity, obtaining the sensational and thrilling dips demanded, yet not reaching that extreme which would pitch the passengers from the cars.[2]

Miller had patents on Racing Coasters, brakes for both cars and tracks, car bar locks, *Bobs* flexible cars (fig. VIII:5), flange locks on tracks, and roller coaster and dome structuring. Miller even had a Ferris wheel patent (#1,539,094) that, if built, would have rivaled Herman's *Wonder Wheel* at Coney Island, Brooklyn. Miller's Ferris Wheel cars not only turned on axles, they nightmarishly rolled on tracks within the giant wheel's structure.

Miller, too, was prolific with roller coasters scattered over the world, many of which are listed in this

(VIII: 1). *The Speed Hound.* Burke Glen, Pa. Courtesy Roy Eddy

(VIII: 2). John Miller was the genius and father—the Thomas Edison—of the high speed roller coaster. Courtesy Frederick Fried Archives.

THIS beautiful suburb of Chicago was settled in a dense forest in the early pioneer days; hence the name *Homewood*. It has two banks; has all required business facilities; and is a thriving place. Elevation somewhat higher than Chicago.

THE MILLER Office and Study (Telephone No. 107) is on the old Vincennes Road portion of the Dixie Highway and only a very short distance from the Illinois Central Electric fast trains, of which one hundred are available daily.

### JOHN A. MILLER
of (P. O. Box No. 48) HOMEWOOD, ILL.

#### CONSULTING DESIGNER AND PATENTEE
GENERAL PRACTICE IN DESIGNS FOR AMUSEMENT PARKS AND EQUIPMENT

Miller Roller Coasters : Miller Patented Dome Truss Ball Rooms and Carrousel Buildings : Miller High Chutes, Roller Curves, Rapids Gorge and Old Mill Water Rides : Mysterious House that Jack Built : Funway Stunts and Fun Houses, Mirror Maze Houses : Miller Special Designed Covered Walks, Concession Buildings, etc. : Complete Park Plans.

W. N. N. Y. CITY 11-1-28

### JOHN A. MILLER of HOMEWOOD, ILLINOIS
## PATENTS INDEX (U.S.A.) N.Y-11/1/28

| No. | DATE | No. | DATE |
|---|---|---|---|
| RE-ISSUE 13,588 | July 1, 1913 | 1,476,995 | Dec. 11, 1923 |
| 979,875 | Dec. 27, 1910 | 1,501,060 | July 15, 1924 |
| 979,982 | Dec. 27, 1910 | 1,501,061 | July 15, 1924 |
| 979,983 | Dec. 27, 1910 | 1,536,122 | May 5, 1925 |
| 979,984 | Dec. 27, 1910 | 1,536,448 | May 5, 1925 |
| 1,037,957 | Sep. 10, 1912 | 1,539,094 | May 26, 1925 |
| 1,037,958 | Sep. 10, 1912 | 1,562,035 | Nov. 17, 1925 |
| 1,038,174 | Sep. 10, 1912 | 1,562,036 | Nov. 17, 1925 |
| 1,038,175 | Sep. 10, 1912 | 1,591,722 | July 6, 1926 |
| 1,062,838 | May 27, 1913 | 1,593,587 | July 27, 1926 |
| 1,062,839 | May 27, 1913 | 1,605,369 | Nov. 2, 1926 |
| 1,076,779 | Oct. 28, 1913 | 1,606,769 | Nov. 16, 1926 |
| 1,319,888 | Oct. 28, 1919 | 1,606,770 | Nov. 16, 1926 |
| 1,373,754 | Apr. 5, 1921 | 1,607,771 | Nov. 23, 1926 |
| 1,380,730 | June 7, 1921 | 1,613,118 | Jan. 4, 1927 |
| 1,380,731 | June 7, 1921 | 1,629,520 | May 24, 1927 |
| 1,380,732 | June 7, 1921 | 1,645,202 | Oct. 11, 1927 |
| 1,409,750 | Mch. 14, 1922 | 1,656,218 | Jan. 17, 1928 |
| 1,409,751 | Mch. 14, 1922 | | |
| 1,415,187 | May 9, 1922 | N.Y. City - 11/1/28 | |
| 1,438,452 | Dec. 12, 1922 | | |
| 1,448,763 | May 20, 1923 | | |
| 1,448,764 | May 20, 1923 | | |

(VIII: 3). A list of 41 Miller patents, December 27, 1910, through November 1, 1928.

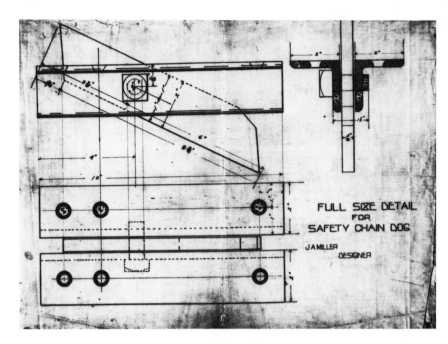

(VIII: 4). The original drawing (Robert Cartmell collection) for Safety Chain Dog by John Miller. 1910. The Safety Dog (See also Appendix: I: drawing) prevents cars rolling backward if the chain should break. Miller's many safety devices led the way to modern, high speed roller coasters.

(VIII: 5). *John A. Miller's Sensational Serpentine Train of Cars,* (n.d.).

chapter. He did own a few coasters outright but most often they were simply built under the Miller name or with various partners. John Allen, the designer most responsible for the "Coaster Boom" in the 1970's, said of Miller's 1924 *Whirl Wind* coaster (fig. VIII:6) at Olympic Park, Maplewood, New Jersey: "For the small plot of land it occupied, in my opinion, it was the finest roller coaster ever built."[3]

Compared to other figures in this book, background on John Miller is sketchy and this seems to be the way he wanted it. Said Andy Brown:

> None of the guys thought it was that important. The rides were the thing, not when or where you were born. We were just too busy putting up rides and Miller didn't give a damn about such things.[4]

He was born in 1872 in, according to patents, Illinois. Judging from the photo in Andy Brown's collection, Miller was building roller coasters at a very early age (fig. VIII:7). It is known that at the age of 19, he started working with La Marcus Thompson and almost immediately became his chief engineer. This meeting must have been similar to the joining of minds of Orville and Wilbur Wright or Picasso and Braque. Thompson and Miller, between them, initiated almost every important roller coaster idea. Their drawings flooded the Patent Office. It's almost as if, in an age before responsible insurance companies, they treated amusement parks as giant laboratories and patrons as guinea pigs. This statement, however, is deceiving and unfair. Thompson and Miller were not only tracking greater thrills, they were creating safety devices to make such rides

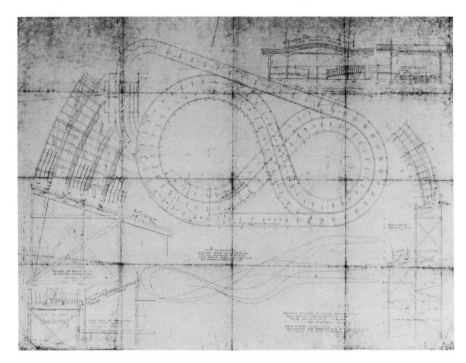

(VIII: 6). *The Whirl Wind*. Olympic Park, Maplewood, N.J., 1924. Original 1924 plan. John Allen called *The Whirlwind* the finest roller coaster ever built for the plot of land it occupied.

possible.

During this time, Miller also worked closely with Frederick Ingersoll and Josiah and Fred Pearce (Chapter IX) (fig. VIII:8). Even before La Marcus Thompson's retirement in 1918, Miller worked free lance with over a dozen important patents in portfolio. In 1911, he was consultant to Philadelphia Toboggan. Over the next few years, Miller designed for this company around 15 coasters including the magnificent *Giant Coaster* at Paragon Park, Nantasket Beach, Massachusetts (fig. VIII:9).

In January, 1920, John Miller formed a fruitful partnership with Harry C. Baker (fig. VIII:12). Baker was former manager of Rexford Park, Schnectady, New York, and a successful contractor specializing in roller coasters. The handsome Miller & Baker catalogue of 1923 opens:

### GREETINGS
#### Miller & Baker, Inc.

Designers and Builders of Amusement Parks, Miller patented Under Friction and Under Friction Locking Device Coasters, Miller Dome roof Carousel Buildings and Dome Roof Dance Pavilions, Old Mills, Mill Chutes, Fun Houses, Miller's Tandem Seat Serpentine Coasters, Mechanical Devices of every description, Equipment and Machinery for all Amusement Park Devices and Sales Agent for the Dodgem, the Whip, and Aeroplane Swings.

MAIN OFFICE:
Suite 3041, Grand Central
Terminal, New York City, N.Y.

CENTRAL OFFICE:
P.O. Box 48
Homewood, Illinois

WESTERN OFFICE:
Care of Chas. Paige. 2628 Palm Court
Los Angeles, California.[5]

The same catalogue lists the following roller coasters:

Big Dipper, River View Park, Chicago, Ill.
Big Dipper, Riverside Park, Des Moines, Iowa.
Big Dipper, Venice Pier, California·
Big Dipper, Woodlawn Beach, Buffalo, N.Y.
Deep Dipper, Liberty Heights Park, Baltimore, Md.
Deep Dipper, Frederick Road Park, Baltimore, Md.
Deep Dipper, Rockaway Beach, Long Island, N.Y.
Lightning Dipper, Riverside Park, Springfield, Mass.
Lightning Dipper, Sea Breeze, Rochester, N.Y.
Krug's Flyer, Toronto, Canada.
Pippin Dips, River View Park, Chicago, Ill.
Pippin Dips, Lagoon Resort, Salt Lake City
Deep Dips, Fort Wayne, Ind.
Deep Dips, Lawrence, Mass.
Deep Dips, Mid City Park, Albany, N.Y.
Deep Dips, Ingersoll Amusement Center, Detroit, Mich.
Deep Dips, Columbia Park, Hoboken, N.J.
Deep Dips, Olympic Park, Newark, N.J.
Thunderbolt Coaster, Revere Beach, Boston, Mass.
Sky Rocket, Pleasure Beach, Bridgeport, Conn.
Sky Rocket, Coney Island Park, Cincinnati, Ohio
Thriller, Palisades Park, N.J.
Thriller, Auburn, N.Y.
Jack Rabbit, Kennywood Park, Pittsburgh, Pa.
Jack Rabbit, Rockford, Ill.
Cascade Dips, Cascade Park, New Castle, Pa.
Deep Dipper, Riverview Beach, Pennsville, N.J.
Deep Dipper, Island Beach, Burlington Island, N.J.

(VIII: 7).  The young John Miller. Site and date not specified.

(VIII: 8).  Roller coaster. Blue Grass Park, Lexington, Ky., 1910.

(VIII: 9). *Giant Coaster*. Paragon park, Natasket Beach, Mass., 1910. Courtesy Charles J. Jacques, Jr./*Amusement Park Journal*.

(VIII: 10). *The Dare-Devil*. Sites and date not specified. *The Dare-Devil* continued the tradition of circus derived ideas. Photo credit: Chicago Historical Society.

Miller's Latest Sensational Ride of Rides
A SHORT SNAPPY RIDE .·. FULL OF THRILLS

Operating 2 twelve-passenger trains. 40 trips per hour for each train. Total capacity nine hundred and sixty passengers per hour.

Beautiful shamrock cars travel a circular and whip motion, caused by its three-point unbalanced load, while traveling through "The Dip" and banking at the curves

"IT'S THE JAZZ RIDE"

DIP-LO-DO-CUS

(VIII: 11). *Dip-Lo-Docus*. Sites not specified, c. 1923. The name came from a prehistoric 84 foot monster-reptile in the Carnegie Museum, Pittsburgh, Pa.

Deep Dipper, Electric Park, Kansas City, Mo.
The Thriller, Arnolds Park, Dickinson, Iowa.
Big Dipper, Sant Mateo, California
Big Dipper, Idora Park, Oakland, California
Deep Dipper, Santa Monica, California
Thunderbolt Coaster, Rockaway Beach, N.Y.
Sky Rocket, Salisbury Beach, Mass.
Big Dipper, Habana Park, Havana, Cuba
Deep Dipper, Hillside Park, Belleville, N.J.
Big Dipper, Gordon Gardens, Cleveland, Ohio
Deep Dipper, Suburban Gardens, Washington, D.C.
Deep Dipper, Erie, Pa.
Big Dipper, Luna Park, Detroit, Mich.
Deep Dipper, Keansburg, N.J.[6]

Miller experimented with many odd-ball rides including the *Dare-Devil* (fig. VIII:10), a ride continuing the tradition of circus derived rides (Chapter VI). Most spectacular was the *Dip-Lo-Docus* (fig. VIII:11). The Miller & Baker 1923 *Dip-Lo-Docus* catalogue describes the ride:

> The name of this new riding device, the DIP-LO-DOCUS is derived from that pre-historic land reptile of gigantic proportions that centuries ago roamed the greater part of tropical South America.
> There is a specimen of this monster reptile in the Carnegie Museum, measuring 84 feet in length and 12 feet in height at the hind legs.
> ...Mr. Miller selected this giant prehistoric animal as the name of his new invention for several good reasons, the most important being the intense interest now prevalent the world over in all things of a prehistoric nature, and rarely a day passes that some mention is not made in the press of the country of some new discovery being made somewhere, and the publicity given to these discoveries will surely react to the benefit of the DIP-LO-DOCUS Coaster, and will also add greatly to the interest manifested in the new device, if

for no other reason than to simply satisfy that natural curiosity we all possess.

> ...Very little, if any, of the structure of the DIP-LO-DOCUS coaster will be visible to the public owing to practically all that part of the structure that would ordinarily show being covered with sheet metal, which is painted in high bright colors, representing the tropical regions formerly traversed and frequented by this most picturesque monster animal.
> ...Each car is so constructed as to contain three separate sections, each section seating two passengers, giving each car a seating capacity of six passengers. The load being centered upon three points causes an unbalanced condition while the car is travelling over the undulated tracks and banked curves, which in turn causes the car to revolve from its own weight. It is this feature of the DIP-LO-DOCUS, the travelling over the summits into the dips and onto the stright-away at a high rate of speed, and experiencing the thrills and sensations of that pleasing, teasing, jazzy motion obtained by the revolving of the car, all of which is crowded into one ride, that will make the DIP-LO-DOCUS the sensation of the amusement park world.[7]

Several *Dip-Lo-Docus* were built, the most famous being at Olympic Park, Maplewood, New Jersey, where Miller's masterpiece, the *Whirl Wind* coaster also stood. (Olympic Park has to be historically the most neglected of America's great parks.[8] It also housed what was possibly Philadelphia Toboggan's finest carousel. The park closed in 1965.)

Miller and Baker ended their partnership in 1923. Miller established his business at the Homewood, Illinois, address while Harry C. Baker went on to build, among others, two of the finest roller coasters: The *Cyclone,* Coney Island, Brooklyn, and the *Blue Streak,* Woodcliffe Pleasure Park on the Hudson,

Poughkeepsie, New York, both discussed in Chapter IX. Baker, too, went into business with his own line of thrill rides naming them *Whippet Coasters* and occasionally *Cyclone Coasters*.

In Illinois, the John A. Miller Company, Inc. produced one great roller coaster after another. Miller was almost the "Golden Age of Roller Coasters" by himself. The opening parallel with Thomas Edison is not far-fetched. Yet, unlike Edison, Miller did not have a "think tank" with other inventors working for him. He had a uniquely inventive mind and was something of a loner needing only business partners, in most cases, to handle mundane ledger work and mail. True to form, in Illinois, Miller hired Elwood Salisbury from Ingersoll as his vice president.

Miller, too, was greatly responsible for the survival of coasters during the Depression. His association with the Dayton Fun House and Riding Device Manufacturing Company (later National Amusement Device Corporation) helped roller coasters through that bleakest of periods from 1929 to World War II.

The greatest invention to come from the Dayton collaboration was the *Flying Turns* (fig. VIII:26-28) and Miller's partnership with Norman Bartlett. The ride continued the flying tradition mentioned in Chapter VI. Bartlett was a former World War I Canadian Royal Air Force pilot working with Custer Specialty Company in Dayton. Andy Brown describes the meeting of Miller and Bartlett:

> This guy called me named Bartlett and made a date with Miller and he told me to come in and see this thing. All the guy had was a moving picture of a toboggan slide in Canada. That's all he had and I don't think he knew the difference between a ten-penny nail and a two-by-four. We planned the first *Flying Turns* over at Fun House — that's where Lawson built all of Miller's equipment. I helped build the first one over at Lakeside Park. Bartlett was really bright.[9]

A ride on the *Flying Turns* started like a roller coaster with the usual chain lift. It differed in that cars on swiveling rubber wheels ran through a cylindrical chute made of cypress wood, in the manner of a bobsled. Passengers shot around the severest of banks, some nearly perpendicular. The ride revitalized the figure-eight pattern with a vengeance.

The first *Flying Turns* opened at Lakeside Park, Dayton, in 1929. It used single cars. A more famous *Flying Turns* opened the following year at Euclid Beach in Cleveland, Ohio. This multi-car version was so popular that it became a symbol of Euclid Beach.

The most vicious *Flying Turns* was the *Lake Placid*

*Bobsled* (fig. VIII:29) at Palisades Park, Fort Lee, New Jersey. Many considered it more lethal than either of the *Cyclone* roller coasters at the same park. It was so severe, additional wheels had to be added to prevent cars from somersaulting (fig. VIII:30).

During the early 1930's, the Philadelphia Toboggan Company obtained exclusive rights to the Bartlett/Miller ride with plans to build many *Flying Turns* in the East. Because of the Depression, only one version, at Rocky Point Park, Warwick, Rhode Island, saw the light of day.

Bartlett and Miller's business went into receivership in 1932, and Miller lost yet another partner. Bartlett continued building *Flying Turns,* including rides at the 1933 and 1939 World's Fairs (fig. VIII:31). The 1939 World's Fair plans were later executed in North Tonawanda, New York, home of Herschell-Spillman carousels.

Miller, earlier, had formed a partnership with Charles Rose, but this too folded in 1932.

Miller's final years are mysterious. He built a *Triple Racer* in 1936 in both Dallas and Louisville. The roller coasters actually had *three* trains racing on three parallel tracks over hills and curves (fig. VIII:32,33). His last years seem to have been spent in and out of Mexico (fig. VIII:34) "developing devices for a syndicate."[10] These activities have been the subject of much speculation and several ghost stories.

John Miller died June 24, 1941, in Houston, Texas, while planning a roller coaster for that city. He was almost completely forgotten after that date.

It is ironic that one of Miller's least memorable roller coasters became one of his most famous, the *Thunderbolt* at Coney Island, completed in 1927 (fig. VIII:35). The Woody Allen character in the movie *Annie Hall* lived in a house beneath the *Thunderbolt* during his Brooklyn childhood. The periodic rumbling and shaking of furniture and china was the subject of many laughs in the movie. The house actually exists belonging first to *Thunderbolt* owner George Moran and later his son, Fred. Beams of the roller coaster actually are part of the house's structure.

Miller's masterpieces were the rides he built through ravines. These include the *Jack Rabbit* and *Pippin* (later converted by Andrew Vettel to the *Thunderbolt)* at Kennywood Park, Pittsburgh. The finest ravine coaster was his *Cyclone* at Puritas Springs in Cleveland (fig. VIII:36). This monstrous ride hid its dips beneath tree tops placed in the park's ravine. Its camouflage was such that only the loading platform could be clearly identified. The brutal parts

(VIII: 12). Harry C. Baker. Site and date not specified. The gentleman in the background is roller coaster designer, Harry Traver (Chapter X).

were cleverly hidden from the public. The savagery of its ride earned the Puritas Springs coaster a place on the Smithsonian Institution's listing of *Great Lost Roller Coasters*. Ruins of this legendary roller coaster can still be found on the few remaining acres that have escaped development.

In addition to the Baker-Miller rides previously listed, Andy Brown's catalogue of blueprints lists the following John Miller roller coasters. They are categorized by city since, in many cases, dates or names were either illegible, erased, or not part of the plans:

Atlanta, Ga.; *Dips Coaster*; Lakeside Park; 1915
Atlanta, Ga.; *Dips Coaster*; Sunset Park; 1922
Anderson, Ind.; *Dips Coaster*; Mounds Park; 1907
Allentown, Pa.; Central Park
Baltimore, Md.; *Racer*; Riverview Park
Baltimore, Md.; Hollywood Park
Baltimore, Md.; Wonderland Park
Battle Creek, Mich.; *Dips* (moved from

Hammond, Ind.)
Boston; *Racing Coaster*; Revere Beach; 1911
Bronx, N.Y.; Bronx Park
Brooklyn, N.Y.; *Dragon's Gorge*; Coney Island; 1905
Brooklyn, N.Y.; *Rocky Road to Dublin;* Coney Island; 1905
Buffalo, N.Y.; Erie Beach
Chicago; *Derby Racer;* Riverview Park; 1912
Chicago; *Jack Rabbit;* Riverview Park; 1913
Chicago; *Racer;* White City; 1909
Cleveland, Oh.; *Big Dipper;* Gordon Gardens
Cleveland, Oh.; *Scenic Railway;* Euclid Beach; 1907
Cleveland, Oh.; Luna Park
Cleveland, Oh.; Puritas Spring Park
Cincinnati, Oh.; *Dips Coaster;* Chester Park; 1927
Clementon, N.J.; Clementon Lake Park
Dayton, Oh.; *Thriller Coaster;* Lakeside Park
Denver, Colo.; *Dips Racer;* Lakeside Park; 1910
Detroit, Mich.; Edgewater Park
Detroit, Mich.; *King Bee;* Granada Park; 1923
Detroit, Mich.; *Daredevil;* Granada Park; 1925
Detroit, Mich.; *Dips Coaster;* Jefferson Beach; 1927
Detroit, Mich.; *Steel Coaster;* Steel Coaster Park
Farmington, Ut.; Lagoon Resort
Fort Dodge, Iowa; *Ideal Coaster;* 1925
Geauga Lake, Oh.; *Dips Coaster;* 1925
Hammond, Ind.; *Dips Coaster;* Palace Gardens; 1924
Holyoke, Mass.; *Dips Coaster;* Mt. Tom Park; 1915
Hot Springs, Ark.; Washington Park
Indianapolis, Ind.; *Dips Coaster;* Riverside Park; 1924
Jackson, Mich.; *Jack Rabbit;* Hague Park; 1915
Jacksonville Beach, Fla.; Oceanview Park
Lancaster, Pa.; Rocky Springs
Lincoln, Nebr.; Capital Beach
Louisville, Ky.; *Racer;* Fontaine Ferry Park; 1911
Long Beach, Calif.; *Jack Rabbit;* 1914
Mansfield, Oh.; White Maple Park
Milwaukee, Wis.; *Dips Coaster;* Fair Park; 1924
Muscego Beach, Wis.
Minneapolis, Minn.; Excelsior
Nantasket Beach, Mass.; *Dips Coaster;* Paragon Park; 1915

Nashville, Tenn.; *Dips Coaster;* State Fair
  Grounds; 1925
New Castle, Pa.; Cascade Park
North Bergen, N.J.; Columbia Park
Oakland, Calif.; *Ideal Coaster;* Idora Park
Ocean View, Va.; Ocean View Park; 1909
Omaha, Nebr.; Krug Park
Omaha, Nebr.; Lakeview Park
Paul, Canada; *Dips Coaster*
Philadelphia, Pa.; *Mountain Ride;* Willow
  Grove Park; 1905
Pittsburgh, Pa.; *Racing Coaster;* Kennywood
  Park; 1927
Pittsburgh, Pa.; *The Speedoplane;* Kennywood
  Park; 1911
Pittsburgh, Pa.; *Pippin;* Kennywood Park; 1924
Redondo Beach, Calif.
Reading, Pa.; Carsonia Park
Rotan Point, Conn.; *Dips Coaster*
Russel's Point, Oh.; *Roller Coaster;* 1924
St. Joseph, Mich.; *Figure 8 Coaster*
San Diego, Calif.
Savin Rock, Conn.; White City
Saginaw, Mich.; Riverside Park
St. Louis, Mo.; *Racer;* Forrest Park Highlands
St. Louis, Mo.; *Mountain Ride;* Forest Park
  Highlands; 1911
St. Louis, Mo.; Creve Cour Park; 1901
St. Louis, Mo.; Chain o' Rocks; 1925
Spokane, Wash.; Natatorium Park
St. Paul, Minn.; *Dips;* Wildwood; 1925

Toronto, Canada; Hanlon's Point
Toronto, Canada; Canadian National Exposition
Tulsa, Okla.; *Dips Coaster;* 1924
Vancouver, Canada; *Dips Coaster;* Stanley
  Park; 1913
Vancouver, Canada; *Greyhound Coaster;*
  Stanley Park; 1913
Washington, D.C.; Glen Echo Park
Westhaven, Conn.; *Dips Coaster;* White City;
  1914
Wichita Falls, Tex.; Lakeside Park
Youngstown, Ohio; Idora Park[11]

Sadly, among Andy Brown's blueprints were many so badly faded that identification was impossible. It is hoped that they will have not disappeared completely when memories of the last riders die; and that they can be found through other sources such as postcard collections or in basements of local historical societies.

John Miller was the most innovative and influential figure in the history of amusement parks. Aurel Vaszin, founder of International Amusement Devices, said, during a 1974 interview in his Dayton office (a portrait of Miller conspicuously hanging over his desk):

...Miller, Miller, Miller. He was everywhere. We were all influenced by him. Joe and Al McKee, Charlie Paige, Nash, Shirley Watkins, Eddie Pratt, Keenan, Baker, so many others. I can't remember them all. Master Miller. He was a genius. He was the master.[12]

(VIII: 13).  An advertisement for John Miller's *Ideal Ride* for recreation parks. (n.d.).

(VIII: 14). *Hummingbird*. Riverview Beach, Pennsville, N.J. 1922.

VIII:15). *Thunderbolt*. Revere Beach, Boston, Mass., 1926.

(VIII: 16).  Roller coaster. Peoria, Ill., 1926.

JOHN A. MILLER-DESIGN

(VIII: 17). *Racer*. Kennywood Park, West Mifflin, Pa., 1927. Miller's great *Racer* still thrills passengers at Kennywood. It is the only continuous-track racing coaster standing today. The ride is an ingeniously convoluted figure eight; cars race side by side but are really on different loops of the same track.

(VIII: 18). Roller coaster. Lake Worth Park, Fort Worth, Tex. 1927.

(VIII: 19).  Roller coaster. Pleasure Beach, Blackpool, England, 1927.

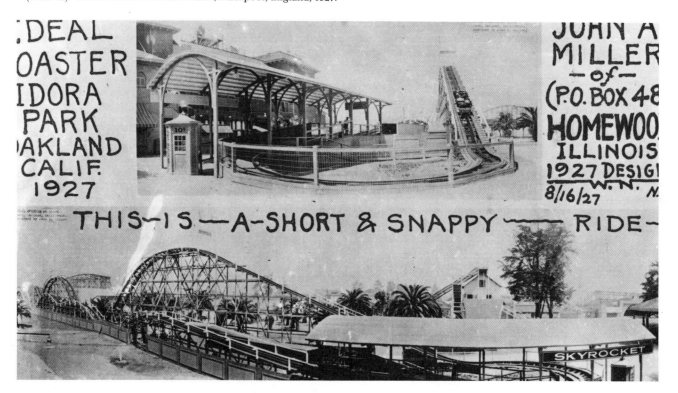

(VIII: 20).  *Ideal Coaster.* Idora Park, Oakland, Calif., 1927.

JOHN A. MILLER of [P.O.BOX 748] HOMEWOOD, ILLINOIS

ESTIMATE DATA SHEET:::::::::::::::::::::::Typed NY 10/1/27-WN

SEPT. 23, 1927 - ESTIMATE FOR 2000 FT. TRACK
Cost of 2000 foot Ozark Park Coaster
Miller 1927 Design Car and XXXXXXX Track Structure
--------000000000000--------

| | |
|---|---|
| PayRoll, Labor, Carpenters, Painters-----------------$ | 5,500.00 |
| Lumber from Minnesota Transfer------------------$ | 5,000.00 |
| 4-Coaster Cars, Three Seated--------------------$ | 2,000.00 |
| 1-36" Chain Idler, and 5-18" Idlers------------$ | 234.00 |
| 1-Shaft, 3-7/16" and bearings------------------$ | 66.00 |
| 3-Safety Chain Dogs for Hoist------------------$ | 45.00 |
| 25-Sets Squeeze Brake Units--------------------$ | 464.50 |
| 1-64" Spur Gear, Cut Teeth, with special Shock-Sleeve and Hub-------------------$ | 308.00 |
| 1-8" Fabroid Pinion for Motor------------------$ | 85.00 |
| 1-40 H.P. Motor with Starter-------------------$ | 800.00 |
| 1-Sprocket and 400 feet Hazel Chain------------$ | 460.00 |
| Electric Wiring, Labor, Lights-----------------$ | 1,000.00 |
| Steel Track Guards and Brake Lining------------$ | 1,500.00 |
| Paint for one Coat-----------------------------$ | 300.00 |
| Bolts, Nails, Screws, etc.---------------------$ | 600.00 |
| Tools, Drills, Ropes, etc.---------------------$ | 200.00 |
| Cement for Walls in Dips and Footings----------$ | 400.00 |
| Freight and Drayage----------------------------$ | 500.00 |
| Compensation Insurance and Builders Risk-------$ | 500.00 |
| Roofing, Ten Squares---------------------------$ | 30.00 |
| | $ 19,992.00 |
| John A. Miller, Plans, License-----------------$ | 2,000.00 |

J.A.MILLER Estimate, Including License:- 21,992.00 FOR 2000 FEET OF TRACK

§ When the Construction payments were added up the cost complete including Miller license and services was *11.00 per foot of track. ◀SAME AS ESTIMATED

TO THE LEFT IS THE COST OF IT AND ABOVE IS THE COASTER WHICH E.E.ELDER BUILT AT ST. LOUIS, MO., OZARK PARK, AS PER PLANS BY: JOHN A. MILLER of (P.O.BOX #48) HOMEWOOD, ILLINOIS. It is cheaper to build Miller way. N. NY-2-20-28 W.

(VIII: 21). Roller coaster. Ozark Park, St. Louis, Mo., 1927.

GEAUGA LAKE COASTER CLEVELAND, OHIO.

DESIGNED AND PATENTED BY JOHN A. MILLER of HOMEWOOD ILLINOIS.

A STREAMLINE JOHN A. MILLER PATENTED COASTER WITH ITS RACY LINES LENDS BEAUTY TO THE LANDSCAPE AND IS FULL OF THRILLS FOR THE PATRONS

(VIII: 22). Roller coaster Geauga Lake, Aurora, Oh., 1927.

(VIII: 23). Roller coaster. Riverside Park, Winnipeg, Canada, 1928.

(VIII; 24). Roller coaster. Jacksonville Beach, Fla., 1928.

(VIII: 25). *Deep Dipper.* National Amusement Park, Pittsburgh, Pa., 1928.

(VIII: 26). *Flying Turns*. Lakeside Park, Dayton, Oh., 1929. The Dayton ride was the first *Flying Turns*. This toboggan-like coaster was the creation of Norman Bartlett and John Miller.

(VIII: 27). *Flying Turns*. Euclid Beach, Cleveland, Oh., 1930.

(VIII:28). *Flying Turns*. Coney Island, Brooklyn, N.Y. The improved Flying Turns featured trains rather than individual cars.

(VIII: 29). *Lake Placid Bobsled.* Palisades Park, Fort Lee, N.J. 1937. The Palisades ride is considered Bartlett's finest.

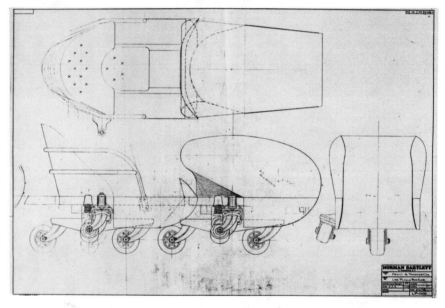

(VIII. 30). *Lake Placid Bobsled* car. Palisades Park, Fort Lee, N.J. 1937. Courtesy Arrow Huss, Inc.

(VIII: 31). Plans for the Flying Turns. 1939 World's Fair, New York, N.Y. Plans dated 1938. Courtesy Arrow Huss, Inc.

(VIII: 32). Triple Racer. Dallas Exposition, Dallas, Tex., 1936. Courtesy Charles J. Jacques, Jr./*Amusement Park Journal.*

(VIII: 33). Triple Racer. Fontaine Ferry Park, Louisville, Ky., 1936. Courtesy Charles J. Jacques, Jr./*Amusement Park Journal.*

(VIII: 34). John Miller in Mexico, 1939.

(VIII: 35). *Thunderbolt.* Coney Island, Brooklyn, N.Y. 1927.

(VIII: 36). Scale model of John Miller's Puritas Springs *Cyclone*, Cleveland, Oh., 1927. Model built from HO gauge scale lumber by James Kelly, Kirtland, Oh., Photograph by Tom Prusha.

(VIII: 37). The last known photograph of "The Master", John Miller. 1941.

# Chapter IX
## Coasters of the Roaring Twenties:
## The Golden Age

It was the "Fastest and Crassest" of all ages said *Vanity Fair,* of that decade aptly named THE ROARING TWENTIES. This remarkable magazine (March, 1914, through February, 1936), perhaps the most accurate mirror of that hectic era, went so far as to call the 1920's "The Roller Coaster Years".[1] Although the comment was meant to reflect the decade's up and down outlook, it was indeed an insightful comment. In every respect the 1920's were the glory years of roller coasters, their Golden Age, and perhaps the finest rides ever built came from this near lunatic decade.

It was an age of heroes, legends, and stars: Babe Ruth, Bobby Jones, Bill Tilden, Jack Dempsey, Isadora Duncan, Houdini, Greta Garbo, D.H. Lawrence, Lawrence of Arabia, Will Rogers, the Gershwins, Valentino, Chaplin, the list goes on and on.

Yet it can be argued the biggest star of the 1920's was the roller coaster. They were as popular as vaudeville and cinema. The term roller coaster and its erratic course came to describe everything from psychiatry to the stock market. The likes of Lindbergh, Capone, and Chaplin clamored to ride this premiere thrill machine.

Experiments at amusement parks continued in earnest but in a different way. Up to the 1920's, there were many ideas and patents but few saw the light of day. The beginning of the 20th century saw many "starts", but they remained merely flourishes that had been halted by World War I (1914-18).

The end of the war combined with John Miller's safety patents (Chapter VIII) proved the ideal combination to test the limits of roller coasters. Designers now reveled in novel and bloodcurdling ideas, and the public of the 1920's, rather than cringing at their audacity, jubilantly encouraged the construction of the new monstrous roller coasters. In a sense, designers were given free license by both parks and public.

The search was on for the ultimate roller coaster and only building codes, insurance companies, and a few glimpses of reassuring sanity kept rides short of mayhem and outright danger. It is conservatively estimated that 1,500 roller coasters were standing in

the 1920's, each identifiable, like signatures, from across the park as the work of one company or designer.

Amusement parks seemed to be everywhere, even in the remotest villages, and traces of forgotten parks from the 1920's are still surfacing to this day. Coney Island, though badly in need of cosmetics, continued to dominate and remained the giant of the amusement industry. However, serious competitors prospered during this era, such as, Euclid Beach (Cleveland), Elitch Gardens (Denver), Kennywood Park (Pittsburgh), Coney Island (Cincinnati), The Pike (Los Angeles), and many others, each with several roller coasters.

Coney Island's most prominent competitor was located in Chicago. Billed as the "World's Largest Amusement Park", Riverview Park became a roller coaster paradise in the 1920's.

### Riverview Park

It is appropriate that perhaps the strongest symbol of amusement parks in the 1920's was located in Chicago, the city most often associated with the Roaring Twenties, speak-easies, and Prohibition.

Riverview (fig. IV:1-7) was as wild as Chicago itself. The park often advertised that at one point eleven roller coasters stood on its grounds. The claim is perhaps stretched since this included the *Shoot-the-Chutes, Flying Turns,* and kiddie coasters; but there is little argument that by the 1920's there were never fewer than six coasters in operation at the park until its closing in 1967.

Located on the opposite side of Chicago from White City, on 72 acres at Belmont and Western on the North Side, Riverview Park opened in 1904 when George Schmidt purchased a shooting range/picnic grove and used goat cart rides as the main attraction.

Some Riverview historians claim Schmidt built the first modern roller coaster although there is little evidence that a coaster stood at the park before 1907. At any rate, many "modern" roller coasters existed over the country, particularly at Coney Island, before Schmidt purchased Riverview. It cannot be denied, though, that the park became the premiere testing ground for roller coasters. Traver, Church, Miller, Pearce, and others set up temporary offices at

Riverview and personally supervised board-by-board construction of their latest designs. This was a tremendous bonus for roller coasters. Now it was not just word of mouth trading of ideas but actual observation of construction methods and designing procedures.

Coasters appeared and often quickly disappeared at Riverview only to surface under a different name several months later. If an accident occurred (Riverview had one of the best safety records in history), Schmidt often closed the ride for a short period, waited for the public to forget, and opened the ride under a different name. The two finest roller coasters were the *Fireball* and *Bobs*.

The *Fireball* (fig. IX: 5) began as the *Blue Streak* but was revamped many times before its final shape in 1963. Riverview fans still claim the *Fireball* was the fastest roller coaster ever built, perhaps remembering the park's exaggerated claim of 100 mph (65 mph was a more accurate reading).

The *Fireball* did have a first drop that made 100 mph seem entirely possible and the park achieved this by very clever means. The Chicago building code of the time stated tracks could not be more than 72 feet high. The *Fireball (Blue Streak)* was one of the first rides to defeat this by digging beneath the ground to allow an even greater drop. (The original Coney Island *Cyclone* and the recent *American Eagle*, Gurnee, Illinois, are other examples of this underground system.)

Riders, too, remember the *Fireball*'s bright, fire engine red cars and the sinister, yawning dark tunnel at the base of the first hill where cars shot under the station.

The *Bobs* (fig. IX: 6,7) was Riverview's masterpiece. Many claim the search for the ultimate roller coaster was over when the *Bobs* opened its gates in 1924. A Prior/Church/Traver gem (see Chapter X), the Riverview *Bobs* was a disputed 87 feet high (the building code was apparently not enforced), had 3,253 feet of track that ran over 16 hills and 12 curves, and started with an improbable and probably park-exaggerated 67 degree drop. It is estimated 30 million people took the *Bob*'s two minute and fifteen second ride.

And the ride was lethal. Said Garry Cooper of his ride in the 1960's:

(IX: 1). Riverview Park, Chicago, Ill., 1904-1967. Riverview Park was a coaster buff's paradise with as many as eleven roller coasters running at the same time. *Artwork* by Don Lindstrom.

(IX: 2). Building the Shoot-the-Chutes. Riverview Park, Chicago, Ill., c. 1910. Courtesy Chicago Historical Society.

(IX: 3). *Figure Eight.* Riverview Park, Chicago, Ill., Courtesy Chicago Historical Society.

(IX: 4). Aerial view of Riverview Park, Chicago, Ill., 1931. The famous *Bobs* roller coaster can be traced through the center foreground shed with the Grecian columns. To follow its layout see fig X:7. Courtesy Chicago Historical Society.

(IX: 5). *Fireball* (formerly *Blue Streak*). Riverview Park, Chicago, Ill., Patrons and advertisements claimed it traveled the unlikely speed of 100 m.p.h. The first drop made it seem possible. Courtesy *Chicago Sun Times*.

(IX: 8). Tray depicting the reckless spirit of Coney Island, Brooklyn, N.Y. in the "Roaring Twenties."

(IX: 6). *Bobs*. Riverview Park, Chicago, Ill. This amazing Frederick Church/ Harry Traver creation is considered by many to be the finest roller coaster ever built. It survived 43 legendary years (1924-67). Courtesy Frederick Fried Archives.

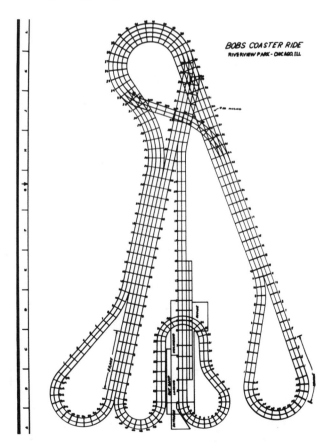

(IX: 7). Layout of the *Bobs*. Courtesy Chicago Historical Society.

It begins quickly, faster than other roller coasters, because this is the King. Down and through the short first tunnel, racing already, even though it doesn't have to, not yet, because the first hill is yet to be scaled. And then you see it, soaring unbelievably, so steep that you are nearly on your back once the train begins the ascent. Already people are nervously giggling, and every so often someone too impractical to save his utterances for later, screams. We are going up and there is no way to stop the ride. We will have to endure it, and to do that we will have to scream as loudly as we can, as often as we can.

The camaraderie is evident. We are pilgrims embarking on a journey. We are nervous, and we grin with gritted teeth into the winds. No one has ever worried about dignity on the *Bobs*. Now we are right at the top, just a long burr on the *Bobs'* savage back, about to be . . . flung down!

Down! Up! Fierce screeching turns! Banking so steeply that we crash screaming against each other, now tearing straight on, the undersides of the tracks we've been on seconds before just inches above our heads, then wrenching left, shooting ahead, then dipping down and up thinking, Geez, if I hadn't been holding on . . . and now flying around a steeply banked turn over the heads of a hundred people in line scanning our faces for panic or nausea, then into the twisting bowels of the *Bobs* again thinking, that's the turn that's in the ads, that's the turn! and on and on and on, lights flashing and the night a wild windstorm as we're twisting, swerving, swooping, wrenching, rearing, roaring towards the end.[2]

This is the same roller coaster that opened in 1924, giving us some idea of rides in the 1920's. It is unfortunate the *Bobs* was torn down in 1967 (Chapter XI) thereby losing a yardstick by which to measure recent roller coasters. From photographs alone, it seems rides of the 1920's must have been the most savage ever built. Yet, these remain memories and defenders of contemporary coasters claim such stories merely fiction. A classic still exists, however, from the 1920's that seems to put arguments to rest and it remains the standard that we measure all coasters against.

### Coney Island Cyclone

Coney Island, Brooklyn, continued to dazzle. It was among America's favorite tourist attractions and a must for foreign visitors. Maxim Gorki wrote in 1903 of its spectacle:

When nights falls, a phantom city of lights rears itself skyward on the ocean. A myriad of glowing sparks scintillate in the darkness, tracing with exquisite subtlety against the dark background of the sky stately turrets of wondrous castles, palaces and temples of coloured crystal. A golden cobweb quivers in the air, weaves itself into a translucent pattern of fire and hangs motionless admiring the beauty of its reflection in the water. Enchanting and incomprehensible in this fire, which burns but does not devour; inexpressibly beautiful in its magnificent, barely perceptible shimmer that creates a magical spectacle of a city of fire amid the bare expanses of sky and ocean. Over it hovers a ruddy glow, and the water gives back its contours, merging them in fantastic splashes of molten gold . . .[3]

Yet, the amusement complex was becoming fraz-

zled in the 1920's. Coney Island was referred to as "The Old Courtesan." Concessionaires, with little outside control, were now dominating the area.

Roller coasters would quickly come and go at Coney Island. There was even an attempt with the *Cannon Coaster* (fig. IX: 9) to leap cars over a gap in the tracks. Fortunately, loaded with sandbags instead of people, the idea didn't work. The gap was later filled with mundane tracks and the ride, boring in every other respect, drew crowds because of stories of innumerable casualties during its gap-in-the-track test runs.

The most successful concession was the great Coney Island *Cyclone* (fig. IX: 11-14).

The Rosenthal brothers, Jack and Irving, grabbed a 19 year lease on a 75 x 500 foot lot on the corner of Surf Avenue and West End Street in early 1927. They immediately tore down the resident *Giant Coaster* (fig. IX: 10) and started planning the finest roller coaster in the world. It was to be the highest and was to have spiral turns. Vernon Keenan was to be the designer, Bill McKee, superintendent, and the Harry C. Baker Company was put in charge of construction with the National Bridge Company supervising iron work. They immediately ran into trouble.

Windstorms lashed Coney Island and it was one of the resort's poorest seasons. Construction was almost impossible in such gales and the project seemed jinxed. Through what amounts to heroism, the *Cyclone* opened six weeks behind schedule on June 26, 1927, and was one of Coney Island's biggest successes. The Rosenthal's $100,000 investment was returned in just a few weeks. "It's one grand thing after another. The latest ride sensation that has swept the Island is the *Cyclone*," reported a July 9, 1927 *Billboard*. "It lives up to its title and has already established an enviable reputation as a thriller. It is accumulating the shekels abundantly. Large crowds are in evidence until the 2:00 a.m. curfew. ...It simply wows the spectator and is a bally par excellence."[4]

The coaster's giant sign caused as much excitement and its ten-foot letters with 500 light bulbs made C-Y-C-L-O-N-E a permanent part of Coney Island's landscape.

Success continued until the Rosenthals decided to take over management of Palisades Park (Chapter XI) in 1934. Chris Feucht, designer of the *Drop-the-Dip* (Chapter VI), was induced from retirement to run the *Cyclone* in partnership with George Kister.

Over that ten year period, the *Cyclone* was becom-

(IX: 10). *Giant Coaster*. Coney Island, Brooklyn, N.Y. Courtesy Staples and Charles Ltd.

(IX: 9). *Cannon Coaster*. Coney Island, Brooklyn, N.Y. The *Cannon Coaster* attempted to hurdle a break in the rails and became famous because it failed. The gap was later completed with mundane tracks.

(IX: 12). Chris Feucht (top) reworking the *Cyclone*. Coney Island, Brooklyn, N.Y., c. 1937. Chris Feucht's ingenuity turned the *Cyclone* into the great roller coaster we know today. Courtesy Brooklyn Library.

(IX: 11). *Cyclone*. Coney Island, Brooklyn, N.Y. The Rosenthal Brothers/Vernon Keenan Cyclone on its opening day, June 26, 1927. Note Luna Park and L.A. Thompson's *Scenic Railway* in the background. The *Cyclone* is the ride all coasters are measured against. Courtesy Frederick Fried Archives.

(IX: 13). *The Cyclone*. Oil on canvas, 24″x30″, 1970. Former circus barker, undertaker, and newsstand manager Vestie Davis (1903-1978) became a painter at age 44. Several of his remarkable canvases are of the Coney Island *Cyclone*. See also fig. IV: 28. Collection of Joan and Darwin Bahm. Courtesy Museum of American Folk Art.

ing rougher and producing more bruises than customers thought necessary. Attendance was down and the structure needed prompt repair. Chris Feucht (fig. IX: 12) redesigned many features of the coaster and turned it into the ride we know today. He single-handedly saved the *Cyclone* from the junk heap.

Feucht was almost lost during early repairs. While working on the chain lift of the first hill, he was caught from behind by an empty train and dragged up the tracks under the first car. He remembers:

> I held on as well as I could but my head kept bumping against the wooden cleats of the catwalk and I was afraid I'd be knocked unconscious and lose my grip. Eight seconds more and I would have gone over the top and down the eighty foot drop. You know how fast the train goes down there? It's about 60 miles an hour. Well, I was almost there when the man at the brake levers on the ground realized something was wrong and pressed the button shutting off the power. When I felt the train stop and realized I was saved, I passed out cold.[5]

The *Cyclone* to this day ranks with the finest in the world even among the current multi-million dollar megacoasters. It is the subject of much artwork, particularly folk artists (fig. IX: 13, 14).

Designer Vernon Keenan, after the success of the *Cyclone,* joined Harry Baker to build one of the most debated roller coasters of the 1920's, the *Blue Streak* at Woodcliffe Pleasure Park on the Hudson,

Poughkeepsie, New York (fig. IX: 15). The ride remains controversial because little information can be found on either the roller coaster or the park except the unbelievable hoopla found in *Billboard* magazines of 1927. The city of Poughkeepsie seems to have forgotten about the park. The *Blue Streak* was either 127' or 140' high, either measurement making it the highest roller coaster until the 141' high *Beast* at Kings Island, Cincinnati.

Vernon Keenan II writes of his father in a June 9, 1974, letter:

> After the Crash of 1929, my father went to work for Mr. Hall as manager of the Crystal Beach Park. I spent many days in the park, of course, and remember the excitement of the *Cyclone.* Shortly after, my father built a coaster at the Chicago World's Fair. I believe I was the first to ride this when some of the workmen let me take the place of one of the sandbags they were using to test it before putting it into operation. (This coaster was later reassembled at Riverview Park in Chicago and my son and I used to ride it there.) My father also built a coaster at the New York World's Fair in 1939, I believe.[6]

Vernon Keenan, along with John Miller and a few others, were the exception to the rule. They were isolated designers in an industry coming to be dominated by large companies and families. Like most businesses up to the present time, the loner was being replaced by the organization.

(IX: 14). *Cyclone.* Anonymous sculptor, wood, 9"H x 11¼"L x 1½" W, 1978. Courtesy Allen and Liucija Ambrosini.

(IX: 15). *Blue Streak*. Woodcliffe Pleasure Park on the Hudson, Poughkeepsie, N.Y., 1927. The *Blue Streak* at 127' or 140' was the highest coaster in the world for fifty years. See also Frontispiece. Courtesy George Siessel and Joe Heflin

(IX: 16). Philadelphia Toboggan Company. Germantown, Pa., early 1920s. Courtesy Charles J. Jacques, Jr./*Amusement Park Journal*.

### The Philadelphia Toboggan Company

Two companies came to dominate roller coaster design in the United States during the 1920's: National Amusement Device (Chapter XI) and Philadelphia Toboggan, that remarkable company that to this day is most associated with roller coasters.[7] They have outlasted all rivals.

The founders of Philadelphia Toboggan were Henry B. Auchey and Chester E. Albright. Auchey ran Chestnut Hill Park in Philadelphia but was unhappy with the quality of amusement rides. He opened the Philadelphia Toboggan Company in 1904 (fig. IX: 16) at 130 East Duval Street in nearby Germantown selling primarily Carousels. The term toboggan referred to the slides and roller coasters also manufactured by the company. PTC prospered, building around 75 Carousels (the last built in 1936) and, to date, close to 150 roller coasters. In 1973, the company moved to Eighth and Maple Streets in Lansdale, Pennsylvania, and is still producing coaster cars but designing fewer roller coasters since John Allen's death in 1979 (Chapter XII).

Philadelphia Toboggan's greatest showcase was Coney Island, Cincinnati, Ohio (Chapter XI). The company built, among other devices, the 1925 *Wildcat* and the mysterious *Twister* (also 1925), a completely enclosed roller coaster with curves reputedly banked at 28 degrees (fig. IX: 18). If proof was needed of the quality of PTC coasters, prospective buyers were simply given a pass to spend the day at Coney Island with few strings attached.

PTC's roster lists many designers including McKee, Watkins, Hoover, Allen, and a freelancing John Miller. It was Herb Schmeck, however, that must be given credit for the company's success, particularly in the 1920's. Schmeck worked under John Miller on the *Giant Coaster,* Paragon Park,

Nantasket Beach, Mass., in 1917-18 (fig. VIII: 9). Absorbing the ideas of the master, Schmeck took over PTC in the early 20's and turned the company into one of the Miller Company's chief rivals.

To compete with the Traver/Prior/Church roller coasters (Chapter X), PTC manufactured their own pretzel-like roller coasters and named them *Wildcats*. They were extreme. Two of the finest were located at Rocky Springs, Lancaster, Pennsylvania, and Lakeside Park, Dayton, Ohio. Both demonstrated the severity of PTC designs.

Tall tales come and go, but the abundance of stories about the roller coasters from the 1920's is unequalled, particularly tales of the wildest rides ever built. The Traver/Prior/Church coasters are usually mentioned in hushed tones and most buffs today say they wish they had ridden the Crystal Beach *Cyclone* or Rye Beach's *Aero-Coaster*. One fanatical group, however, claims Rocky Springs's 1928 *Wildcat* made all other rides look pale in comparison (fig. IX: 22).

Roller coasters built in natural ravines seem to rate among the best ever built. John Miller's Puritas Springs's *Cyclone,* the *Blue Streak* at Woodcliffe Pleasure Park, Poughkeepsie, and Kennywood's *Thunderbolt* were a few. But in this special category, Rocky Springs's *Wildcat* appears the most ominous. The ride has been surveyed from every angle and the most accurate say the first hill was 90'3" dropping into a wooded hollow at 60 degrees, the steepest wooden coaster incline ever built. The second hill was higher than most coasters of the time at 72 feet.[8]

Perhaps not in the same category as Rocky Springs is the Lakeside Park, Dayton, Ohio, *Wildcat* (fig. IX: 23). (See also Chapter XI.) Built 1929-30, the ride was dwarfed in size and reputation by the nearby *Flying Turns*. Still, coaster connoisseurs found the ride much more terrifying than its illustrious

(IX: 17). Coney Island. Cincinnati, Oh., 1925. Coney Island became the showcase of Philadelphia Toboggan coasters. Courtesy B. Derek Shaw.

(IX: 18). *Twister*. Coney Island, Cincinnati, Oh., 1926. Courtesy Charles J. Jacques, Jr./*Amusement Park Journal*.

(IX: 19). Erie Beach Park. Ontario, Canada, 1928. Courtesy Charles J. Jacques, Jr./*Amusement Park Journal*.

(IX: 21). Salisbury Beach. PTC, Salisbury Beach, Mass., 1927. (rebuilt by Dodgem Corporation). Courtesy Charles J. Jacques, Jr./*Amusement Park Journal.*

: 20). Shady Grove Park. PTC, Connellsville, Pa., 1925. Courtesy Charles Jacques, Jr./*Amusement Park Journal.*

(IX: 23). *Wildcat.* Lakeside Park, Dayton, Oh., 1929/30. Spectators would gather at night to watch sparks fly off the second hill's severely banked tracks. Note the chutes (right) of Bartlett and Miller's first *Flying Turns.* Courtesy Charles J. Jacques, Jr./*Amusement Park Journal.*

(IX: 22). Climbing the 1928 *Wildcat*, Rocky Springs Park, Lancaster, Pa. Rocky Spring Manager Ben Brookmeyer (bottom to top) and ACE members B. Derek Shaw, Jim Roberts, and Don Newtig scale the ruins of the *Wildcat,* October 1982. The great ride was bulldozed two years later. Photograph by Wayne Stuber.

neighbor and its amazing, curving second hill a rival of Traver/Prior/Church's best. Overall, it was probably a better paced ride than the Rocky Springs's *Wildcat* but lacked its crushing first hill and grandeur of site.

Perhaps even more dominant than the major companies from the beginning of the century into the late 1920's were concessionaires.

Often single figures or families would take over the task of designing, building, hiring crews, and supervising construction of coasters for themselves or other parks. Often, too, as John Miller, they would free-lance and would work for companies such as Philadelphia Toboggan. These small firms are so numerous that it's impossible to mention them all, but three families deserve special credit: The Pearces, Vettels, and Looffs.

### The Pearce Family

The Pearce family contributed mightily to the amusement park industry. They have 30 listed roller coasters; unfortunately, most of them have disappeared without benefit of plans or photographs.

The Pearces started in 1902 at Exposition Park, Conneaut Lake, Pennsylvania, where Josiah Pearce owned and ran a small steamboat. Son, Fred Pearce, then 17, became its captain. By 1905, the Pearces had moved into the park business when Josiah Pearce and Sons (Josiah with Fred and brother, J. Eugene) built an *Old Mill,* a tunnel of love type ride at Exposition Park.

Fred moved that year to Fairyland Park in Paterson, New Jersey, where he built both a Figure Eight and an unnamed roller coaster. He left after five years of operating the rides. The Pearce family then moved exclusively into park construction and operation with the building of rides as the business's backbone.

In 1918, following Josiah's death, Fred (fig. IX: 24) took over the firm.

(IX: 24).  J. Eugene Pearce (left); Fred Pearce. Dallas, Tex., 1930. Courtesy Fred W. Pearce.

Their biggest single park job was Jefferson Beach, Detroit, built in 1927 at a coast of $1,250,000. Other complete parks include Pleasure Beach, Bridgeport, Conn., Walled Lake Park near Detroit, Chain of Rocks Park, St. Louis, and Excelsior Park, Minneapolis.

Among roller coasters credited to the Pearce family are: Ocean View Park in Virginia (fig. IX: 25); the *Big Dipper* at Chippewa Lake Park (Ohio); a Racer at Revere Beach, Mass.; another Racer at Lakeside Park, Denver; a 4,000 foot long coaster at Capitol Park, Lincoln, Nebraska (completely destroyed by a tornado); and most famous, the massive *Trip Thru the Clouds* (fig. IX: 26) of 1915 at Riverview Park, Belle Isle Bridge, Detroit. It measured over one mile carrying six trains running at twenty second intervals. The first hill was over 90 feet (1915!) and required a crew of 20 to run it. *Trip Thru the Clouds* was destroyed in 1924.

Fred Pearce is well remembered for several other contributions. The invention of pressure-treated creosoted lumber that protects against wood rot and decay made construction cheaper and consequently more coasters available to the public.

Pearce was one of the first to realize the historical importance of amusement parks and was an early officer of W.F. Mangels's ill-fated American Museum of Public Recreation at 2875 West 8th Street, Coney Island, Brooklyn. He died July 9, 1958, and was succeeded by Fred Pearce, Jr.

(IX: 25). *Leap the Dips.* Ocean View Park, Norfolk, Va., (n.d.). Courtesy Fred W. Pearce.

(IX: 26). *Trip Thru the Clouds.* Riverview Park, Belle Isle Bridge, Detroit, Mich., 1915-24. The ride's front sign reads "Biggest Roller Coaster in the World," which *Trip Thru the Clouds* was in every statistical respect. It was Fred Pearce's masterpiece. Courtesy Fred W. Pearce.

### The Vettel Family

Erwin (fig. IX: 27) and Edward A. Vettel were authentic coaster pioneers and several of their rides stand today. Erwin's son, Andy, who still lives at Kennywood Park, Pittsburgh (he is responsible for their sensational *Thunderbolt*), when asked about his family history, said this in a 1974 interview:

> My father and his oldest brother started back around 1898. Something like that. Figure Eights. They both used to work for the T.M. Harton Company. Harton was something like Philadelphia Toboggan, building coasters all over the world. This was back in the early 1900's. My dad and uncle were building for them. Some rides were kept as concessions but most of them were like John Allen. They'd sell a design and send a man to supervise the building. That's what Harton did with my dad and uncle.
>
> We all followed the family tradition. Edward's son, Ed, is at Ponchartrain; and my brother, Robert, is out at Westview. The family has seen a lot of roller coasters. Near here we had the old *Leap-the-Dips* at Cedar Point and the coaster at Conneaut is still standing. Dad worked mostly out of Westview Park on the other side of town where Harton was.[9]

Westview Park's great roller coaster was the T.M. Harton/Vettel *Dip-the-Dip* (fig. IX: 29) later called the *Dips*. It was a magnificent ride that lasted 70 years before its deplorable destruction in 1980. Another Vettel family coaster, the beautiful *Zephyr* (fig. IX: 30) at Ponchartrain Beach, New Orleans, was bulldozed under in 1983. The *Zephyr* was built by Edward and son, Ed, in 1933. It will always be remembered for its psuedomoderne, art deco train car replica loading platform and the forbidding tunnels skillfully distributed throughout the ride.

An equally wonderful Vettel roller coaster stands in Denver at Lakeside Park. The Edward A. Vettel designed *Cyclone* (fig. IX: 31) follows the path of the park's old *Derby Coaster*. It's a showcase of Vettel family trademarks in its combination of hills, curves, and elegant structuring as are the cars which could easily be displayed in a museum.

### The Looff Family

Another important contributor was Arthur Looff, son of the great carousel designer, carver, and manufacturer, Charles Looff. Arthur, born June 11, 1888, joined his father's firm at the age of 16 but immediately concentrated on building and designing other rides for the expanding factory such as Ferris Wheels, swings, and roller coasters.

In 1910, Charles Looff moved most of his business from Riverside, Rhode Island, to California, first in Ocean Park and later to Long Beach. In 1916, Charles and Arthur opened the great Santa Monica Pleasure Pier near Linda Vista Park Palisades. The Arthur Looff designed *Blue Streak* roller coaster extended into the ocean (fig. IX: 32), and the site became one of the premiere amusement areas, along with Venice and Long Beach, of the Los Angeles area.

The Hippodrome building with its carousel still stands today and is often seen on television and in movies.

Arthur Looff's greatest roller coaster was the *Giant Dipper* (fig. IX: 33) at Santa Cruz Beach just outside San Francisco. It seems appropriate the ride was the creation of a carousel family since it is among the most beautiful standing today (the Smithsonian listed it as "The Most Beautiful" in 1976;[10] *Oui* magazine called it the "most sensuous" in 1977.[11]) It is also a superb ride and is seen on many "top-ten" roller coaster lists.

The *Giant Dipper* and Coney Island *Cyclone* remain proof from the 1920's that coasters from that era more than hold their own against the giants of today. Yet even they were overshadowed in their own time by those ultimate terror coasters, the nightmare rides of the Traver Engineering Company and Prior and Church.

IX: 27). Erwin Vettel. *c.* 1900. Courtesy Andrew Vettel Collection and Courtesy Charles J. Jacques, Jr./*Amusement Park Journal.*

(IX: 28). *Scenic Auto Dip*. Canadian Exposition, Toronto, Canada, c. 1905. The T.M. Harton Company built roller coasters across the United States and Canada at the beginning of the century. The Vettels became Harton's trouble-shooters and helped supervise construction of the company's ''High-Grade Park Amusements.'' Courtesy Andrew Vettel Collection.

(IX: 29). *Dip the Dip* (later *Dips*). West View Park, Pittsburgh, Pa., 1910-80. Courtesy B. Derek Shaw.

(IX: 30). *Zephyr*. Ponchartrain Beach, New Orleans, La., 1938-83. Courtesy *New Orleans Times-Picayune*.

(IX: 33). *Giant Dipper*. Santa Cruz Beach, Santa Cruz, Calif. 192
Courtesy Santa Cruz Beach.

(IX: 31). *Cyclone*. Lakeside Park, Denver, Colo. 1940. The Edward
Vettel *Cyclone* displays long, elegant lines and the beautiful (often
red and yellow) cars are of museum quality.

(IX: 32). *Blue Streak*. Santa Monica Pleasure Pier, Santa Monica, Calif., 1916. Courtesy Cameo Production

# Chapter X
## Traver, Prior and Church

Those looking for the wildest, scariest, most forbidding roller coasters ever built need look no further than this chapter. The monstrous, brutish rides of Traver, Prior and Church have had every adjective — adjectives usually reserved for horror films — applied to them. Figure X:3 gives an idea of their severity.

They represent the extremes of the 1920's and probably of all-time. Traver's *Cyclones* could not be built today because of insurance risks and the realization by park managements that most families would not ride them. Yet, as an indication of the reckless spirit of the 1920's, their construction was not questioned in 1927.

Today the severity of Traver's rides is cause for argument. Some believe they were indeed too dangerous and that bloody noses and broken ribs are not a sign of entertainment and any notion of rebuilding them is foolhardy.*

---

*The two sides of the argument are best shown in: PRO: Munch, Richard. *Harry G. Traver: Legends of Terror.* Mentor, Ohio: Amusement Park Books. 1982.
 CON: Heflin, Joe, "Traver Cyclones: Reexamination," *Coaster World,* Volume IV, issue 3, Fall 1983, pp. 8-13.

(X: 2). Harry Guy Traver (1877-1961). His triplets, the *Cyclones* at Crystal Beach, Revere Beach, and Palisade Park, are the pinnacles of roller coaster ferocity. The Crystal Beach *Cyclone* is the ride most coaster buffs say they wish they had ridden. Courtesy June Schetterer.

(X: 1). *Bobs.* Riverview Park, Chicago, Ill. 1924-67. The *Bobs* was the earliest collaboration of Church and Traver and to many, their masterpiece. The columns (right) can also be found in the aerial view of Riverview Park, fig. IX: 4. Courtesy Frederick Fried Archives.

Further debates rage over who really built and designed some of these monsters. Who was the real villain / saint? All the files, plans, and signed drawings of the Traver Engineering Company have been destroyed. Without such documented evidence, it is difficult to say who designed or built many of these roller coasters. Traver and Church worked together on several rides, then separated and produced individual masterpieces. Traver built some Church designed coasters, Traver designed and built some Traver coasters, and Church designed and built some Church rides.

Arguments say that Frederick Church is the real "Evil Genius" behind the *Bobs* type coaster and there is evidence to support this. The wonderful Rye Beach *Aero-Coaster* is now recognized as completely his.

But how can you ignore Traver's contributions. He was brilliant as indicated by Patents 1,805,266 (May 12, 1931) and 1,806,102 (May 19, 1931) (fig. X: 4,5).* He was a spectacular showman and the 1920's and roller coasters themselves benefitted from his influence. His rides have taken on legendary status and are so special they deserve this chapter separated from other roller coasters of the Golden Age.

### Harry Guy Traver

"Seagulls got me into this crackpot business", Harry Traver (fig. X:2) is recorded to have said. Traver was working on a cattle boat to Europe early in his career (1901) and was recuperating from an attack of diptheria. He was daydreaming on the deck while watching seagulls circle the ship's mast. In his mind the graceful swoops of the birds turned into suspended cars swinging around a tall pole. The image stuck and Traver turned the idea into the Circle Swing — his first and most popular ride (fig. X:6).

Harry Guy Traver was born in Gardner, Illinois, November 25, 1877. His father was a farmer and Harry received his early education in Gardner. He graduated from Davenport (Nebraska) High School in 1894 and later studied at both New York University and College of the City of New York.

---

*Even the honesty and originality of Traver's contributions are in question. Harry Davis, during a March 1978 interview, said that Traver "...couldn't design a sour apple. All he could do was get some ideas. He had some crazy ideas." Davis further said that Traver put all company patents under his name whether he helped with the design or not. Yet Anna Cook, Administrative Manager of Palisades Park, remembers, during a July 1983 interview, that Traver did all his drawing, planning, and designing.

His career followed a rocky path. In 1895 he became a teacher for three years back at Davenport. This was followed by a job as mechanical engineer with the General Electric Company at the 1898 Omaha Exposition (fig. X:7). Traver then worked for the Denver Tramway Company (1898-1900) and the Harris Safety Company, New York City, as shop superintendent (1901-1902). It was at this time that he reportedly designed and built the first mechanically drawn fire engine for New York City's Fire Department. All of this was the finest training for his eventual entry into the amusement park business.

With the idea of the Circle Swing as impetus, Traver began designing and building amusement park rides in 1903. He transferred his belongings from New York City to Beaver Falls, Pa., in 1919 and organized the Traver Engineering Company. Harry Traver built a remarkable business turning out such rides as Laff in the Dark, Bug Ride, Turtle Chase, and Scooter Ride. A January 5, 1924, *Billboard* magazine reports,

With the completion of the paint shop of the Traver Engineering Company at Beaver Falls, Pa., the plant will be the largest in the world devoted exclusively to the manufacture of amusement devices....[1]

(X: 3). The original and often quoted column of Robert Garland in the June 14, 1928, *New York Telegram*. Courtesy June Schetterer.

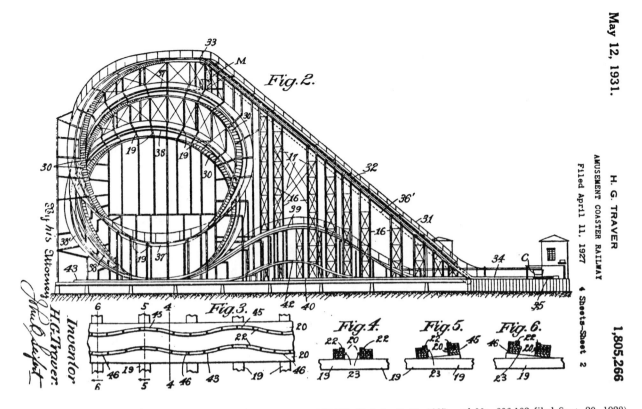

(X: 4, 5). These elaborate nine and six page patents (No. 1,805 266 filed April 11, 1927; and No. 806,102 filed Sept. 20, 1928) list many features and the layout of Traver's great *Cyclone* roller coasters.

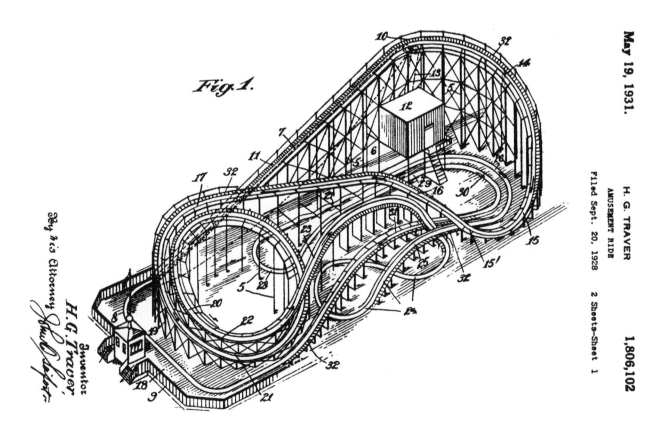

It was also in 1924 that the first prominent notice of Traver roller coaster appears. Dated August 23, the *Billboard* article states:

> *BOBS* Coaster, Chicago. It was designed by Fred Church and built by the Traver Engineering Company. The dips are all on steep spiral curves banked up to 45 degrees. Only the patented train can be used on these special dips. "Prior and Church patented," this is the first coaster built with tracks banked high enough on curves to prevent passengers falling out.[2]
> (See fig. X:1.)

Business boomed for the company including, in 1926, the construction of a *Cyclone* (the first use of the name) coaster for the Sesquicentennial Exposition in Philadelphia. The promotional material heralds the coaster as "...Strong as the Rock of Gibralter, patrons come 100 miles to ride this coaster. Dips are all on curves banked up to fifty degrees."

In 1927, Traver's infamous triplets were born: The Crystal Beach *Cyclone* (Ontario, Canada), Revere Beach's Lightning (Boston, Mass.), and Palisades Park's *Cyclone* (Fort Lee, N.J.). A new standard was set for roller coaster savagery. Here is a description of the Crystal Beach *Cyclone's* opening from a December 31, 1927, *Billboard:*

> ...If you don't think so, ask G.E. Hall of Crystal Beach who installed one of Harry G. Traver's super-stupendous gravity rides, the *Cyclone,* which on the opening day, it is estimated, drew 75,000 people to Crystal Beach. Hall states that the crowds were so great that they broke down the rail-

ings in order to get a close-up of the *Cyclone.* One man, in particular, was so vividly impressed that he rode it 67 times. It took him three hours to accomplish this feat. The second day two boys rode it 52 times which cost them $26.75.[3]

There might be doubts over opening day attendance but not the *Cyclone's* ferocity. The ride is now a legend and the coaster most buffs wish they had ridden. It is the ultimate terror ride. (fig. X:8-13).

The monster reputation frightened many patrons from testing the ride. This, ever rising insurance costs, and frequent maintenance led to the *Cyclone's* demolition on September 16, 1946.

The *Lightning* and Palisades's *Cyclone* were more or less duplicates of the Crystal Beach *Cyclone,* equally violent but not as well publicized. For a description of the Palisades coaster, see Robert Garland's *New York Telegram* report (fig. X:3).

Harry Davis (fig. X:14), a supervisor at the Traver Company, worked with the *Lightning* (fig. X:15) at Revere Beach and gave this description during a 1978 interview:

> ...But I went up and helped Jim Mitchell at Revere Beach. I helped Jim break in his cars and we thought we had a stinker. We couldn't get those cars to come in no way. We'd haul them in with block and tackle. Those G#☆!! cars just wouldn't come in. Woke up one Sunday morning and it was just raining pitchforks—just coming down in

(X: 6) Circle Swing. Mid-City park, Albany, N.Y., c. 1905. The Circle Swing was Traver's first and most popular ride. Originals can still be found in some parks today.

(X: 7). Harry Traver's identification card for the Trans-Mississippi International Exposition in Omaha, Nebr. 1898. Courtesy June Schetterer.

(X: 8). *Cyclone*. Crystal Beach, Ontario, Canada, 1927-46. Perhaps the most ferocious coaster ever built; The front cars twisted into a severe bank before the rear cars were atop the first hill. Builders could not put brakes outside the loading platform because there was not a level spot on the tracks. The *Cyclone* is the only roller coaster known to have had a nurse and a first aid station at the exit exclusively for its passengers. Courtesy Harry Davis.

(X: 9). *Cyclone*. Crystal Beach, Ontario, Canada, 1927-46. At the base of the first hill. Courtesy Harry Davis.

(X: 10). *Cyclone.* Crystal Beach, Ontario, Canada, 1927-46. Looking down the chain lift over the *Cyclone* complex to the still standing *Giant Coaster.* Courtesy Harry Davis.

(X: 11). *Cyclone.* Crystal Beach, Ontario, Canada, 1927-46. The final curves into the unloading platform. Tracks at the base of the first hill can be seen in the background. Courtesy Harry Davis.

(X: 12, 13). *Cyclone.* Crystal Beach, Ontario, Canada, 1927-46. Traveling into and around the infamous figure eight, the most horrifying section of the *Cyclone.* Courtesy Harry Davis.

X:13

(X: 14). The brains and muscles of the *Cyclone*: (Left to right) Harry Davis, Ralph Chambers, and the two Mitchell brothers, James and John, all posing on Crystal Beach's *Cyclone* tracks. Courtesy Harry Davis.

(X:15). *Lightning*. Revere Beach, Mass., 1927-1933. Courtesy Joe Heflin.

(X: 16, 17). *Zip*. Oaks Park, Portland, Oreg.c. 1927-34. Courtesy Harry Davis.

The *Lightning* and Palisades's *Cyclone* had even shorter lives than the Crystal Beach *Cyclone* with demolitions in 1933 and 1934 respectively.

An oddball *Cyclone* type roller coaster was Traver's *Zip* (c.1927), Oaks Park, Portland, Oregon. It appears to have been an abbreviated form of the notorious triplets. The two photographs (fig. X:16,17) from Harry Davis's collection show a ride bordering on the macabre. There was a stunned silence when slides of these photos were shown at the 1979 American Coaster Enthusiasts' meeting in Cincinnati—as if some primeval nightmare had been projected on the screen. The *Zip* was totaled in 1934.

Traver had many patents that were never built. Patent 1,713,793 (May 21, 1929) (fig. X:18) is the most representative of this inventive and often bizarre mind. It reads in part:

> ...It is a further object of the invention to provide in apparatus of this character means to effect illusory representations to passengers, as giving an illusion of the car passing through episodes in action, such as a forest fire, a rain storm and of a car revolving about the track as it moves along the same.

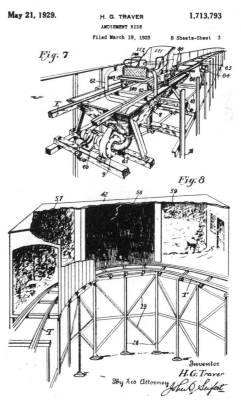

(X: 18). Traver's odd roller coaster Patent No. 1,713,793 (filed 1925) had a forest fire, rain storm, revolving cars, seats tilting backward, electric shocks, and blasts of confetti, in addition to the coaster ride

torrents—and I beat it down the hall of this hotel we were staying in and hammered on Jim's door. We got a half dozen or so of the gang that were working on the thing and by ten o'clock that morning we had the cars coming clear through like nobody's business. We were using sandbags instead of people.

We rolled a couple of cars out, Jim and I, and we decided we would ride the thing. So we got in, went over to hit the chain, and started up, and got to the top and ☆G#!!, I'd have given $50 to be out of that thing. It looked like four miles to the bottom. Jim told me afterward, brother, if I could have crawled out, I'd have been out. And we were the first ones to ride in it—Jim Mitchell and I. But after that, after I'd ridden the G#☆!! thing, I couldn't lay straight in bed at night.[4]

It is a further object of the invention to provide an improved passenger carrying car for amusement rides, wherein the seat is provided with a backward tilting back support, which seat back is normally releasably retained in back supporting position and adapted to release as the car moves along the track to cause the passenger to assume a partly inclining position, and after the seat has been tilted cause it to immediately be returned to back supporting position.

Further objects of the invention relate to noise making means to be actuated by the car as it passes along the track, such as the making of a clattering noise as the car rides down dips in the track, and also the means to impart an electric shock to a passenger of a car as well as when the passengers leave the ride.

Another object of the invention relates to the provision of a blower which is set in operation and stopped by the movement of the car along the track, and the blower arranged to direct the blast of air therefrom laden with comminuted material, such as confetti, against the passengers in the cars as they move along the track, a collector being provided for said material from which it is drawn by the blower to be used repeatedly.[5]

Harry Traver's most famous roller coaster was the *Cyclone Racer* (fig. X:19), Long Beach, California.

Built in 1930, it was Traver's favorite ride and his only Racing Coaster. The *Standard Star* (New Rochelle, New York) reports:

It was at the *Cyclone Racer* where a young man got off, got down and kissed the platform at the end of the ride. And it was also there where a passenger insisted on paying twice for one ride—'It was two rides—my first and last' he declared fervently.[6]

To the disgrace of Long Beach, the *Cyclone Racer* was destroyed in 1968 to make room for the *Queen Mary*.

The Great Depression wiped out the Traver Engineering Company. In 1932, Traver began an association with the Midway Recreation Corporation, Chicago, primarily in the construction and operation of scooter rides and roller coasters for the 1933 Century of Progress Exposition. His connection with World's Fair rides continued through the 1934-36 Brussels Exposition, the 1936-38 Paris Ex-

(X: 19). *Cyclone Racer*. The Pike, Long Beach, Calif., 1930-68. The *Cyclone Racer* was Traver's favorite and his only racing coaster. Courtesy George Metivier/Long Beach Historical Society.

position, and the 1939 World of Tomorrow Exposition (New York City).

Traver's inventive skills and lifetime interest in aviation (see also Chapter VI) met their test during World War II. He worked with General Motors, Lawrence Aeronautical Corporation, and Columbia University. During this time he designed torpedo controls and improved rocket launchers. This activity culminated in the award of a bronze plaque by Columbia University and the Navy Department for exemplary service.

After World War II, his efforts were again directed to the amusement park business. He established Traver Enterprises and planned the design and construction of kiddie rides for Playland, Rye Beach, New York. This work and his interest in anthropology (he authored a book tracing the history of mankind) absorbed his final years. It is a tragedy he witnessed the destruction of his major rides before his death September 27, 1961.

### Prior and Church

The race is on to find material on Frederick Church. There are mad scrambles, but little has surfaced other than some records in California. It appears the important documents disappeared with the burned Traver files.

Yet, the Traver masterpieces were obviously based on the brainstorms of Frederick Church. The aforementioned *Billboard* article (August 23, 1924) notes the *Bobs* ran on Church patented cars. Traver's later *Cyclone* coasters could not have run without these articulated cars. Further, the great *Cyclones* were, without question, based on Church *Bobs* designs.

(X:20). *Race Thru the Clouds.* Venice Amusement Park, Venice, Calif., c. 1924. The office of the great designer, Frederick Church (with partner Thomas Prior) is circled. Some of the finest and most thrilling roller coasters were planned here. Courtesy Mike Chew.

(X: 21). *Aero Coaster.* Rye Playland, Rye, N.Y., 1928-57. Perhaps the "Ultimate Roller Coaster," Frederick Church's *Aero Coaster* combined speed, height, safety, pacing, fright, and magnificent curves better than any ride in history. Courtesy Rye Playland.

Church and Prior worked for years in Venice, California, with offices near the entrance of their *Race Thru the Clouds* roller coaster (fig. X:20). Frederick Church was the designer/planner, and Thomas Prior was the needed business partner to guide fortunes along.

The *Aero-Coaster,* Rye Beach, N.Y., (fig. X:21) was Church's great, great masterpiece. Traver for years was listed as collaborator although an August 11, 1928, *Billboard* simply listed him as agent. During the summer of 1983, coaster buff, Joe Heflin, in a sweltering attic at Rye Beach, found signed plans for the *Aero-Coaster.* They showed once and for all that Harry Traver had nothing to do with the *Aero-Coaster's* design and construction. Frank W. Darling, who took over L.A. Thompson's company in 1915 and ran Rye Beach, is listed as contractor.

First named *Aeroplane Dips,* then *Aero-Coaster,* and finally *Airplane Coaster,* it is probably the greatest body wringer ever built. Both John Allen and Andrew Vettel remember getting nosebleeds on the ride. Here is what Louis Botto writes in the May 21, 1978, *Sunday News Magazine* (New York):

> The Airplane Coaster was 92 feet high and was constructed as a series of whiplash curves. When the car reached the top of the first hill and started its descent, it took a sharp curve, then plunged straight down into a tunnel ten feet below ground. That was nothing. The second hill was built like a whirlpool. At the top, the car made an immediate curve, then reached down a spiral track banked

so steeply that you were thrown to one side, rattled and knocked almost senseless as it shook the breath out of you. The rest of the ride consisted of shattering drops and twists. We were never able to ride this coaster twice in succession. It jangled your nerves so that you had to recuperate on the carousel.[7].

The *Aero-Coaster* was dismantled in 1957.

Confusion it appears will reign for many years over the contributions of Frederick Church and Harry Traver. Several recently discovered coaster plans have moved authorship from the Traver Engineering Company to Church, adding strength to the Church camp. In fact, it is often sarcastically remarked that the only difference between Traver and Church is that Traver used steel structuring while Church used more forgiving wood. Such simplistic barbs only deny Traver's unique contributions. Both Traver and Church contributed mightily to roller coasters. Both are symbolic of the superb rides of the 1920's.

Joe Heflin's list of Traver, Prior and Church roller coasters is the most accurate to date:

Documented Traver Engineering Designed and Built Rollercoasters

*Cyclones:*

Philadelphia Sesquicentennial (1926); moved to Fair Park, Birmingham, Alabama (1927); moved to Century of Progress, Chicago (1933)

Crystal Beach, Canada (1927)

Revere Beach, Mass. (1927)

Palisades Park, Ft. Lee, N.J. (1927)

Oaks Park, Portland, Oregon (1927)

Harry Traver along with Leonard Thompson (of Blackpool, England), had a Cyclone coaster in Paris in 1937.

*Jazz Railways:*
Rocky Glen Park, Scranton, Pa. (1925)
Fair Park, Birmingham, Alabama (1927); from Philadelphia Sesquicentennial (1926)
Exposition Park, Bombay, India (1928)
May also have been erected at parks in Toronto and Detroit (1925), and New Orleans (late 1920's).

*Whirlwind Racer* (3rd Rail Racing Coaster)
Midland Beach, N.Y. (1929)
Exhibition Park, Philippines (1929)
Jantzen Beach, Portland, Oregon (1929)
May also have been erected at Woodlawn Park, Trenton, N.J. (1929)

Documented Prior and Church Designed, Traver Engineering Built Roller-coasters, 1930 and Earlier:
*Bobs:*
Riverview Park, Chicago (1924)
Palace Gardens, Belle Isle, Detroit, Michigan (1925)
Savin Rock, Conn. (1925)
Revere Beach, Mass. (1925)
Eastwood Park, Detroit, Michigan (1928)
Ponchartrain Beach, New Orleans (1928)
Cedar Point, Sandusky, Ohio (1929)
Forest Park, Genoa, Ohio (1929)
Willow Beach, Toledo, Ohio (1929)
Belle Vue Gardens, Manchester, England (1929)
Waukesha Beach, Milwaukee, Wisc. (1930)
Long Beach, Calif. (1930)

Documented Prior and Church Designed and Built *Bobs* Coasters:
1. Ocean Park, Ca. 1923
2. Lincoln Park, Los Angeles, Ca. 1923
3. Venice Beach, Ca. 1924
4. Redondo Beach, Ca. 1924
5. Chutes Park, San Francisco, Ca., (1924/25)
6. Santa Monica, Ca. 1924/1925
7. Mission Beach, San Diego, Ca. 1925
May also include Honolulu, Hawaii and Bohemia Park, Los Angeles, Ca. 1925

Documented Prior and Church Designed, but Builder Unknown Coasters:
Hastings Park, Vancouver, British Columbia (1927/28)
Santa Monica, Calif. (1930)

Documented coasters that incorporate Prior and Church patents:
1. Santa Cruz *Giant Dipper,* 1924/25
2. Jantzen Beach, Portland, Or. 1928/29
3. Hastings Park, Vancouver, B.C. 1928

Documented Fred Church designed and built coasters:
Rye Playland, Rye, N.Y. *Airplane,* 1928

Note:
At least three other Traver built *Bobs* coasters were installed in "eastern" parks (east of the Mississippi River) prior to 1929; they are unknown as of this writing (5/24/83). Also the *Tornado* at Coney Island, designed by Prior and Church, was built by the La Marcus Thompson Co. (1926).

Manila, Philippines: *Whirlwind Racer* (Traver, 1929)
Kings Park, Norfolk, Nebraska: (John A. Miller) (1929)
Manions Park, St. Louis, Mo. (John A. Miller) (1929)
Muskego, Beach, Milwaukee, Wis. (John A. Miller) (1929)
Casino Park, Mansfield, Ohio (John A. Miller) (1929)
Pearce Park, Wall Lake, Mich. (John A. Miller) (1929)
Milton Dam, Ohio (John A. Miller) (1929)
Lakeside Park, Battle Creek, Mich. (John A. Miller) (1929)
Island Park, Portsmouth, Rhode Island (Harry Baker)
Joyland, Clearwater Beach, Florida
Moxahala Park, Zanesville, Ohio: (John A. Miller)
Munich, Germany Fair: (Steel coaster, 2800' and portable, manufactured by Rupprecht)
Dreamland on the Bay, Love Point, Md. (near Balt.)
Ontario Lake, New York
Lake Hopatcong, N.J.
Exposition Park, Ft. Dodge, Iowa
Warners Park, Chattanooga, Tenn. (PTC)
Boardwalk, Jacksonville, Florida
Cedar Point, Sandusky, Ohio: *Cyclone* (OPENED in 1929)
Rosedale Park, Rosedale, Ky.
Crescent Park, Providence, Rhode Island: Comet
Neptune Park, Alameda, Calif.: (John A. Miller)
Lakeside Park, Wichita Falls, Texas: *Skyrocket* (John A. Miller, 1929)
Shady Grove Park, Uniontown, Pa.: (PTC, 1929)
Memorial Park, Williamsport, Pa.
Jefferson Beach, Detroit, Mich.: *Thunderbolt*
Columbia Park, North Bergen, New Jersey: a second coaster to go along with Baker's
Cenaqua Park, Detroit, Mich. (1929)
Fernbrook Park, Wilkes-Barre, Pa.
Dominion Park, Montreal, Canada
Bitter Lake, Seattle, Wash. (1930) (coaster was reportedly 4000' long; cost $75,000)
Oak Park, Houston, Texas (1930)
Lake Ariel Park, Scranton, Pa.
Erie Beach, Ontario, Canada: *Wildcat*
Lakeside, Dayton, Ohio: *Wildcat* (to go along with Flying Turns)
Jantzen Beach, Portland, Oregon: *Whirlwind Racer* (1929, Harry Traver)
Woodlawn Park, Trenton, New Jersey: *Whirlwind Racer* (possibly Traver, but no documentations) (opened 1929)
Edgewater Beach, Detroit, Mich.: Coaster was built but had to be demolished before it opened; it seems that part of it was built on land that did not belong to the park!!!) (1929)

Total number of coasters found: 117

It will be some time before this jigsaw puzzle is completed. Future roller coaster historians with the aid of newly discovered drawings, files and letters, such as fig. X:22, can supply missing pieces and reveal individual glories. It will take a Sherlock Holmes. It's worth the effort: The *Bobs, Aero-Coaster,* and the *Cyclones,* after all, have become the measuring standard for roller coasters since the 1920's.

MILFORD STERN PRESIDENT AND MANAGER

TELEPHONE EDGEWOOD 1661

## Palace Gardens Company
### OPERATING
## Palace Gardens Amusement Park
#### 7400 JEFFERSON AVENUE EAST
#### DETROIT, MICH.

March 30th, 1925

Mr. Fred A. Church,
c/o Prior & Church,
Venice, California

Dear Mr. Church:-

Beginning last Thursday we ran a pilot car over the new ride. For the first half dozen trips it was necessary to pull it over two or three of the humps, but after that, loaded with cement bags the car went the whole length of the ride herself. Then Bill Gierke added on one car after another to the pilot until by Saturday noon he had a full train of ten cars making the ride, beautifully and smooth and quietly as if it had been running for weeks.

Finally at about 2:00 o'clock Saturday afternoon Bill and I and a few of the men sat ourselves in the cars and took the ride twice in succession. We were delighted, completely captivated by it because it gives one the grand thrill and sensation so much desired by coaster riders.and at the same time has none of the nauseating effects of some of the giant rides. As far as I am any judge, this coaster will prove to be the biggest attraction of its kind that ever appeared in Michigan.

I congratulate you sincerely upon your remarkable achievement.

We are planning to open up the ride to the public next Sunday afternoon if the weather permits.

With kindest personal regards, I am

Cordially, yours,

*Milford Stern*

President,

PALACE GARDENS COMPANY.

MS/EDM

(X: 22). Letter to Frederick Church from Milford Stern, March 30, 1925. Courtesy Frederick Fried Archives.

# Chapter XI
## 1930-1972:
## Innovations and the Struggle to Survive

My heart was flying
Up, like a rocket ship
Down, like a roller coaster
Back, like a Loop-the-loop
And round, like a merry-go-round
...You'll never know how great a kiss can feel
—When you stop at the top of a Ferris wheel
When I fell in love
Down at Palisades Park[1]

  "PALISADES PARK"
  *Chuck Barris*

It was the bleakest of times for roller coasters. Over 2000 parks disappeared and almost as many coasters from 1930-1972.

The 1930's were the bleakest. The Great Depression caused most of the carnage but it wasn't the only destructive force. Greed, real estate interests, fire, arson, apathy, neglect, and more neglect figured in this deplorable period.

No one seemed to care. Invaluable records, blueprints, and negatives were intentionally destroyed. If lucky, they survived molding away in basements. Simply put, amusement parks and roller coasters were treated as an embarassing part of our American heritage.

Hidden behind this wall of destruction were important innovations and many parks survived the era. Kennywood, Elitch Gardens, and Cedar Point are thriving as never before. The saving, positive aspects (to be discussed in Chapter XII) also overlapped this period. But on the whole, 1930-1972 was a dark, unrewarding time for amusement parks.

It is not the intent of this book to dwell on devastation. Indeed, it is hoped the book is a joyous celebration. But the wholesale slaughter of roller coasters, cannot be ignored. If Chapter VII was an orgy of roller coasters, this chapter could easily be their dirge.

If anything symbolizes the dual aspects of this era, innovation and the struggle to survive, it is Palisades Park. Located on the Hudson across from Manhatten, it prospered into the 1970's. Palisades was innovative, offering boundless park invention and the finest of roller coasters. After all, during this time, it

had a Traver *Cyclone* (Chapter X), Bartlett's *Lake Placid Bob Sled* (Chapter VIII) and for nearly forty years another *Cyclone* that was called "The Favorite of the New York Yankees" (fig. XI:1). Both *Cyclones* were listed as legendary roller coasters by the Smithsonian Institution and there is argument that the Bartlett ride should have been listed high among them.

Palisades was ruthlessly leveled to make way for an apartment complex in 1972. Its demise appeared to be the tombstone of amusement parks. It wasn't, but more on this later in the chapter.

### Mechanical Gadget Resort

Coney Island, as usual, had its own unique history. It boomed and thrived while the money resorts closed during the Depression. Coney Island was where people had fun and rode roller coasters and neither fire nor windstorm could tame that great amusement area (fig. XI:2,3).

Steeplechase burned in 1907 in an eighteen-hour conflagration. George Tilyou was a fighter and erected a sign the next day:

I have troubles today
That I did not have yesterday.
I had troubles yesterday
That I have not today.
On this site will be erected shortly
A better,
Bigger,
Greater
Steeplechase Park.
Admission to the Burning Ruins—
10 cents

A bigger, better Steeplechase was built but more fires followed. Steeplechase's great pavilion was razed in 1965 leaving only its chimney as souvenir.

Dreamland burned May, 1911, in a fire unequaled in New York history. A million light bulbs exploded, the shooting-gallery's ammunition recocheted, the towers melted, and flames could be seen over Brooklyn from Manhattan and spotted from liners miles out to sea. Dreamland never opened again.

(IX: 1). *Cyclone*. Palisades Park, Fort Lee, N.J., 1926/34-1972.

(XI: 2). Above. Fire at Luna Park, Brooklyn, N.Y., 1905. The first large fire at Luna park. Coney Island was haunted by such devestation. Courtesy Brooklyn Library.

(XI: 3). Right. Fire at Steeplechase Park, Brooklyn, N.Y., Sept. 14, 1939. 50,000 visitors watch as another fire destroys 3 roller coasters and a *Flying Turns*. Courtesy International News Photo.

(XI: 4). Crowd at Coney Island, Brooklyn, N.Y., 1938. Police estimated this July 4, 1938, crowd at well over one million. Courtesy International News Photo.

(XI: 5). Aurel "Dutch" Vaszin was founder of National Amusement Device and a major force in the survival of roller coasters through the Great Depression.

Luna Park suffered fire in 1905, again in 1906, but survived. The fire of 1945 closed its doors forever.

An early seed to Coney's downfall was planted in 1920 with the completion of the subway. It opened the gates to crowds of such monstrous proportions that photographers traveled from over the world to record its beaches (fig. XI:4). Lines to the *Thunderbolt, Tornado,* and *Cyclone* reached three to five hours long. With rerides permissible, lines barely moved and during July heat waves, tempers flared. Several murders were recorded when the foolish dared cut in line.

Standing in line is part of a roller coaster ride, but waits of such frustrating length were a dangerous annoyance. Such bottlenecks were ingeniously overcome in the 1960's and are discussed in Appendix I.

Coney Island lost the fight when politicians stepped in. Robert Moses, who despised Coney Island, became Parks Commissioner in 1938 and began systematic destruction of the area. He believed, "No one was interested in a mechanical gadget resort like Coney Island", and in 1949 rezoned the land for housing projects. They ate the parks away. Coney Island became a ghostly shell. Author Mario Puzo put it this way:

> There was a time when every child in New York loved Coney Island, and so it breaks your heart to see what a slothful, bedraggled harridan it has become, endangered by the violence of its poor and hopeless people, as well as by the city planners who would improve it out of existence. If I were a wizard with one last magic trick in my bag, I would bring back the old Coney Island.[2]

(XI: 6). National Amusement Device offices and factory (center complex). Dayton, Ohio, late 1930s. With the establishment of N.A.D. offices, Dayton became a roller coaster capital from the 1930s into the 1950s.

### National Amusement Device Company

With parks collapsing and rides bulldozed across the country, how did roller coasters survive? One of the reasons can be found in a spot far removed from Coney Island's millions in Dayton, Ohio. Here, Aurel Vaszin, John Miller, and the National Amusement Device Company, against all odds, created some of the finest roller coasters in the world (fig. XI:5,6).

With its steel mills and bridge building facilities,

it's easy to understand why T.M. Harton and Frederick Ingersoll located in Pittsburgh. But why and how did conservative Midwest Dayton become a roller coaster center? Perhaps the answer is that Dayton, in the field of technology, was not at all conservative. It was a community that, after being ridiculed for ignoring the Wright brother's experiments, actually encouraged innovation. National Cash Register settled here and built a factory copied the world over. Wright-Patterson Field still designs and tests the most radical aircraft. One of the first wind tunnels was built here. Also located at Wright-Patterson Field is the Air Force Museum as well as Project Blue-Book and its catalogue of UFO's.

Dayton, too, had historically important Lakeside Park where John Miller and Norman Bartlett opened the first *Flying Turns* in 1929 (Chapter VIII). On the same grounds, Philadelphia Toboggan had one of its most splendid and ferocious *Wildcat* roller coasters (fig. IX:23). Customers would stand at the bottom of the first hill at night to watch sparks fly off the tracks.

Aurel "Dutch" Vaszin started The Dayton Fun House and Riding Device Manufacturing Company in the 1920's. When John Miller later added his inestimable know-how, the company evolved into Philadelphia Toboggan's chief competitor. The two

(XI: 7). The filming of *Cinerama* on the *Atom Smasher*, Rockaway's Playland, Rockaway Beach, Queens, N.Y., 1951.

companies helped roller coasters survive and deserve the highest accolades from coaster buffs.

National Amusement Device appeared prominently in the public eye when its Vernon Keenan designed *Atom Smasher* roller coaster opened the film *Cinerama* in 1952 (fig. XI:7,8). The movie was the novelty sensation of the year. Three cameras pro-

(XI: 8). The original 1952 advertisement for *Cinerama*. On the *Atom Smasher*, Rockaway's Playland, Rockaway Beach, Queens N.Y. *Cinerama* helped keep the roller coaster alive through the doldrums of the 1950's.

jected a roller coaster ride, the finale of Act II from *Aida* performed at the La Scala Opera House in Milan, Italy, the Vienna Boys Choir, a B-52 flying through the Grand Canyon, and others on a giant curving screen that surrounded and enveloped its customers.

The screen ride helped revive interest in roller coasters and is probably the most exciting and sensational action sequence ever put on film. The movie ride was so thrilling, coaster buffs were disappointed when they later rode the coaster at Rockaways' Playland, New York. The counterfeit, it seems, outdid reality.

In addition to running National Amusement Device, Aurel Vaszin managed nearby Forest Park ("Frankie's Forest Park") and ran his own coaster on the grounds. His most famous contribution was the wonderful art deco train that so trademarks roller coasters of that era (fig. XI:9).

The company built only a few roller coasters (the exact number is not clear) but they seemed many during a time when such rides were a rarity. The following are considered National Amusement Device's[3] finest:

*Sterling's Million Dollar Coaster,* Rocky Glen Park, Moosic, Pa. (fig. XI:10). This classic "out and back" opened in 1945 and carried over one-million

passengers its first three seasons. Designed by Vernon Keenan with contributions from Ackley, Bradley, and Day and Associates, the coaster was 4700 feet long and 96 feet high. It was squeezed between Glen Lake and the Wyoming Valley and Lackawanna Railroad tracks. According to B. Derek Shaw, it was partially built from the lumber of Fernbrook Park's roller coaster, Shavertown, Pa. It was called *Million Dollar Coaster* because park owners Ben and Mae Sterling liked the title (it cost $100,000.00). The ride was dismantled during the winter of 1957-58.

*La Montana Rusa(?),* Guatemala City, Guatemala. Over a mile long at 5800 feet, it has reached mythical—Olympian—status. The coaster's only known photograph is figure XI:11, found in the trash at National Amusement Device's old factory. It lasted only four years, 1953-57, before the Guatemalan government actually used it for firewood. Those that have ridden it say it was the finest ravine ride ever built, Puritas Springs and Rocky Springs not excluded.

*La Montana Rusa,* Chapultepec Park, Mexico City (fig. XI:12,13). For many years this wonderful racing coaster was the highest standing at 110 feet. Built in 1963 and designed by Edward Leis, it still rides beautifully and many consider it the best on the

(XI: 9). Classic National Amusement Device car. 1940's. These magnificent cars are among the most beautiful ever built and deserve museum status.

(XI: 10). *Sterling's Million Dollar Coaster*. Rocky Glen Park, Moosic, Pa. 1945-57/58. Courtesy Rygel Studio, Wyoming, Pa.

(XI: 11). *La Montana Rusa.* Guatemala City, Guatemala, 1953-57. For over a quarter-century this was the longest roller coaster ever built at 5800 feet.

(XI: 12). *La Montana Rusa.* Chapultepec Park, Mexico City, 1953. "The Russian Mountain" is the prototype for many coasters including *Screamin' Eagle* (Eureka, Mo.) and *Colossus* (Valencia, Ca.)

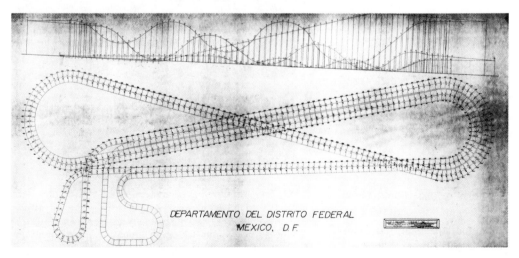

(XI: 13). Original plans for *La Montana Rusa.* Chapultepec Park, Mexico City, 1953.

North American continent. The coaster is chameleon-like in that it changes garish color every year. It is also famous for fainting passengers since Mexico City is a lightheaded 7350 feet above sea level.

*La Montana Rusa* is National Amusement Device's most influential roller coaster. *The Screamin' Eagle* (Eureka, Mo.) and *Colossus* (Valencia, Calif.) are partially based on the Mexico City ride.

### Thunderbolt

The most famous use of National Amusement Device cars is the *Thunderbolt,* Kennywood Park, Pittsburgh.

In 1968, Andy Vettel, son of coaster designer Erwin Vettel, remodeled Kennywood's 1924 John Miller *Pippin* coaster. He retained the ravine section, reworked the upper hills, and produced one of the great roller coasters of this century (fig. XI:14).

The Thunderbolt is unique even among ravine coasters. The general observer, seeing only the top section, is usually puzzled over the coaster's reputation. The valley is cleverly hidden by trees and fences. Often riders only become aware of the ravine when their car plunges into the trees from the unloading platform.

The key to the *Thunderbolt* is a chain lift at the middle rather than the beginning of the ride. Midway through the *Thunderbolt,* after having left the chain lift, cars bruisingly whirl through turns that so jumble directions, the disoriented rider loses track of the ravine. Without warning, the train again drops into the valley, this time with severe plunges of 80 and 90 feet.

The Kennywood *Thunderbolt* has the highest finishing hills ever built and was listed in my June 9, 1974, *New York Times* article as the ultimate roller coaster.

Kennywood Park should also be listed among the reasons roller coasters survived during this bleak era. When experts were screaming of the coaster's death, they continued to build and maintain them. Many parks turned their backs on roller coasters, but not Kennywood.

### Demolished Parks

If statisticians are generous, records could show 120 roller coasters built between 1930 and 1972 including 72 by the Philadelphia Toboggan Co. This may seem a large number but compared to the 1500

destroyed, it is a depressing total. It wasn't just small parks being obliterated, the majors were treated just as shabbily. Seventy miles from National Amusement Device, on the banks of the Ohio River near Cincinnati, was one of the most joyful parks to see the light of day—Coney Island. One of my treasured childhood memories was going up the Ohio on the *Island Queen* steamboat. Can you imagine taking a paddle wheeler to an amusement park and arriving there to ride the *Shooting Star* and *Wildcat* roller coasters?

The park opened in 1886 as Ohio Grove, "The Coney Island of the West", and after the first season, just Coney Island. The park suffered flood after flood including one 52 feet deep in 1937 (fig. XI:15). Yet Coney Island always seemed to emerge a better park. It was a classic, beautiful, well-scrubbed park, but the floods plus greater and greater crowds closed the gates September 6, 1970.

In Coney Island's case the loss was not a total tragedy. Taft Broadcasting Company transported much of the park to higher and drier land as part of the Kings Island complex. Kings Island's *Racer* is

(XI: 14). *Thunderbolt.* Kennywood Park, West Mifflin, Pa., 1924/68—.The Kennywood *Thunderbolt* was listed as the "Ultimate Roller Coaster" by the *New York Times* in 1974. Shown here are cars taking an immediate plunge from the loading platform into a ravine.

considered the start of the "Coaster Boom" (Chapter XII), but no matter how wonderful the new park, it's impossible to forget the *Shooting Star, Wildcat, Island Queen,* and beautiful Coney Island.

Other parks were not as fortunate as Ohio's Coney Island. *They are gone forever* and all had several roller coasters on their property.

After announcements to the contrary, Chicago Riverview Park (the world's largest amusement park) closed its gates in 1967. Articles have appeared yearly lamenting its death. Seven roller coasters, including the legendary *Bobs,* were erased by bulldozer. Now sitting blandly at Western and Belmont is a shopping center, a factory, and lots of parking space.

After seventy-four years of entertainment, Cleveland's Euclid Beach closed in 1969 and has been replaced by high-rise apartments. The *Thriller, Flying Turns, Aero Dips,* and *Racing Coaster* were obliterated.

Most saddening was the West Coast (fig. XI:16). Santa Cruz's *Giant Dipper* and San Diego's *Earth-*

*quake* still stand, but it seems as if a phantom bulldozer started rolling in Southern California, worked its way up the coast to Washington, and splintered every coaster along the way. Roller coasters in Oceanside, Venice, Ocean Park, Long Beach, Santa Monica, Grover City, San Francisco, Oakland, Eugene, Portland, Seattle, Bellingham, and others, were mangled. Harry Traver's wonderful *Cyclone Racer* at Long Beach was destroyed to make way for the *Queen Mary* in 1968. The park itself, The Pike, soon followed in 1979.

Perhaps most disgraceful was the destruction of Palisades Park. New Yorkers still gnash teeth at the thought.

The Schenck brothers leased a park in Fort Lee, New Jersey, around 1913. It had a few rides, commanded a magnificent view of the Hudson and Manhattan, and was nicely located across from the 125th Street Ferry. The Schencks named their purchase after area cliffs and quickly turned Palisades into a well run and profitable park.

(XI: 15). Ohio River flood at Coney Island, Cincinnati, Oh., 1939. Courtesy Cincinnati Historical Society and Jim Payer.

The Schenck brothers became major forces in the film industry with Joe heading MGM and Nick, Twentieth Century-Fox. With their sights now in California and Beverly Hills real estate, the Schencks lost interest in their park.

The Rosenthal brothers began careers in the park business by renting beach umbrellas. In 1917, they very successfully ran amusements in Canarsie, New York. Ten years later the brothers sold their belongings and moved to Coney Island to build the legendary *Cyclone*. They made enough money on their roller coaster to buy all the Schenck rides and the property at Palisades in 1934. Amusement park historian Lou DuFour said, "...From then on, it was among the most beautiful and profitable funparks on the North American continent, and an industry showplace."[5]

Everyone built roller coasters at Palisades: John Miller (one as early as 1904), Traver, Ingersoll, Bartlett, Thompson, and National Amusement Device. It was a roller coaster buff's paradise. The rides always seemed higher and more threatening over Palisades's cliffs.

When Traver's *Cyclone* (Chapter X) was destroyed in 1934, a nearby wooden coaster took over its name. Designed by John Miller and assisted by Erwin Vettel, the wooden ride opened as the *Skyrocket* in 1926. A 1934 fire badly disfigured its structure. From that moment on, every board, bolt and track of this ride, now renamed the *Cyclone,* was Joseph McKee's. He redesigned and reworked the ride and operated it.

McKee, who started at Pittsburgh's Luna Park in 1905, built over 300 roller coasters. "I invented the first S-turn back in 1910 at Lakeside Park, Denver," said McKee, "and the only reason I did was that I had to — had to get around a building that was in the way....We learned from each other, we took from each other too. I've invented, I guess, about a hundred things to do with roller coasters since I started out. But do you think I've patented one of them? I never owned a patent in my life."[6]

McKee will always be remembered for the layout and maintenance of mint-clean Palisades Park. The *Cyclone* was his gem and it was often called "McKee's Coaster."

"McKee's Coaster" was levelled in 1972 (fig. XI:17,18). It was despicable. Palisades was sold by Irving Rosenthal for $12,500,000.00 to the Centex Winston Corporation, and a huge apartment complex now squats on Palisades's site.

Promises were made. On August 27, 1972, *New York Times* said:

> The Palisades Amusement Park, only a memory of roller coaster rides and summers past since its facilities and land at Fort Lee, N.J. were sold last year, will be resurrected on a Morris County site 50 miles west of New York City, under plans announced yesterday by a new management.[7]

John Allen was to build his last roller coaster there.

Nothing came of it.

(XI: 16). Aerial view of Santa Monica Bay, California, early 1920s. The West Coast from California to Washington was strewn with roller coasters. At least 8 can be found in this promotional photo. Largest piers, from top to bottom: The piers of Looff, Ocean Park, and Venice. Courtesy Santa Monica Public Library.

(XI: 17, 18). Bulldozing the *Cyclone*, Palisades Park, Fort Lee, N.J., 1972. The demolition of "McKee's Coaster" seemed to be the death-knell of roller coasters. Its demise actually overlapped the "Coaster Room." Courtesy *Bergen Evening Record* and Jim Payer.

# Chapter XII
## Kings Island, Disneyland, and Metal Coasters

This chapter could easily have been named "The Second Golden Age of Roller Coasters." To the amazement of doomsayers, multi-million dollar roller coasters appeared in every section of the country. It was a magical time. For roller coaster buffs, it was like falling into Pinocchio's Pleasure Island without dire consequences, limitless tickets in hand.

April 29, 1972, is usually given as the day when the gloom of Chapter XI ended and the new Golden Age began. On that day Kings Island, Cincinnati, opened its *Racer* (fig. XII:1). New-and better-coasters had opened immediately before the *Racer*, such as Kennywood's *Thunderbolt* and Elitch Gardens's *Mr. Twister*, but for some reason they didn't carry the impact of Kings Island's new roller coaster.

The *Racer* was gorgeous in every sense. On opening day, its structure was blinding white looking like one of the Seven Wonders of the World. It was not a tame ride; then again it didn't scare families away. The ride was *fun* to both hard core coaster buffs and first-time riders.

Kings Island wisely traded on the beauty and nostalgia of demolished Coney Island (Chapter XI). They salvaged several rides from the old park and strategically devoted a section to the memory of Coney Island (fig. XII:2). It helped make mammoth Kings Island more intimate.

While the *Racer* is certainly not the *Shooting Star*, it is a remarkable roller coaster. It brilliantly added modern technology to a 19th century ride and brought back the idea of Racing Coasters.

But most of all the *Racer* was photogenic. It was the first major ride to take worldwide advantage of television. How awesome it looked on TV. Word spread as fast as the 6:00 news and the ride became a celebrity.

Almost overnight roller coasters became part of television commercials. They starred in films such as *ROLLERCOASTER* with Richard Widmark and George Segal.

The "Great Ride" was again part of American summers.

National Amusement Device's *La Montana Rusa,*

(XII: 1). *Racer.* Kings Island, Cincinnati, Oh., 1972. The beautiful *Racer* was the beginning of the Coaster Boom. It was also the beginning of the roller coaster as TV star. Courtesy Kings Island.

Mexico City, was the *Racer's* forerunner, an influence acknowledged by designer John Allen during a 1973 interview.[1] Allen admits looking at Kennywood's *Racer* but deciding against the continual track idea. But Kings Island's coaster was different from the others. It made racers look sparkling new and offered its own brilliant inventions. The splitting loops midway through the ride are a stroke of genius and, when viewed from the top of the first hill, a great architectural vista that makes riders forget the 89 foot plunge (fig. XII:1).

### John Allen

*Racer* clones soon appeared at Kings Dominion *(Reble Yell,* Doswell, Va.) and Carowinds *(Thunder*

*Road,* Charlotte, N.C.). All were designed by John Allen (fig. XII:3), *the man, without argument, most responsible for the Coaster Boom.* A quiet, sometimes gruff, unassuming man, he seemed an unlikely target for the barrage of publicity aimed at him during the 1970's. His nature seemed the opposite of a roller coaster with its inherent wildness and carnival atmosphere.

Allen's calmness was amazing, as can be seen in this 1973 interview:

> When we built the racing coaster at Kings Island, Mr. Gary Wachs, the President of the company, stood over on the platform where we were ready to try a train. We hadn't run anything yet. Everyone was running around getting everything ready and he said to me, "John, you're the calmest one on the platform. Don't you have any feeling of trepidation about the thing? How sure are you that it's going to work?" I said, "I'm not , but I may as well be calm whether it's going to work or not. Getting excited won't make it go." Being an expert has its problems in the sense that you have to act like an expert. And many times I don't feel like an expert. I have butterflies in my stomach. I wonder if I've done everything right. Maybe the Japanese sold me a calculator that works backward or something.[2]

John Allen was born May 21, 1907, in Philadelphia. He attended Temple University where he was told he would never make it as an engineer. After ventures in the radio and amplification business, he started at the bottom with Philadelphia Toboggan during the Depression. He ran the coaster at Holyoke, Massachusetts, during the summer of 1934 and studied its structure microscopically.

He moved back to Philadelphia with his wife and son and became Philadelphia Toboggan's main troubleshooter. One of his odder jobs was building an apparatus in 1953 that pulled golfers from the 18th hole to the top of an exhausting 280 foot hill where the Oreland (Pennsylvania) Country Club stood. Another of his trouble-shooting duties was a complete reworking of Crystal Beach's legendary *Cyclone* (Chapter X) by integrating much of the *Cyclone's* wood and steel bracing into a new PTC/Schmeck roller coaster. The 1947 *Comet* (fig. XII:4) was an immense success resulting in perhaps the best "out-and-back" standing today.

John Allen became president of Philadelphia Toboggan January 18, 1954, during the company's fiftieth anniversary. Over the next twenty-five years he designed approximately two dozen coasters. His first major roller coaster was the *Skyliner* at Roseland Park, Canadaigua, New York, in 1960.

Allen doggedly revived interest in roller coasters, and his Kings Island *Racer* threw the doors wide open. He continued to build "megacoasters" (a term coined in the late 1970's) after Kings Island, including *The Great American Scream Machine* at Six Flags Over Georgia, Atlanta, and *The Screamin' Eagle* at Six Flags Over Mid-America, Eureka, Missouri.

Not everyone was pleased. Criticism filtered back to Allen (he read every letter) that his rides were too glass-smooth, too family oriented, lacking the thrills of rides from the 1920's. Such comments never bothered him. He liked a good argument. He always countered by saying you could never make a ride too smooth and "The older I get, the wilder my rides."[3] John Allen liked to have it both ways.

It remains a puzzle though, to even his staunchest fans, that what is considered Allen's most tepid coaster, *The Screamin' Eagle,* was his favorite ride. Conversely, what most coaster buffs consider his greatest, the *Mr. Twister* at Elitch Gardens, Denver, was Allen's least favorite.

When the *Mr. Twister* opened in 1964 it was quickly labeled a dud. The coaster derived its name from two 360 degree turns and apparently the ride had little more. The hills were negligible and the speed a snail's pace. John Allen returned in 1965, at the park's request, to rework the ride. He discovered the first hill was incorrectly angled at 42½ degrees rather than the planned 45 degrees. Allen immediately corrected this, added a higher first hill, performed known and unknown wizardries, and transformed the *Mr. Twister* into a masterpiece, a roller coaster that is listed among history's finest (fig. XII:5)

From a helicopter, *Mr. Twister* looks like a cat's cradle. Another roller coaster, the *Wildcat,* (1935), weaves in and out of *Mr. Twister's* structure turning that section of the park into a gargantuan labyrinth. There is lumber and track everywhere making it difficult to predict what's coming next no matter how many times you've ridden the coaster.

John Allen always seemed proudest of his contributions to roller coaster technology:

> I was the first to use specifications rather than drawings in the planning of roller coasters. It made life a lot easier. We were the first to design the big hills in the shape of parabolas, the way objects naturally fall, instead of part of a circle.. I was the first to go from wooden to aluminum cars. Maybe that was my best contribution.[4]

John Allen died August 17, 1979, in Philadelphia and in memory of him, this book is dedicated.

## *Disneyland*

What John Allen is to roller coasters, Walt Disney is to amusement parks. Disney was the savior of amusement parks and the industry has boomed since the opening day of Disneyland on July 17, 1955. It is questionable whether Kings Island's *Racer* would be standing today without the example of Disneyland.

This is ironic. Disney was known to hate amusement parks. Richard Schickel writes:

(XII: 2). Entrance to *The Racer* in the Coney Island section at Kings Island, Cincinnati, Oh., Courtesy Kings Island.

(XII: 3). John Allen in front of the *Scremin' Eagle*, Six Flags over Mid-America, Eureka, Mo. 1976. John Allen is the man most responsible for the Coaster Boom. His "Megacoasters" led the way to what many call "The Second Golden Age." Courtesy Six Flags Over Mid-America.

...Disney...had trouble in logically articulating just what he had in mind and just how his amusement park would be different from all other amusement parks. All he knew for certain was that he did not want to imitate the existing pattern because, as he had discovered when visiting them with his daughters years before, they were "dirty, phoney places, run by tough-looking people." There was, he said, "a need for something new, but I didn't know what it was."⁵

That something new was the "theme park" showcased by Disneyland in Anaheim, California. Only a few people believed in "Walt's crazy ideas" and to the shame of the industry (and many bankers),

those contacted at amusement parks told Disney "He was nuts." But then they underestimated his promotional ideas and what could be done with television.

Disney had the idea brewing in his mind 15 to 20 years before ground was broken in Anaheim. The thought became serious when Disney built a miniature railroad in his back yard and later decided it should surround a park. Realizing he had the best staff in the world for designing a new amusement park at his movie studios, a staff not weighed by traditional carnival ideas, he established a design

(XII: 4). *Comet.* Crystal Beach, Ontario, Canada, 1947/48. The *Comet* used metal and wood from Crystal Beach's legendary *Cyclone.* Herb Schmeck, with the aid of John Allen, produced a towering giant that is among the best standing today. Courtesy Crystal Beach.

(XII: 5). *Mister Twister.* Elitch Gardens, Denver, Co. 1964/67-. The *Mister Twister* was not John Allen's favorite but is considered by coaster experts his masterpiece.

team called WED (Walter E. Disney). Outside consultants were either of little help or not trusted. WED didn't know how roller coasters, Ferris Wheels and dark rides worked, so they invented their own.

WED based the new park on the studio's themes and characters, and the result was the most successful amusement park ever built. Disneyland recorded over one million visitors between its July 17, opening day, and September 30, 1955, and almost four million its first fiscal year. Every part of Disneyland was related and calculated like a vast preplanned movie set. The idea was contagious and theme parks appeared everywhere including the chain of Six Flags parks, several Busch Gardens, and the Taft Broadcasting chain. Older parks were revitalized and some, for the first time in years, applied cosmetics to rust, cobwebs, and peeling paint.

To coaster buffs, Disney's finest contribution was the *Matterhorn* ride (fig. XII:6) that introduced an entirely new track structure to roller coasters. The ride opened at Disneyland in 1959. Manufactured by Arrow Development Company, Mountain View, Calif., its tubular rails and nylon wheels are now part of every Loop, Corkscrew, and Mine Train in the world. The *Matterhorn* introduced a new type of scenic coaster and its quiet wheels made plummeting through enclosed spaces a less ear-shattering experience. The construction made just about any configuration possible on a roller coaster without straining riders' backs and necks.

The *Matterhorn* seemed to be Disney's ultimate roller coaster, but WED had bigger plans for their new toy. *Space Mountain* and Walt Disney World were already on the drawing boards (Chapter XIII).

### Metal Coasters

The terms wooden coaster and metal coaster first appeared in the early 1970's. They were handy labels for comparing traditional coasters to the Wild Mouse, Wildcat, and later Corkscrews, Loops, and Shuttle Loops.

As soon as the terms became popular, anti-metal coaster factions appeared. The wooden camp resented the new thrillers, considering them, with some justification, an inferior ride. They thumbed their noses at the new "metal prefabs", never including them on top ten roller coaster lists cropping up all over the country. Many buffs claimed metal rides were not roller coasters, saying they belonged with Rotors, Whips, and other carnival attractions. The *Mind Bender,* Six Flags Over Georgia, Atlanta,

(XII: 6). *Matterhorn.* Disneyland, Anaheim, Calif., 1959. With the *Matterhorn* Disney and Arrow Development Company pioneered the immensely popular tubular track/nylon wheel metal coaster. They pointed the way to future Loops and Corkscrews. Courtesy © Walt Disney Productions.

changed a few opinions, but the staunchest still labeled metal coasters a glorified trick.

This is a shame. Wooden coasters owe several of their nine lives to the publicity these new rides produced. The metal coasters created customers. They looked spectacular and became calling cards of many amusement parks. A Corkscrew at night could be seen for miles from highways and, like the sound of all calliopes, could pull the curious through the gates.

For a decade, metal coasters, in the form of the Wild Mouse (fig. XII:7), Galaxy, Wildcat or Jumbo Jet, kept the idea of roller coasters in the air. These metal rides are still the only coasters in most European countries and deserve their due.

The term metal coaster, however, is deceiving after the Wild Mouse era since metal scaffolding has little to do with the ride and feel of Corkscrew and Loops. The term has come to include the tubular rail/nylon wheels construction derived from Disneyland's *Matterhorn.* Its ride is extremely smooth — the opposite of the ungiving, bruising ride of the older metal rides.

Many historians feel the term metal coaster is too inclusive and that there should now be three classifications: wooden coasters, metal coasters, and tubular coasters.

And the metal coaster is not new, at least not its scaffolding. They existed around the beginning of the century as prefabricated roller coasters that could be moved from carnival to carnival in Germany (fig. XII:8). Parts were carefully coded so that the rides could be bolted and screwed together at new locations.

Metal coaster technology is difficult to trace, but almost certainly the elevated train and subway contributed their share.

The precedent for high metal structures started with *Harvey's West Side and Yonker's Railway.*

Built in 1867 by Charles T. Harvey, it was sometimes called the "long-legged railway" or "railway on stilts." It was the first "El" in the world and used engine drawn cables for power, with tracks sitting on wrought iron columns. It ran one quarter mile along Greenwich Avenue between the Battery and Morris Street. Charles Harvey (fig. XII:9) in suit and tall hat maneuvered the first experimental run without protective railing. It was so successful, more cars were added and tracks were extended another quarter mile to Cortland Street. Speeds hit up to ten miles per hour.

(XII: 7). *Wild Mouse.* Palisades Park, Fort Lee, N.J., c. 1958. (Partially designed by Joseph McKee). Courtesy Charles J. Jacques, Jr./*Amusement Park Journal.*

(XII: 8). Portable roller coaster at the Oktoberfest, Munich, Germany, 1906. Courtesy Frederick Fried Archives.

The road survived financial ruin, rust, and auctions. The El eventually reached Central Park and in May to June, 1876, carried 345,000 passengers. That year it was purchased by Cyrus Field who doubled the fare and rebuilt the tracks.

The world's first subway was a 3.7 mile section of the London Underground from Farrington to Bishop's Road, Paddington. It was begun in 1860 and completed in 1863.

The three mile *City and South London Railway* of 1890 was the first electrically run underground railway. It was powered by an electric third-rail or shoe. Roller coasters tested the idea resulting in the Third Railers described in Chapter VI.

The idea of Loop Coasters had been lying dormant for nearly seventy years. Several minds, as so often happens with "original" inventions, thought of combining the *Matterhorn* track system with the 1901 Loop-the-Loop at the same time. New technology now permitted high-capacity trains and everything from triple loops to near pretzels.

Two companies, Arrow Development and Intamin AG, led the way.

ARROW DEVELOPMENT COMPANY: The significance of Arrow is only now being realized. Their *Matterhorn* track construction at Disneyland was a pivotal invention opening the way for Corkscrew and Loop Coasters. Their contributions to 20th century amusement park technology are formidable.

Arrow was founded by Ed Morgan, Walter Schulze, and Karl Bacon in 1946. Their intention was not to build amusement park rides but to "tackle difficult and unusual mechanical engineering tasks."[6] They built the first of several carousels in 1947. In the early 1950's, Disney commissioned Arrow to build rides for his new park. In addition to seven rides at Disneyland, Arrow built the transportation systems for *It's a Small World, The Haunted Mansion,* and *Pirates of the Caribbean* at Walt Disney World.

The new theme parks bombarded Arrow with orders for the latest innovation. Karl Bacon developed the Flume Ride in 1963 and the Runaway Mine Ride (fig. XII: 10) appeared in 1966.

Karl Bacon, around 1968, also came up with the idea of the Corkscrew coaster (fig. XII: 11,12). After much experimentation on their factory grounds in Mountain View, California, Arrow opened rides in Old Chicago, Nashville's Opryland, and Knott's Berry Farm at Buena Park, California, in 1975. The Corkscrew's tracks contained two 360 degree rolls in the shape of a helix, used polyurethane wheels, and ran top speeds at 45 miles per hour. The ride was a sensation, and openings at Myrtle Beach and Cedar Point soon followed.

(XII: 9). *Harvey's West Side and Yonker's Railway.* New York City, 1867. It was the first "El" and the precedent for metal transportation structures. The apparatus was also called the "long-legged railway" and "railway on stilts". Courtesy Museum of the City of New York.

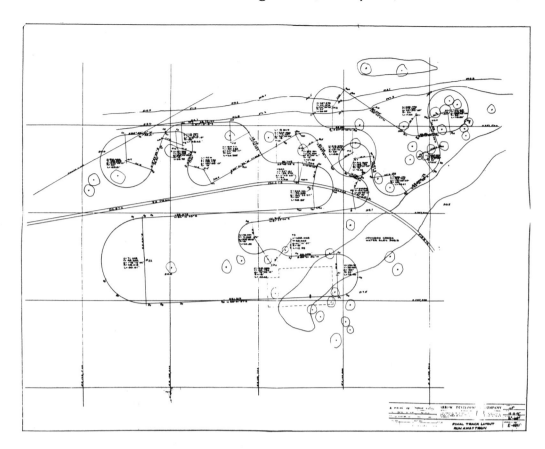

(XII: 10) Layout of Runaway Mine Ride. Six Flags over Texas, Arlington, Texas, drawing dated 1965 (ride opened 1966). Courtesy Arrow Huss, Inc.

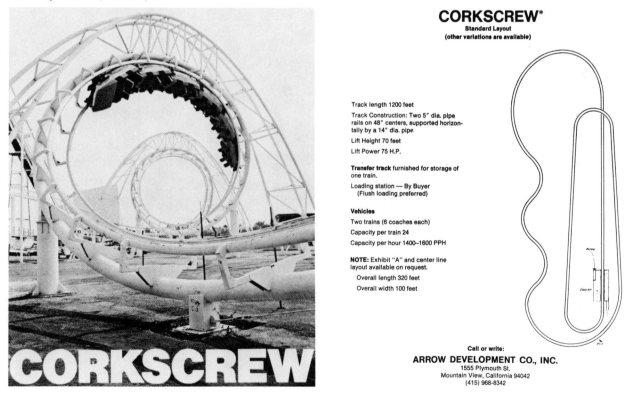

(XII: 11, 12). *Corkscrew*. Original ad depicting standard layout and cars being tested on Arrow's Mountain View, Calif. grounds. Rides opened in Chicago, Nashville, and Buena Park, Calif., in 1975. Courtesy Arrow Huss, Inc.

The low capacity bugaboo of the old Loop-the-Loops was overcome. Using the two six-car trains with four passengers per car, the Corkscrew had a capacity of 1500-1600 an hour.

The Corkscrew in 1974 sold for $700,000.00 with installation an extra $250,000.00 to $300,000.00.

With Arrow rides being installed over the world, the original Mountain View facility became cramped and could not accommodate its numerous projects. In 1978, an additional facility was opened in Clearfield, Utah. Today, all manufacturing takes place on Clearfield's 238,000 square-foot grounds.

In 1981, Huss Trading Corporation (Europe) purchased Arrow Development and formed Arrow Huss, Inc.

INTAMIN AG: Intamin delivered the first Loop Coaster since the beginning of the century,[7] by the freighter *Westfalia,* to Magic Mountain (now Six Flags Magic Mountain), Valencia, California, in 1975. It was called *The Great American Revolution* (fig. XII:13). The following year Intamin introduced the Shuttle Loop at Kings Dominion (Va.).

Intamin has built over 75 roller coasters since 1968. Their most famous ride, and probably the best metal coaster standing today, is the *Mind Bender,* Six Flags Over Georgia, Atlanta (Chapter XIII).

With offices in Zurich, Switzerland, Intamin uses three factories in Europe. The Schwartzkopf factory, Intamin's largest, in Munsterhausen, West Germany, specializes in roller coasters. Schwartzkopf assembles and disassembles prefabricated rides at the factory (fig. XII:14) and rejoins them on park grounds like a giant erector set.

Intamin seems to have taken roller coaster technology to its zenith, refining trial and error formulas of the 1901 Loop-the-Loop and producing rides of such complexity that even hardened Coney Island showmen would have called impossible.

Reinhold Spieldiener's Shuttle Loop is Intamin's zenith. Cars are catapulted from 0 to 60 miles per hour in three seconds through a mammoth 46' x 72' loop where they somersault up a vertical ramp 145 feet high. The cars then roll backward through the entire ride. (fig. XII:15).

The catapult is similar to those on aircraft carriers. The Shuttle Loop uses a five-ton fly wheel which engages a cable that instantly drives the train forward.

The problem of circle versus ellipse discussed in Chapter VI was re-examined. Intamin tested over twenty different formations. The Klothoide curve was their final answer and is the formation used on

(XII:13). *The Great American Revolution.* Magic Mountain, Valencia, California, 1975. Intamin's was the first major Loop Coaster since the beginning of the century. Courtesy Six Flags Magic Mountain.

Shuttle Loops (if you drive a car with the steering wheel locked at constant turn, you will be driving a Klothoide curve).

Intamin found the trouble with early Loops was that the g.-forces were too high (almost twelve g.'s) and they caused excessive strain on riders' backs and necks. The Shuttle Loop uses only six g.'s.

Everything is calculated on Intamin's rides, even center of gravity. The center of gravity on the *Mind Bender*, for instance, is not the bottom or top of the roller coaster but the rider's heart.

(XII:15). *Tidal Wave*. Marriott's Great America, Santa Clara, Calif. Courtesy Marriott's Great America.

(XII: 14). Schwartzkopf Factory. Munsterhausen, West Germany. Rides at the factory are prefabricated later to be assembled like a giant erector set at the park. Courtesy Astroworld..

# *Chapter XIII*
# The Coaster Boom

While the risks and credits for the coaster revival belong to John Allen, Kings Island, Disney, and others, the Coaster Boom belongs to riders. A roller coaster, after all, is worthless to parks without paying customers to cover costs, pay salaries, maintenance, and make profits.

Yet the Coaster Boom came about not because of mundane ledger books, but because a few outside the amusement industry loved roller coasters. Their enthusiasm spread. In every case it was a lifetime love affair, the enjoyment and fun to be described in Appendix I, and not the mercenary incentives often found throughout this book. Newspapers, quick to react, coined the term "coaster nuts" or "coaster buffs."

Almost before the paint was dry on Kings Island's *Racer,* jazz musician Jim Payer of San Francisco started a tour of 14 roller coasters from California to Massachusettes over a period of 9 days. Payer's schedule was a whirlwind to itself:

> July 15, 1972: *Giant Dipper,* Santa Cruz, Calif.; July 16: *Giant Coaster,* Lagoon Park, Salt Lake City; July 16: *Cyclone,* Lakeside Park, Denver; July 17: *Roller Coaster,* Joyland, Wichita, Kansas; July 17-18: *Zephyr,* Pontchartrain Beach, New Orleans; July 19: *Racer,* Kings Island, Cincinnati; July 20: *Racer, Jackrabbit, Thunderbolt,* Kennywood Park Pittsburgh; July 21: *Giant Coaster, Comet,* Crystal Beach, Ontario, Canada; July 22: *Giant Coaster,* Paragon Park, Boston; July 23: *Comet Coaster,* Lincoln Park, North Dartmouth, Mass.

Payer estimated 117.11 miles of coaster riding over the nine days. The tour was covered by newspapers and television stations and was the earliest notice of a roller coaster buff.

Payer was one of the earliest collectors of roller coaster memorabilia. His mother had ridden many roller coasters, and he took his first ride at the age of eleven on Edward Leis's (designer of *Montana Rusa,* Mexico City) *Comet Coaster,* Lincoln Park. "I returned to the park about a month later," said Payer, "and rode the coaster 55 times in a row."[1] Payer made sure his "first coaster" was the last ride on his tour.

Of greater international impact was the printing of my *New York Times's* article, "The Quest for the Ultimate Roller Coaster" in 1974.[2] It triggered a giant roller coaster snowball that is still gathering speed into the 1980's. The article was a turning point and its influence, through the worldwide distribution of *The New York Times,* has proven enormous. The piece has been reproduced in countless publications from Australian newspapers to the U.S. Armed Forces' *Stars and Stripes* in Europe and Japan.

In 1971 I was art critic for the *Albany-Times-Union* (Albany, New York). The idea of a casual piece on amusement parks crossed my mind while daydreaming behind my steering wheel counting all the roller coasters I had ridden (around 150 at the time).

At the age of six, I rode my first roller coaster, the *Whirlwind Dipper,* Santa Monica, California. Being an "army brat," I was able—or forced—to travel extensively. When arriving at a new post, I would immediately use the yellow pages to find the nearest amusement park. In this way I was able to accumulate a large collection of amusement park memorabilia, many roller coaster rides, and a lifetime of park and coaster experiences.

The idea then of an amusement park/roller coaster article for the newspaper seemed an offbeat idea and, after a few days of research and a dozen or so phone calls, I typed up a short piece. The editor hated it and threatened not to publish the piece claiming inadequate readership. At the last minute, the newspaper reneged and "Amusement Parks in the United States" was published March 7, 1971.[3]

The response was something of a shock. The *Albany-Times Union* was swamped with mail from amusement park-starved writers. The mail was so great that another article was published two weeks later.

From this response it seemed a major, national article was in order, but I was not sure how to construct or write the story. Instead, I approached the Smithsonian Institution about an exhibition on the history of roller coasters, and they wholeheartedly backed the show as part of their Bicentennial series. With some funds now available for research, I started tracking material and interviewing anyone connected with roller coasters. It was a supremely frustrating task. Very little was written on the subject. Encyclopedias barely noted their existence. In most cases, files of existing companies were in slapdash order. Often documents, photographs, and blueprints were burned, and it was impossible to explore every trail, basement, and attic.

It was now imperative to write an article in hopes of unearthing roller coaster material. Several fortunate events occured. John Allen told me of many roller coaster fans writing letters with opinions on his rides. I, too, had met many buffs while traveling from park to park, and this seemed the gist of a good article. It lacked some magical ingredient, however.

At the time, the movie *The Endless Summer* was touring the country. it described surfers traveling the world hunting for the perfect wave. It had crossed my mind several times during my lifetime of travels that I was searching for the perfect roller coaster (it was always at the next park or next state). The movie reinforced and encouraged the idea that all coaster buffs were doing the same.

The thought seemed to be a travel piece and I queried *The New York Times's* Sunday Travel Section during February, 1974. With snow on the ground and worlds removed from roller coasters, it seemed the article would be instantly rejected so I turned to other matters. *The New York Times* phoned that week, told me to get busy, and wanted it for their big June issue.

The article was published Sunday, June 9, 1974, and roller coaster matters were never quite the same. My phone rang from morning to night that Sunday and for over a year the daily mail from coaster fans would not fit in my box. Stage designers, jet-pilots, professional athletes, six-year olds, hundreds of teenagers, grandmothers, students writing theses, the list goes on and on. Over 8000 people wrote.

Almost all the mail said the same thing: *"I thought I was the only one."* The article opened many eyes (see Preface). It's almost as if writers felt less strange or less an outsider knowing other coaster buffs existed.

Perhaps of more importance, "Quest for the Ultimate Roller Coaster" generated interest outside the industry. Many newspaper and magazine articles, TV programs, and films followed its publication. The general public now seemed acutely aware of roller coasters, even respecting them as something beyond amusement park novelties.

In November 1975, the Smithsonian exhibition *Coast-to-Coast Coasters* started traveling the United States. Sites included Boston, New York, Albany, Los Angeles, Chicago, and 55 other cities. The exhibition consisted of 265 photographs on panels with text and was the first published and documented history of roller coasters. Its tour concluded in 1980.

Since 1965, the Coney Island *Cyclone* has fought for its life. During that year, the roller coaster's site was purchased by the city for $2 million with help from the Federal Open Space Program. In 1969 the ride was condemned.

Its owners, through a negotiated lease, fought yearly for its survival but did little to repair the aging hulk. Finally in March, 1972, James Oliver, Director of the nearby New York Aquarium, announced:

> The *Cyclone* will be replaced by a trout stream—complete with fish—a fresh water swamp, a brackish swamp, and a salt water estuary.[4].

But the ride's owners held on to the land tenaciously, aided by a new phenomenon. "Save the *Cyclone*" petitions were appearing from all over the world.

Every year seemed to be the last for the *Cyclone* despite continuing popularity. More mail poured in, peaking in 1974 when SAVE THE CYCLONE buttons and T-shirts appeared in Brooklyn (they have become popular collector's items).

Astroworld's (Houston) manager, Bill Crandall, watched the *Cyclone's* plight with some interest and sent engineer Bill Cobb (fig. XIII:2) to Coney Island to see if the ride could be moved to the Texas park. After all, the London Bridge had been moved from England to Arizona.

It was determined that it would cost more to move the *Cyclone* than build a new one, so the plan was scrapped. Cobb's other duty was to see if the Coney Island ride could open for the next season. For this information, permission was given to duplicate the *Cyclone* at Astroworld.

After weeks of surveying and measuring, it was decided to retain the 53 degree first drop but make the ride higher and longer (92 feet by 3,180 feet). They also reversed the plans (mirror image) to fit the entrance and exit conveniently and profitably into Astroworld's layout. According to Cobb, the new *Texas Cyclone* was closer to the original 1927 plans. "...We found it had been cut down in places, and you didn't get the smooth flow you originally had", said Cobb.[5]

The *Texas Cyclone* (fig. XIII:1,3) opened June 12, 1976, during a huge media blitz which included writer

(XIII: 1). *Texas Cyclone*. Astroworld, Houston, TX. 1976. The *Texas Cyclone* exemplifies the best of the "Coaster Boom." Modeled after Brooklyn's great Coney Island *Cyclone*, it ranks No. 1 on many top-ten lists that surfaced during this era. Height: 922 feet; drop: 53 degrees; length: 3180 feet; designer: Bill Cobb. Courtesy Astroworld.

(XIII: 2). Designer Bill Cobb in front of the *Riverside Cyclone*, Agawam, Ma. 1983. Bill Cobb, working out of Dallas, Tx., produced the *Texas Cyclone* and *Riverside Cyclone* (see XIII: 28-29), two gems of the "Coaster Boom." Courtesy Paul Ruben/*Amusement Park Journal*.

(XIII: 3). Middle section of the *Texas Cyclone*. Astroworld, Houston, TX. This complex roller coaster required 750 working drawings and 400 sheets of design notes before its grand opening day June 12, 1976.

and TV star George Plimpton (and myself) taking the first ride. The roller coaster was covered on national TV, most prominently George Lewis's award-winning coverage of the complete ride for NBC. It seemed almost as much money was spent on publicity as on the ride's construction. It was a big gamble but the risk paid off. The *Texas Cyclone* has held firm as the number one coaster on most lists since its opening, a number of buffs claiming it the finest roller coaster ever built.

Earlier Dewey Albert, owner of Astroland Park in Coney Island, stepped in on June 24th, 1975, and bid $54,000 to lease the original *Cyclone*. The ride was in deplorable shape. Albert engaged Bert Whitworth (he had worked on the *Cyclone* in 1938) as general overseer of the coaster's repairs. The Brooklyn engineering firm of Weinberg and Kirschenbaum was retained to devise new field techniques. Every nut, bolt, plate, and rivet was inspected and repaired. Boards were replaced and tracks and cars were polished to perfection. An additional $60,000 was spent on cosmetic repairs.

Finally, Borough Superintendent of Buildings Philip Olin and a team of experts swarmed over every foot of the coaster and approved the structure. The numerous violations posted by the New York City Buildings Department were removed. The *Cyclone* reopened July 3, 1975, and was a better ride than 48 years earlier. In gratitude, it earned $125,000 that weekend with lines continually two to three hours long.

On June 26, 1977, the Coney Island *Cyclone* celebrated its 50th Anniversary. Cars were painted especially for the occasion (fig. XIII:4). A huge birthday cake was cut at twelve noon and hundreds of champagne corks popped. There were free rides—brakes off—and the famous ten-foot C-Y-C-L-O-N-E letters with their hundreds of light bulbs were again part of the Brooklyn landscape.

It seemed a time for optimism at Coney Island, but disaster struck six months later. December 9th saw the first of a series of suspicious fires that leveled the great 1926 *Tornado* roller coaster. It was one of the few *Bobs* (Frederick Church) type coasters left in the world, and once again, a gloomy pall fell on Coney Island.

Such deplorable destruction was not unnoticed. Conservation was one of the reasons leading to the formation of the roller coaster club, ACE (American Coaster Enthusiasts). Richard Munch, the club's first president, Paul Greenwald, and Roy Brashears

gathered roller coaster buffs together at Busch Gardens, Williamsburg, Virginia, June 9-11, 1978 (fig. XIII:5). Movies, slides, and talks were given through the day into the dawn hours. An added attraction was the opening of the *Loch Ness Monster* (fig. XIII:6), one of Arrow's finest metal roller coasters.

It was the first time a large group of roller coaster fans had met. ACE (P.O. Box 8226 / Chicago, Illinois 60680) now holds one large convention and several mini-conventions yearly across the United States. The club has proven an asset to roller coasters. Members, over 1500 at publication, are uncovering the obscurest of information and are helping preserve both roller coasters and priceless documents, mostly through the club's publications, *ACE News* and *Roller Coaster* (formerly called *Coaster World)*.

Nineteen days after the first ACE meeting, an International Roller Coaster Conference, Coastermania, was held at Cedar Point, Sandusky, Ohio, June 30 - July 2, 1978, sponsored by Bowling Green

(XIII: 4). *Cyclone*. Coney Island, Brooklyn, N.Y. The great and influential *Cyclone* celebrated its 50th anniversary, June 16, 1977, with a huge birthday cake and champagne. Coaster buffs joining the celebration found the *Cyclone* running better than ever.

(XIII: 5). The first ACE (American Coaster Enthusiasts) Meeting at Busch Gardens, Williamsburg, Va. Around 50 attended June 9-11, 1978,) for movies, slides and talks. The club now has over 1500 members. Courtesy Richard Munch.

State University's Department of Popular Culture and Cedar Point. Its purpose was to take a scholarly look at roller coasters while officially opening the park's new Arrow ride, *Gemini*.

Topics of lectures and discussions included: history of coasters (pre-WW II and post-WW II); psychology of why we ride coasters; experiences of marathon riders; coasters as part of modern culture; coasters in television; coasters in movies; coasters in books, novels, and magazines; architecture of roller coasters; and a dozen other subjects.

Pulitzer Prize winner Dr. Russell Nye, Dr. Marcello Truzzi, and other scholars, as well as coaster buffs, gave talks, all carefully taped and documented in Bowling Green's archives.[6]

The most dramatic success of the 1970's was Walt Disney World near Orlando, Florida. The attendance at California's Disneyland made financing of the new park an almost simple matter. By October, 1965, Disney representatives had secretly jigsawed together nearly 43 square miles for the park at a cost of slightly over five million dollars, and Central Florida was

(XIII: 6). *Loch Ness Monster*. Busch Gardens, The Old Country, Williamsburg, Va., 1978. ACE members included the opening of *Loch Ness Monster* in their first meeting. The ride features a steep 114′ first drop and interlocking loops. Height: 130 feet; drop: 55 degrees; length: 3240 feet; designer: Arrow Huss, Inc. Courtesy Busch Gardens.

(XIII: 7) *Space Mountain.* Walt Disney World, Lake Buena Vista, Florida, 1975. The 175 foot high cone houses the most spectacular Scenic Railway ever built. *Space Mountain* includes a complete Milky Way and a fiery re-entry to Earth. Courtesy Charles J. Jacques, Jr./Amusement Park Journal.

never the unnoticed, peaceful retirement area again. Disney World is the largest amusement park ever built. The complex has been compared to New York's Rockefeller Center and designers the world over have studied its efficient layout and traffic patterns. Architect Peter Blake has said: "In great many respects, the most interesting new town in the United States is Walt Disney World."[7]

Disney World opened with great fanfare October 1, 1971. Yet a bigger celebration took place January 15th, 1975, on the same grounds. Five hundred fluttering doves and 50,000 balloons were released, a 2000 piece band marched, and fireworks filled the night skies. The cause of this spectacle was the opening of *Space Mountain* (fig. XIII:7). James Irwin, Lunar Module pilot of Apollo 15, said the ride was "rougher than Saturn V."[8]

This innovative ride continued the explorations of Disneyland's *Mastterhorn,* combining the best of La Marcus Thompson's Scenic Railway and state-of-the-art technology. *Space Mountain* was designed by WED Enterprises and consists of cars traveling inside a 175 foot high cone. This light controlled environment allows the most spectacular of Disney illusions including a complete Milky Way, specially com-

puterized space-travel effects, and even a firey reentry to Earth.

*Space Mountain* runs on the tubular/composite wheel construction of most late metal coasters but, being entirely in the dark, eliminates visual anticipation of curves and drops. You actually feel you are traveling—tumbling—through the stars. It is an original and exciting idea pointing, as will most rides into the 21st century, to both future inventions and to the outlandish creations that flooded the Patent Office from 1900 to 1930.

*Space Mountain* was expensive. The 1975 ride cost more than the entire Disneyland park twenty years earlier.

The roller coaster/amusement park boom matched the strides of *Space Mountain. Time* magazine reported July 4, 1977:

...The major amusement parks will pull in some $960 million this year—more than Americans spend to attend pro football, baseball, basketball and hockey combined.[9]

Earlier destroyed parks were not forgotten during the Coaster Boom. Splendid books on Euclid Beach (Cleveland), Riverview Park (Chicago), Coney Island (Cincinnati), Willow Grove (Philadelphia), Venice and The Pike (Los Angeles), and others have been published, with books promised on Palisades (Fort Lee, New Jersey) and Brooklyn's Coney Island.

The past decade has been a paradise for roller coaster buffs. Coasterites were not just hitchhiking cross-country during summer vacations, but often were traveling all year in carvans, sometimes on organized tours like those visiting cathedrals in Europe.

The first "Top-Ten Roller Coasters" list appeared as part of my June 9, 1974, *New York Times* article, "The Quest for the Ultimate Roller Coaster." Hundreds of lists have appeared since by almost as many contributors.

I was very much against the publication of a top-ten list in 1974 but *The New York Times* convincingly argued such a listing would help promote roller coasters. Still, there are many flaws in such a competition besides the obvious political drawbacks. Every park wants the #1, not the #2 coaster. Is it a good ride from the front or back seat? Was it ridden as most patrons would ride the coaster, or with brakes off to impress coaster buffs? What about metal coasters? Do they warrant a special list? Should *Space Mountain* compete with the *Beast*?

The December, 1977, *Fortune* magazine writes that the saturation point has probably been reached with amusement parks in the United States and parks will now turn to spectacular rides to maintain high attendance.[10] This is proving true and *The Incredible Scream Machine* concludes with pictures of one dozen selected roller coasters built since Kings Islands *Racer* and the beginning of the Coaster Boom (fig. XIII:10-29).

What of the Ultimate Roller Coaster? Was it built back in the 1920's in the form of the *Bobs,* Crystal Beach's *Cyclone,* or *Aero-Coaster*? Or is it standing today as the *Texas Cyclone, Mr. Twister,* or *Riverside Cyclone*?

Will the always promised 200 foot high roller coaster prove child's play in the future? That is, will the ride run along the lines of the KC-135 with its miraculous height and distance figures, nominated by the Fairchild "Free Floaters" (see fig. XIII:8,9) as the Ultimate Roller Coaster.[11]

Roller coasters could appear on vast, orbiting satellites—or on other planets: Isaac Asimov has already designed his amusement park of the future on the moon where the benefits of less gravity turns

**FAIRCHILD**

Fairchild Republic Division   Farmingdale,   New York 11735   (516) 531-0105

June 14, 1974

Professor Robert Cartmell
State University of New York
Art Department
Albany, New York

Dear Professor Cartmell:

In your "quest for the ultimate roller coaster," we submit a candidate which, while technically not a <u>roller</u> coaster, deserves consideration by virtue of its subjective effect on the "rider." Our nominee is the KC-135 aircraft (similar to a commercial 707 jet) flown over the Gulf of Mexico by NASA Manned Spacecraft Center, Houston, Texas for the testing of spacecraft equipment at zero-g. The plane, known affectionately as the "Vomit Comet" achieves a weightless state for periods of 20–30 seconds by flying a series of maneuvers mathematically described as parabolas.

To begin the maneuver, the Comet climbs at a speed of Mach .88, during which the rider experiences forces of about 2g (i.e., his weight is effectively doubled) and he is flattened on the padded floor. As the Comet begins the parabola, in less than one second the rider goes from 2g to zero-g, sometimes with disasterous effect. The plane is now "falling" up until it reaches a peak and then "falls" down. During this zero-g phase, if the rider is not anchored, he is freely floating and unaware of which way is up. As the Comet pulls out of the dive at Mach .88, the rider again is at 2g. The Comet now begins another climb in preparation for a new parabola. As many as 8 consecutive parabolas may be flown before running out of the prescribed course.

The following coaster records may be claimed. Height: start at 25,000 feet, peak at 35,000 feet. Distance: 9 miles horizontally in 70 seconds for each parabola.

The NASA flight director who manages to maintain order and safety through all of this is Don Griggs.

Sincerely,
FREE FLOATERS:

B. Cooper

M. Abbate

L. Peyser

(XIII:8). June 14, 1974. Letter to the author from the FREE FLOATERS describing their ultimate roller coaster (see fig. XIII:9).

rides into mighty, flying leaps.[12]

With these visions before us, it's easy to identify the Ultimate Roller Coaster. Like any quest, the Ultimate will always be in the future, around the next bend, or beyond the next mountain. The seeker, most of all the serious and critical coaster buff, will never be satisfied.

The disturbing thought occurs that roller coasters might eventually disappear. They will be seen as some type of barbaric activity not fit for unemotional, computerized, future societies. This indeed would be unfortunate because a certain joy will have disappeared. To many, when the coaster's silhouette appears against the sky, sagging spirits lift, and all seems well with the world.

They can hardly wait to ride the great monster. The roller coaster is the best of their summers past and present.

The roller coaster is summer itself.

(XIII: 9).  The FREE FLOATERS' ultimate roller coaster, the KC-135. Courtesy the FREE FLOATERS.

(XIII: 10).  *The Great American Scream Machine*. Six Flags Over Georgia, Atlanta, 1972/73. Height: 105 feet; drop: 47 degrees length: 3800 feet; designer: John Allen and PTC.

(XIII: 11).  *The Screamin' Eagle*. Six Flags Over Mid-America Eureka, Mo. 1975/76. Height: 110 feet; drop: 47 degrees; length: 3872 feet; designer: John Allen and PTC.

(XIII:12). Award winning logo for *The Beast*, Kings Island, Kings Mill, Oh., 1979. Courtesy Kings Island.

(XIII:14). *The Beast.* Kings Island, Kings Mill, Oh., 1979. Height: 135 (first drop) and 141 feet; drop: 45 degrees; length: 7,400 feet; designer: Charles Dinn and Kings Island staff. Courtesy Kings Island.

(XIII: 15). *Gemini.* Cedar Point, Sandusky, Oh., 1978. Height: 125 feet; drop: 55 degrees; length: 3935 feet; designer: Arrow Huss, Inc. Courtesy Cedar Point.

(XIII: 13). Layout of *The Beast*, Kings Island, Kings Mill Oh., 1979. Courtesy of Kings Island. ·

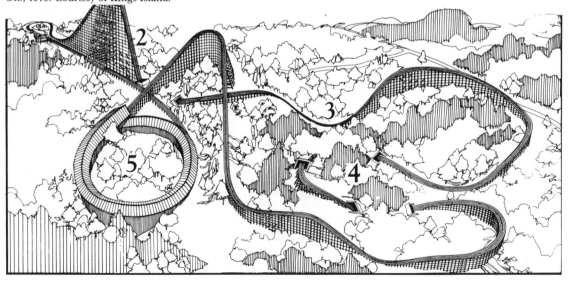

(XIII: 17). *Collossus*. Six Flags Magic Mountain, Valencia, Calif., 1978. Height: 125 feet; drop: 48 degrees; length: 4601 feet; designer: International Amusement Devices. Courtesy Six Flags Magic Mountain.

(XIII: 16). Scale model of *Colossus*. Anonymous builder. Magic Mountain, Valencia, Calif., 1978. Courtesy Six Flags Magic Mountain.

(XIII:18). *Mind Bender*. Six Flags Over Georgia, Atlanta, 1978. Height: 130 feet; drop: not applicable; length: 3235 feet; designer: Intamin/ W. Stengel and Schwarzkopf. Courtesy Six Flags Over Georgia.

(XIII:19). Freefall. Six Flags Over Texas, Arlington, 1980. Height: 128 feet; drop: 90 degrees; length: approx. 400 feet; designer: Intamin AG. Courtesy Six Flags Over Texas.

(XIII: 20).  *Shock Wave*. Six Flags Over Texas, Arlington, 1978. Height: 116 feet; drop: not applicable; length: 3500 feet; designer: Intamin/Schwarzkopf.

(XIII:22).  *American Eagle*. Six Flags Great America, Gurnee, Ill., 1981. Height: 147 feet; (including drop beneath ground); drop: 55 degrees; length: 4650 feet; designer: Figley-Wright Contractors, Inc. for Intamin AG. (See also construction of *American Eagle*, Appendix I, (fig. App. 11-15).

(XIII:21). Scale model of *American Eagle*. Anonymous builder. *Six Flags Great America*, Gurnee, Ill., 1981. Courtesy Six Flags Great America.

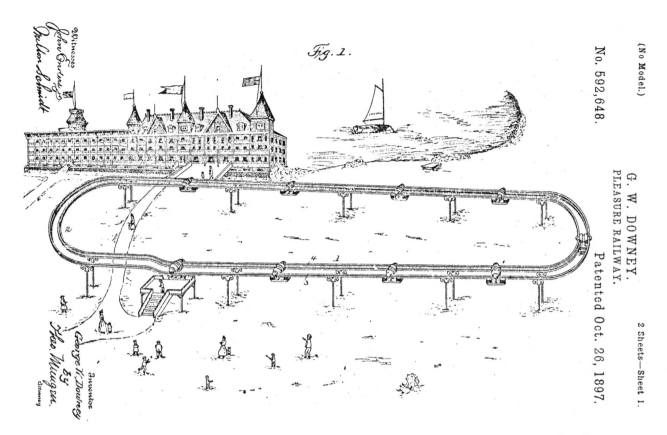

(XIII: 23, 24). Patent No. 592,648, Oct. 26, 1897 by G.W. Downey. *Bisby's Spiral Airship,* The Pike, Long Beach, Calif. (n.d).

Bisby's Spiral Airship,
Long Beach, Cal.

(XIII: 25) The Suspended Coaster has many precedents. The 1897 Downey Patent uses a rolling ball with suspended cars as locomotion.

(XIII: 25). *XLR-8* (Suspended Coaster). Astroworld, Houston, Tex., 1984. Height: 81 feet; drop: not applicable; length: 3000 feet; designer: Arrow Huss Inc. The XLR-8 cars hang from the track. This feature allows cars to bank up and out. Passengers float with these forces giving the sensation of tight turns in a glider. Courtesy Astroworld.

## CAN YOU STAND IT?

(XIII: 26, 27). *King Cobra*. Kings Island, Kings Mill, Oh., 1984. Height: 95 feet; drop: not applicable; length: 2210 feet; designer: Togo, Inc., Tokyo, Japan. Courtesy Kings Island.

(XIII: 28, 29). *Riverside Cyclone*. Riverside Park, Agawam, Mass., 1983. Height: 112 feet; drop: 54 degrees; length: 3600 feet; designer: Bill Cobb; *The Riverside Cyclone* returns to the days of Church/Prior/Traver with the use of steep drops and thrilling curves. Courtesy Paul Ruben/*Amusement Park Journal*.

# Appendix I
## How a Coaster Works / Why People Ride
## Roller Coasters

And, you all know, security
Is mortal's chiefest enemy.
(Hecate in *Macbeth*
Act III, Scene 5)

A second reading of THE RIDE section of this book reveals a strange perhaps humorous, repetition. Many, in the most anguished tones, speak of the roller coaster ride as a religious experience or cataclysmic event:

....This long interval...may be the best rebuttal to atheism ever devised.

....damndest ride this side of Hades.

....You're God's lowliest creature with gravitation gone back on you...

....and before you can remember what comes after "Thy Kingdom Come," shoots you to the stars again.

....It was something dreadful. I was never so frightened in my life and if the dear Lord will forgive me this time, I will never do so again.

There are many riders that find the first trip on a roller coaster as close to death as they want to come. The experience was shattering and they cannot understand why any sane person would submit themselves to such torture again. They emphatically are not in jest. The ride has truly left a lifetime, traumatic scar.

I was interviewed in 1974 for National Public Radio by a war correspondent just back from Vietnam. He had seen the worst of battle and was not easily frightened. After a test run on the Coney Island *Cyclone,* he refused to ride again. His very soul, he said, had been shaken and he had glimpsed death on the first drop. I had to tape the interview with the recorder strapped to the seat on my right, microphone in hand, *without the interviewer,* answering listed questions and describing the ride to an empty seat, pretending the interviewer was next to me. He later dubbed in the questions safely back in the Washington, D.C. studios.[1]

Many feel this way about the machine. The parks, however, seldom help in comforting these passengers. They seem to go out of their way to add to their terror. The entrance to any coaster is strewn with warnings: IF YOU HAVE A PACEMAKER OR ARE PREGNANT, DO NOT ATTEMPT THIS RIDE; WE ARE NOT RESPONSIBLE FOR LOST VALUABLES; DON'T STAND; YOU CANNOT RIDE IF YOU'RE UNDER FIVE FEET. A few even say FOR SAFETY REASONS, YOU MUST HAVE A RIDING PARTNER. Patrons often wear a park button saying I SURVIVED THE CYCLONE, etc.

A look at some names owners give their roller coasters reveals the park's intentions:

Beast; Circle of Death; The Great American Scream Machine; Mind Bender; Loch Ness Monster; Thunderbolt; Cyclone; Tornado; Hurricane; Typhoon; Comet; Shooting Star; Judge Roy Scream; Wildcat; Thunder Road; Lightning; Whirlwind; Mile Sky Chaser; Fireball; The Limit; King Cobra; Scorpion; and many, many more.

Before the coaster at Astroworld (Houston) was officially named *Texas Cyclone,* an open competition was held to name the ride. A sampling of submitted names shows the contestants' attitudes to roller coasters:

Bayou City Bruiser; Spine Tingler; Dastardly Devil; Rail to Hell; Evil Weevil; Texas Twister; The Hair Riser; The Chiller Thriller; The Nerve Racker; The Fright Train; The Armageddon; The Body Snatcher; The Great White Wail; The Wipe Out Machine; The Nightmare; The Rattlesnake; Hell on Wheels; Calamity Coaster; The Devil's Playmate; Screamin' Meanie; Astrofear; Suicidal Rail; Jaws...

Every park, too, has hair-raising stories of accidents on roller coasters and like most tales, each telling twists and exaggerates a little more, turning a splinter into a massacre. A favorite, heard in almost every park across the country, is the opening of a brand new coaster taking its first run with a fully loaded train (each rider usually a celebrity). The coaster returns with every passenger's neck broken.

Some variations say all riders had heart attacks or expired from shock. The story tellers sincerely believe it happened even though proof has never surfaced of this horror occuring anywhere.

What mystifies the frightened rider is not just "Why do people ride roller coasters?" They are equally confounded by the laughter and high spirits of many passengers after a ride, that these riders will not only get on again but will stand in line for hours to do so. Why are they thrilled and elated by this ultimate terror, instead of shaking in the nearest corner?

But is the roller coaster really the ultimate terror? Is it in the same category as skydiving, parachuting, or Grand-Prix racing? Not even the most die-hard coaster buff would claim that it is, for the roller coaster is *much safer* than these truly dangerous pursuits. Besides, a great deal of the roller coaster's fright depends on illusion and clever pacing. Ignorance of this and of the coaster's workings contributes greatly to the ride's terror.

Many believe a car can fly off the tracks. It is helpful then, before turning to why people ride roller coasters, to probe the mechanics of the ride.

### How A Roller Coaster Works

It's fun to do things you're not made to do, like going to the moon or living under the ocean. I was playing when I invented the aqualung. I'm still playing. I think play is the most important thing in the world....For two decades now I haven't tried to hold onto anything. I just feel open to life and embrace whatever comes.[2]

Jacques Cousteau

If, to seek its level
Water can all the time
Descend
What God or Devil
Makes men climb
No end[5]

Kenneth Burke, *Rhetoric of Religion*

A certain amount of danger is essential to the Quality of life.[4]

Charles Lindbergh

The roller coaster is a simple, efficient machine as one might expect from an invention evolving over several centuries from Russian Ice Slides to high speed, megacoaster. It is so efficient that Albert Einstein used it as the perfect example of "Energy conversions in a mechanical system" in his *Evolution of Physics*.[5]

The roller coaster moves by gravity and momentum, usually requiring outside power but once during its run. The principal thrill of the ride is acceleration, going from a near standstill to over 50 miles per hour in five seconds or less. This is most often accomplished on the first drop. The car then uses this tremendous forward power to complete its run through curves and lesser hills. The roller coaster is self-contained, being nothing more than a huge circular track with variations.

To make up for certain restrictions, since the roller coaster really can not travel 200 miles per hour, designers rely on illusion (see also Chapter VI) to make the ride more frightening. "We build in psychology," said John Allen in 1973. "We build in anticipation. Part of the appeal is the imagined danger. That's why many passengers start screaming before the ride even takes off."[6]

The following are some of the features John Allen mentioned during this September 1973 interview:

— Being slowly towed to the top of the first hill intensifies its height. Cars could be rapidly drawn to the top but this would destroy an important illusion. A slow ascent makes the hill seem even higher. It allows passengers to sightsee, alarming them into realizing objects in the landscape are becoming smaller. The ultimate tantalizer is to dangle cars at the highest point before the great plunge.

— As much as possible, make the drop seem straight down or, better yet, make it appear that the cars are curling under the tracks. This is the roller coaster's most famous illusion, yet the drops are seldom near 90 degrees. Both the first drops on the Coney Island *Cyclone* and *Texas Cyclone* are 53 degrees, 37 degrees short of a straight drop. The illusion is usually most successful in the back cars because these passengers can see the forward cars curling over, down, and under (?) the tracks in front of them.

— The proximity of the lumber structure makes cars seem as if they're travelling at tremendous speeds. A car bulleting through a forest seems to be going faster than on a flat, featureless road. This is one of the disadvantages of the new metal coasters. Their structure is such that the trains, without reference points (nearby lumber, for instance) seem to be going slower than wooden coasters, when in most cases they are actually going faster.

Tunnels serve purposes other than being dark and eerie. They too distort time not only be proximity but by their abrupt transitions from light to dark to light.

— Even wind is part of the roller coaster's arsenal. After a few rides, it is obvious why a windshield is not placed on a coaster and why the best cars are open. The sound and feel of wind whoooooshing past the unprotected rider makes the speed seem tremendous and the trip more exhilerating. Those that have ridden enclosed cars feel cheated without knowing why. The speed seems snail-like because the wind is barely heard.

— The momentum of the train decreases after the first drop. A good designer is aware of this and works it to the coaster's advantage by throwing in curves, smaller hills, and even tunnels to hide this decrease. A roller coaster is as contrived as a Broadway play. A remarkable roller coaster has remarkable pacing. It's all choreographed. The *Texas Cyclone,* for instance, has one of its roughest curves five seconds before the cars stop at the unloading platform.

— A good roller coaster will take advantage of many "forces" to thrill passengers. Riders at the top of a second hill will become completely weightless when the train crests. Seconds before, at the bottom of the first hill curling up the second, passengers face severe gravitational stress (around three g.'s).[7] The centrifugal force of curves is another effective weapon and the more imaginative—or sadistic—designer hides the most lethal in darkened tunnels.

If one reason could be given for the success of roller coasters today, it would be the transformation of coaster cars using primitive trolley car-like wheels to the high speed aluminum train equipped with

(App.: 1).  Holy Rollers. *Comet*, Rocky Glen Park, Moosic, Pa. Courtesy Mae Sterling and B. Derek Shaw.

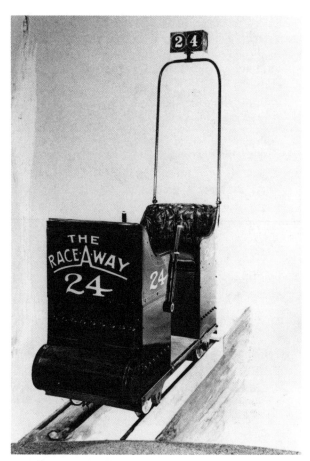

(App.: 4).  Race-a-way car. Race-a-way Amusement Ride Corporation, c. 1895. Courtesy Frederick Fried Archives.

(App.: 2).  Drafting rooms at National Amusement Device, Dayton, Oh. The gentleman second from left is the late Aurel Vaszin, founder and president of the company.

(App.: 3).  Original Thompson/Griffiths Switchback car, c. 1884-5. Courtesy Frederick Fried Archives.

undertrack wheels and lap bars (fig. App.:3,4). Cars are of such importance that they dictate the look of a roller coaster. Andrew Vettel took note of this:

> Each train is different. One that Vaszin built won't do the same thing as one that John Allen built. You've either got to design from the point of view of what the train will do or design the coaster and then make the train do what the coaster does. You've got to go one way or the other. Invariably you design from the car. The train exists so you design the coaster to do what the train will do. For instance, John Allen's train will bank quicker—go into a sharp bank faster because it's smaller and the wheel-base is shorter than Mr. Vaszin's.[8]

The idea of locking cars to the track (fig. App.: 5,6) goes at least as far back as 1912 and John Miller. Its significance cannot be overemphasized. The device was the key (before its invention, cars occasionally did fly to the sidewalks below) to the Golden Age and future multistory, viciously curving, high speed roller coasters.

With contemporary coasters, cars cannot leave the tracks except at points near the loading platform where trains are taken off for repairs and cars added or subtracted.

Yet, in a contrary sense, trains leave the tracks during a ride. If you walk the rails you will notice the metal track tops are glossy except for the rusted lengths at the summits of sharp hills. The shine is caused by the contact and buffing of car wheels. At the top of sharp hills, the cars have momentarily lifted, for a fraction of an inch, off the tracks. The wheels, therefore, have not polished the track surface, resulting in rust. At this point both passengers and cars are weightless with riders held down by the lap bar and cars by undertrack wheels.

Trains are hauled to the top by means of a chain lift usually driven by a 75 horsepower engine (fig. App.: 7-9). If the chain should break, a ratchet (fig. App.: 10) prevents the cars slipping backward. That clanking ratchet noise, along with screams, is the noise most often associated with roller coasters.

Figures App.: 11-15 show the construction of the *American Eagle*. The procedure is similar to building a house using cranes, scaffolding, and heavy equipment. John Allen says:

> We can make figure eights, L-shaped, V-shaped so the coaster fits any size plot of land. Of course, if we have lots of land we can do anything we want. But if we're limited in length or width then this would limit the height, length and so on. We start out with the figure of about 40 feet of running length to one foot of height. So say we have 1400 feet of ground to play with or 2800 feet of track. This would average out to about a 70 foot coaster. It's all pre fab. Everything is cut in advance and you just put the whole thing together like an erector set. Of course you have to

know how many bolts to put in it. One of the innovations that I guess I did as far as the builders are concerned is they no longer build from drawings. You build strictly from specifications.[9]

All roller coasters are "overstructured." Every other upright member (called bents or bent legs) could be removed, and the ride would still withstand a major earthquake.

Wood, up to the invention of the nylon wheeled *Matterhorn* (see Chapter XII), was always the best material for roller coasters. Wood is forgiving and has "give" which is immediately noticeable when the whole coaster structure creaks top to base from the weight of speeding cars. In addition, wood cuts easily to a template.

Metal, in contrast, is stern and ungiving, producing a very rough ride when hard wheels are used. Even Harry Traver (Chapter X) had to combine metal and wood for his *Cyclones*. Complete metal would have been unbearable.

> Metal rides are now more comfortable because of the recent "soft wheels" and tubular tracks. Still, the feeling produced is that of a well paved highway far removed from the clank and clatter of the wooden coaster. It's the preference of propeller driven, barnstorming planes (wooden coasters) over the sleek jet (metal coasters).

Roller coasters must be constantly maintained and have parts replaced. Insurance companies expect tracks to be walked daily from end to end and that empty cars be sent out to test brakes and brake lights each day before customers are permitted to ride (fig. App.: 16). Replacement of wood is a constant difficulty. The roller coaster maintenance crew at LeSourdsville Lake (now called Americana Amusement Park), Middletown, Ohio, claims the wise operator looks for woodpeckers: "They'll find that rotten wood long before you can ever find it. They'll have it bored out with a little nest in it."[10]

Maintenance of a roller coaster is many times more dangerous than the actual ride. Workers are often supported by only a fragile wooden catwalk at dizzying heights. Even the replacement of thousands of light bulbs that run up and along first hills is a grueling, dirty job. Further, workers must be alert to approaching cars even during hours when the park is closed, such as Chris Feucht's near fatal accident while maintaining the Coney Island *Cyclone* (see Chapter IX).

Painting a roller coaster's structure (fig. App.: 17) is perhaps the most backbreaking of jobs. Roller

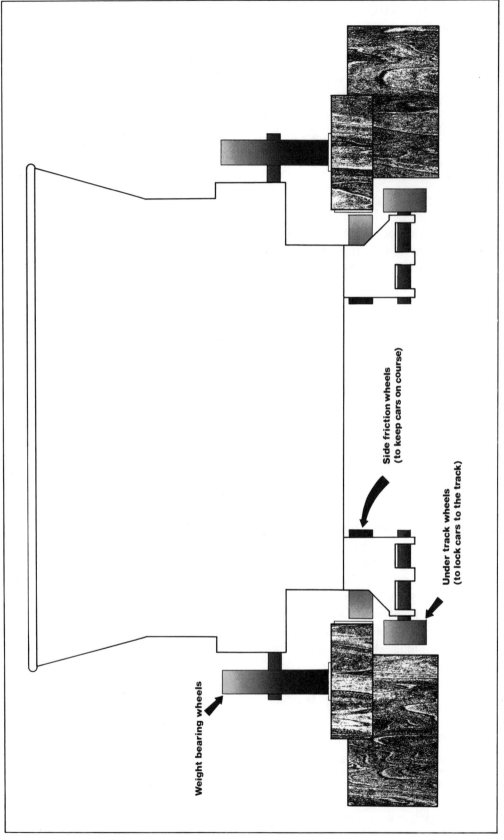

(App.: 5). Drawing of how a coaster car is locked to the tracks (based on original 1916 John Miller drawings).

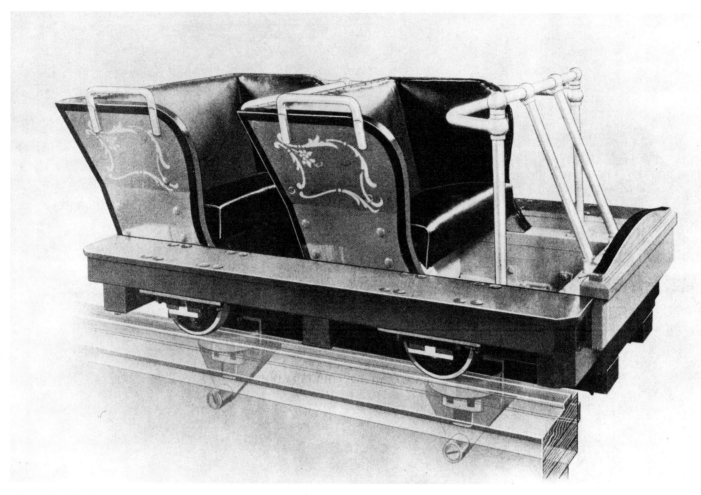

(App.: 6).   Car locked to the tracks. From the 1929 Philadelphia Toboggan Company catalogue. Courtesy Staples and Charles Ltd.

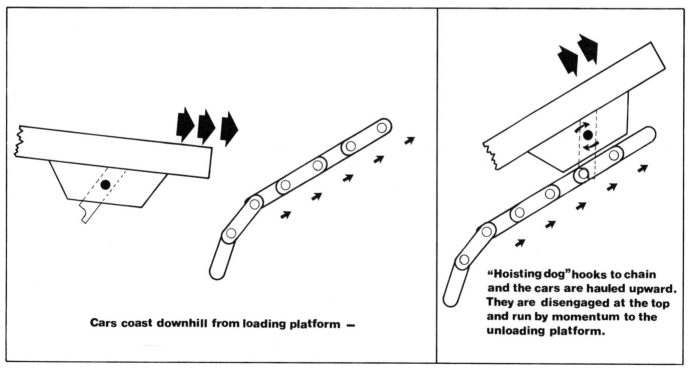

**Cars coast downhill from loading platform —**

**"Hoisting dog"hooks to chain and the cars are hauled upward. They are disengaged at the top and run by momentum to the unloading platform.**

(App.: 7).   Drawing of chain and hoisting dog to pull cars to summit.

(App.: 8). Model of 1904 with giant chain lift wheels. Early experiments used wheels to chain pull cars to the top. Courtesy Frederick Fried Archives.

(App.: 9). Engine and chain at National Amusement Device Co., Dayton, Oh. All roller coaster today use engine propelled chains to haul coaster trains to the summit.

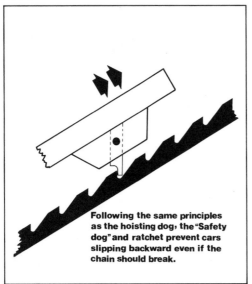

Following the same principles as the hoisting dog, the "Safety dog" and ratchet prevent cars slipping backward even if the chain should break.

(App.: 10).Drawing of safety dog and ratchet mechanism.

(App.: 11,12,13,14,15). Building the *American Eagle*, Marriott's Great America (now Six Flags Great America), Gurnee, Illinois. Sequence dates read July 22, August 5, August 12, August 20, October 7, 1980. The construction of a roller coaster follows the same procedures as a house. Huge cranes have now replaced horses to install massive structures and bracing. Courtesy Great America.

August 12, 1980

(App.: 13).

(App.: 14).

(App.: 15).

Apx. I: 16). Carl Jeske (manager of the *Bobs* for 22 years) and crew loading sandbags. *Bobs*, Riverview Park, Chicago, IL. To test roller coasters, parks substituted sandbags for passengers, a procedure still followed today. Courtesy *Chicago Sun Times*.

coasters are generally white, the cheapest of paints. There are exceptions, notably *Montana Rusa,* Mexico City, which seems to change colors every park season. In 1983 its colors were orange horizontals, yellow verticals, blue diagonals, and lime green track borders.

The *American Eagle,* Six Flags Great America (formerly Marriott's Great America), Gurnee, Illinois, lists the following for its construction:

> -2,000 concrete footings (average of
>     18'' in diameter, 4.5 feet in depth)
> -1,060,000 board feet of lumber
> -60,720 bolts
> -30,600 lbs. of nails (between 15 and
>     16 tons)
> -9,000 gallons of white paint
> -over 20,000 man hours[11]

The purpose of maintenance, of course, is to keep the roller coaster running and as safe as possible. The high speed roller coaster, after all, was made possible by the constant search for safety devices. The majority of John Miller's patents are concerned with reducing hazards and risks to passengers.

Yet, accidents do occur and are the designer's nightmare.

John Allen tells of his worries:

> I've been in this business 42 years, going on 43. Every Fourth of July I'd sit at home in the living room and chew my finger nails down to the elbow waiting for the phone to ring. We counted up that we had 219 devices operating throughout the country and those devices were geared to ride anywhere from 600 to 1300 people an hour. You multiply that by a 10 to 12 hour day, particularly on the Fourth of July. You multiply all that together—600 to 1300 customers and hour times 10 or 12 times 219 devices and that's quite a lot of people. And if that telephone rang I would jump three feet off the ground. It could mean trouble. But it is remarkable. I think the amusement business as a whole has a tremendous safety record compared to others—take for instance elevators, escalators, the airlines, and everything else.[12]

Andrew Vettel:

> There are some pretty dumb people in the world riding on these rides and you have to allow for them. The public has no idea of the unbelievable safety precautions taken on these rides. They can't conceive. If the automobile industry was half as safe as an amusement park you'd have some great cars. You really have to work to hurt yourself in an amusement park. Like standing on a roller coaster. That's like driving down an interstate at 90 miles an hour and deciding to take a nap to see if you can make it. Same thing.[13]

Insurance companies claim the roller coaster is safer than a Merry-Go-Round, a statement scoffed at by the casual park visitor. This is not to say the roller coaster is less hazardous for it is not likely a passenger will be killed on a Merry-Go-Round; but passengers will take a Merry-Go-Round for granted by changing horses while in motion or jumping off the revolving turntable resulting in minor injuries.

*Generally,* people will respect a roller coaster to the point of intimidation, knowing full well the ride can be a killer.

The word *generally* is chosen with care. Accidents—monstrous accidents—do occur on roller coasters. They are almost always the result of showing off, drinking, and in recent years, drugs. There are those riders that feel the roller coaster is not enough, that they have to go one or more steps further to test themselves and prove their mettle to friends. Even "no hands" is not enough. The LeSourdsville maintenance crew had this to say:

> Accidents? A lot of them are suicides. People who commit suicide like to get attention and where else can you get it more than on a ride like this. One time a guy jumped out as it was coming over the hill and he beat the train down and it ran over the top of him. Another time, right about here, this guy was changing seats. He climbed all the way to the back seat and fell out of the last seat.
>
> On the last hill here a guy was standing up in the front seat. Sitting up on the front seat—drunk. The cars hit a tremendous uplift and it flipped him right out onto the golf course. He came back the next year and rode it and I found out he sued the park and the park paid for his doctor bills and everything just to keep the advertisement down. And it was totally his fault.
>
> We had another accident. The operator went to the rest room and left the chain running. Some kids jumped in and let the brake out. They didn't know how to operate the brake so they let it all the way out. When it came back it didn't stop. It went around the corner and flipped the whole back car off. It spilled a couple of people out of the thing, dragged it over the top of the hill and fell into the first dip. Everybody jumped out and took off running and we never found them except for the people that fell off. They were hurt pretty bad. It went around the corner so fast it just dumped them out. Tore the track out too.[14]

I received the following letter from a coaster rider:

> ...Although it's only right that you should consider yourself an expert in the field, you and I have the same hobby, and you aren't the only expert! Have you ever stood up "no hands" in the back? Have you ever sat backwards in the last seat, throwing your legs over the edge? Have you ever sat on top of the back of the last seat, and put your feet up over the bar? If you haven't, you owe it to yourself, because I've done them all and they're really something else! Try it, you'll like it.
>
> ...I hope you will get a kick out of the enclosed picture. ...The person standing up "no hands" in the back is yours truly...The third time that I stood that night, I was lifted up so high that only from my knees down was I inside the car.[15]

With such foolish antics, it is remarkable more accidents don't occur. Yet, there is backlash. Parks, concerned about lawsuits over the slightest scratch, are now installing complicated seat belts and harnesses. The result is an increase in waiting time and a great deal of fun removed from roller coasters. The majority pays for the foolishness of a few. This trend has helped in the creation of the "riskless coaster" where passengers view rather than participate in the ride. Examples of this can be seen in shopping malls where 12 passengers enter a portable "entertainment capsule." Patrons then travel a *simulated* roller coaster trip, viewing a motion picture while the entire capsule rocks and rattles. Often called "mental rides," the Doron SR2 and Kinop's KMS 2000 are the best examples.

Roller coaster accidents and violence occur not just on the ride but in the waiting lines. Parks, particularly Coney Island, report fights—even murder—when the unthinking intruder cuts in line on sweltering summer days. Standing in line for popular rides has always been a major headache to parks, a headache probably going as far back as 15th and 16th century Ice Slides. Customers standing in line one to four hours are not spending money on the park's food, drinks, and souvenirs. It is a costly bottleneck to parks and frustrating to patrons. The tremendously popular *Texas Cyclone* (Astroworld, Houston) is using the following to defeat this snarl:

In anticipation of armies of roller coaster freaks descending upon the *Texas Cyclone,* Astroworld has devised a reservation system for park guests which will reduce waiting time.

Guests who want a ride should go to the *Cyclone* queue building where a ride time will be stamped on the back of their hands. Guests will not be admitted into the queue until that time.

Astroworld managers anticipate the system should mean line standing times of about thirty minutes.[16]

The actual violence of a roller coaster is perhaps best demonstrated by objects, from wigs to false teeth, lost during the ride.

To quote the LeSourdsville crew again:

The coaster is like a treasure chest. Everytime you walk it, you find everything there is—keys, glasses, lots of money, cigarettes. You just pick them up as you go. We've had girls lose their bikini tops. We had a girl one time with a paper dress and nothing under it. I was collecting quarters for rerides. I said where's your money? She said I lost my clothes. It didn't dawn on me what had happened. I said to Bill, come down and look at this. She wouldn't give me any money or get off. She rode two or three more times before we could get a coat for her. Everybody was looking at her.[17]

The reputed violence of roller coasters has been used in attempted shock cures for smoking, stutter-ing, hiccups, and even blindness. Perhaps its ugliest use is recorded in Neil Sedaka's *Laughter in the Rain. My Own Story:*

No wonder roller coasters have always haunted me. When my mother was pregnant, she tried to abort me by riding the *Cyclone* on Coney Island.
I refused to budge.[18]

If part of the terror of roller coasters is in the mind of the rider, or illusion, there still remains a great deal that is excruciating bedlam to some and frightening to many. It is then that the question is asked over and over again, why does anyone volunteer for this savagery, why do they feel obligated to tame that multi-wheeled monster, the roller coaster?

### Why People Ride Roller Coasters

O for a life of sensations rather than thoughts.[19]
    Keats

Whom have we conquered? None but ourselves. Have we won a kingdom? No—and yes. We have achieved an ultimate satisfaction, fulfilled a destiny. To struggle and to understand, never this last without the other.[20]
    George Mallory speaking of Everset.

It is only by risking our persons from one hour to another that we live at all.[21]
    William James

This most difficult question, "Why do people ride roller coasters," has many answers, all probably holding some truth, and almost as many sheer nonsense lacking any substance at all. In the author's eyes, the philobat / ocnophil theory of Dr. Michael Balint described at the end of this chapter is as close as any to cracking the riddle; but even Dr. Balint's conclusions are debatable.

It should be noted at the beginning that it is likely many people would not be as frightened of roller coasters if they knew of their elaborate safety measures—cars locked to the tracks for instance. Yet, this statement does not pretend to be an answer to why people ride. There are still those paralyzed with fright, even with the most thorough explanations of ratchets and brakes. It is similar to a person frightened of heights atop a skyscraper. They are not reassured when told it's physically impossible for the building to tilt at 45 degrees and that it's illogical to believe it will topple into the streets. The frightened viewer still sees and *feels* the structure on the edge of doom.

Before exploring the ideas of Dr. Balint and others (especially of Samuel Klausner and Marvin Zuckerman), it is fun to note some other people's reasons for riding a roller coaster and similar behavior:

(App.: 17). Painting the *American Eagle.* Marriott's Great America, Gurnee, Ill. Courtesy Great America.

The psychoanalytical orientation of most of what we do as adults has roots in childhood experiences. Our styles of living have a characteristic stamp reflected in the ways in which we adjust to growing up—so a rider is seeking a trip back to youth.

At the same time there is a rebellion against authority, against parents who made us behave, against bosses we have to obey, against unfulfilled expectations and unchallenging jobs. So a number of unconscious thought processes are taking place every time you replace routine and boredom with the challenge of thrill-seeking on an amusement park ride.

First, you are tempting fate with a safer bet-taking in effect, the safe risk, the "look ma, no hands" bit that shows you've left the sheltering arms of your parents. Next, you've got a sense of accomplishment, a feeling of conquering the unknown, a well-being state that comes from achievement through daring, a feeling all too lacking in most jobs.

Some people only really come alive when they are in a state of excitement. That's why so many juvenile delinquents steal, to call attention to themselves, to give themselves importance and a high that comes from living dangerously. That same high extends to thrill seekers on amusement park rides.

It is frequently the attraction of opposites—a rebellion against what may be an essentially safe lifestyle so different from the exciting life pictured while growing up. It is a

rebellion against conformity. And when you stand up during a ride, you're showing you've experienced the thrill ride before and want to milk it for even more than before so you won't become satiated. You need that one more jolt.[22]

Dr. Lawrence Balter

We didn't have air conditioning in those days. We went to Coney Island to ride the roller coasters just to cool off.[23]

Richard Stander, Sr.

Of all the formulations of play, the briefest and the best is to be found in Plato's *Laws.* He sees the model of true playfulness in the need of all young creatures, animal and human, to leap. To truly leap, you must learn how to use the ground as a springboard, and how to land resiliently and safely. It means to test the leeway allowed by given limits; to outdo and yet not escape gravity. Thus, wherever playfulness prevails, there is always a surprising element, surpassing mere repetition or habituation, and at its best suggesting some virgin chance conquered, some divine leeway shared.[24]

Erik H. Erikson

It's part fascination with the machine/part daredevil. Show the customer he can become a circus acrobat without getting hurt and they'll line up for hours at the ticket booth dollars in hand.[25]

Andy Brown

Perhaps it's the fact that one can loose a loud and satisfying primal scream while riding a coaster that brings such a feeling of satisfaction.[26]

Vee K. Wertime

Perhaps the clearest thinking can be found in Dr. Marvin Zuckerman's *Sensation Seeking: Beyond the Optimal Level of Arousal.* Dr. Zuckerman's 384 page volume is not recommended reading because of its massive data and clinical detail. Its arguments, however, are most convincing. Dr. Zuckerman, after 30 years of research, concludes, "Sensation seeking is one of man's primary needs and a source of much of our creativity, as well as much of our discontent and destructiveness."[27] Dr. Zuckerman believes sensation seeking is a human characteristic that varies like most personality traits from person to person. Some people are more adventurous than others and need more excitement and strong emotion. Their lives are made more enjoyable by risk, change, and variety. Boredom is a problem for them and they usually seek experiences sometimes to the extreme of fear, anger, bodily pain, and near death. Activities range from jumping into a cold pool, skydiving, roller coasters, sexual exploits, and crossing the Atlantic in a rowboat. A list of Dr. Zuckerman's *signals* to indicate if you are a sensation seeker runs in part:

— You enjoy spicy foods
— You'd like a job that requires lots of traveling
— You sometimes take different routes to a place

you visit often, just for variety's sake
— You would like to experience hypnosis
— You enjoy a scary movie
— You enjoy daring rides at an amusement park[28]

Dr. Zuckerman's thinking is supported by *Time* magazine's cover story, "Risking It All," published August 29, 1983, which describes in detail some of the more death-defying risks and explorations of our time, such as, climbing Mt. Everest without oxygen.

### Philobats and Ocnophils

You feel these free falls in your heart. You are euphoric. When I'm in the jump, I hate to see it coming to an end.[29]

Ben Colli describing his falls by rappeling rope from a 75 story building.

The Child's Toys and the Old Man's Reasons are the Fruits of the Two Seasons.[30]

William Blake

It's an adventure. You don't have to justify it. It's just an adventure.[31]

Peter Bird after 296 days of rowing 9,560 miles alone across the Pacific from San Francisco.

The theories of Samuel Klausner and Dr. Balint follow closely those of Dr. Zuckerman. Klausner and Balint, however, seem to put more emphasis on *pain and pleasure*. Dr. Klausner, while writing "Fear and Enthusiasm in Sport Parachuting," discovered that many parachutists, rather than being victims of stress, were actually seeking it.[32] He later writes:

The basic paradox of the stress-seeker lies in his apparent engagement rather than avoidance of the painful. This paradox may be resolved by the fact that pleasure and pain both draw upon the same reservoir of underlying excitement. Depending upon the intensity of the excitement or upon the conditions surrounding it, the arousal may be appraised as either pleasureable or painful. As one moves through a stress-seeking act, the appraisal may change, so that excitement which at first seemed painful may be experienced as pleasurable.[33]

The roller coaster as pleasure is a notion many people are not willing to accept; yet the term for the roller coaster's site is "amusement park," a term suggesting a playground of enjoyment. A showcase example of the coaster depicted as pleasure, the glowing image of the sybaritic life, has been with us since 1940. Disney Productions, in the movie *Pinocchio*, uses the amusement park, Pleasure Island, with its fantastic, elegant, looping ribbon roller coaster, as *the* symbol of life's wondrous temptations, as pleasure in its most attractive form, to lure and hypnotize the small boys that are later transformed into donkeys. (Was Pleasure Island Disney's earliest

thinking about Disneyland and Disney World?)

The pleasure / pain idea is carried to near formula by Dr. Michael Balint (as described by Klausner):

...He considers, among others, pleasures associated with dizziness, vertigo, loss of stability, and games of chance found in "fun fairs." Here the individual exposes himself to aggression for "fun..." Those who expose themselves to excitement, such as riding a roller coaster, have three characteristic attitudes: (1) they are aware and afraid of external danger; (2) they expose themselves voluntarily and intentionally to this external danger and the fear it arouses; and (3) they have the more or less confident hope that the fear can be tolerated and mastered, the danger will pass and they will return to safety. This mixture of fear, pleasure, and confident hope in the face of an external danger is what constitutes the fundamental element of all thrills. The farther we are from safety, the greater the thrill. Balint calls one who enjoys such thrills a "philobat"...

...Individuals who cannot stand swings or switchbacks, and who prefer to clutch something when in danger, Balint calls "ocnophils." Ocnophils fear expanses, and clinging to "part objects," like a drowning man to a straw, they unrealistically clutch certain limited aspects of the objects in their environment. Their real aim is to be held by the object. The philobat is similar to the individualistic, autonomous stress-seeker. The ocnophil is similar to the self-effacing, dependent stress seeker. For both, the thrill involves pain and pleasure.[34]

If Dr. Balint's writings are carried one extreme step further, they could be interpreted as: One man's pleasure (philobat) is another man's poison (ocnophil).

While this is playing scientific games and proves very little, it would seem any definition of coaster riding would have to take pain and pleasure / pleasure and pain into account mixed with complicated and unpredictable human emotions.

A form of the pleasure / pain principle surfaced at the Coastermania conference held at Cedar Point in Sandusky, Ohio, in 1978 (see also Chapter XIII). Learned scholars carefully presented many heavily weighted reasons why people rode roller coasters. A hostile, oppressive atmosphere began to fall on the entire meeting as one negative theory after another was recited to an audience of mostly coaster buffs. The words, *delight, exaltation, thrill* and *elation*, were not part of these turgid vocabularies. It was as if scholars and journalists alike were suspicious of the simple, positive, and clear-cut. Finally a fan shouted why he thought people rode roller coasters. The audience erupted. They whistled and cheered with strength and relief. It was as if a dam of tension had been broken by a mystical and key word. The fan said he thought people rode roller coasters because they were *fun*.

By nature and emotion (we are not really computers: a robot has yet to *enjoy* a roller coaster), man seems to continually stretch his capacities and mastery of skills. It makes us different from other animals. This drive to cross oceans or scale unclimbable mountains gives us the opportunity to test and find ourselves. It produces an inner radiance, and fun will always be part of it.

# *Appendix II*

Complete listing of Philadelphia Toboggan Company roller coasters 1904-1975 compiled by Charles J. Jacques, Jr. Courtesy Charles J. Jacques, Jr. / *Amusement Park Journal.*

## PTC COASTERS

**1904**

1  PINE BEACH - Norfolk, Virginia — dismantled
2  VINEWOOD PARK - Topeka, Kansas — dismantled
3  ZOO - Columbus, Ohio — Reconstructed at Oletangy Park, Columbus, Ohio — Dismantled
4  ATHLETIC PARK - New Orleans, Louisiana — dismantled
5  PABST PARK - Milwaukee, Wisconsin — dismantled
6  ELITCH GARDENS - Denver, Colorado — dismantled

**1905**

7  DELMAR GARDEN - St. Louis, Missouri — dismantled
8  Ft. George, New York — dismantled
9  EUCLID BEACH - Cleveland, Ohio reconstructed — dismantled

**1906**

10  IDLEWILD PARK - Richmond, Virginia — dismantled
11  CHESTNUT HILL PARK - Philadelphia, Pennsylvania reconstructed — dismantled

**1907**

12  DREAMLAND - Coney Island, New York - Albright designer — burned down in 1913

**1908**

**1909**

13  WILLOW GROVE PARK - Philadelphia, Pennsylvania reconstructed — dismantled

**1910**

14  DELMAR GARDEN - St. Louis, Missouri reconstructed — dismantled
15  ELITCH GARDENS - Denver, Colorado reconstructed — dismantled

**1911**

**1912**

16  PT. BREEZE PARK - Philadelphia, Pennsylvania — dismantled

**1913**

**1914**

**1915**

17  GOLDEN CITY PARK - Canarsie, New York - Joe A. McKee, designer - Joe A. McKee, construction supervisor — dismantled
18  LAKE ORION - Detroit, Michigan - Joe A. McKee, designer - C. Mitchow, construction supervisor — dismantled
19  LUNA PARK - Cleveland, Ohio - Joe A. McKee, designer - Baker, construction supervisor — dismantled
20  WILLOUGH BEACH - Willoughby, Ohio - Joe A. McKee, designer - Baker, construction supervisor — dismantled

**1916**

21  Revere Beach, Massachusetts for Kirby - Joe A. McKee, designer - Edward E. Rhoads, construction supervisor — dismantled
22  SHELLPOT PARK - Wilmington, Delaware - Joe A. McKee, designer - Austin McFadden, construction supervisor — dismantled

**1917**

23  PARAGON PARK - Nantasket Beach, Massachusetts - John A. Miller, designer - William Strickler, construction supervisor
24  ROSS FARMS - Pittsburgh, Pennsylvania — dismantled
25  EUCLID BEACH - Cleveland, Ohio — dismantled

**1918**

26  Rebuilt PT. BREEZE - Philadelphia, Pennsylvania — dismantled in 1923

**1919**

27  WILLOW GROVE PARK - Willow Grove, Pennsylvania - (Forest Ride) — dismantled
28  CLEMENTON PARK - Clementon, New Jersey - John A. Miller, designer
29  LIBERTY HEIGHTS PARK - Baltimore, Maryland - John A. Miller, designer — dismantled

**1920**

30  Buckroe Beach, Virginia - John A. Miller, designer - Herbert P. Schmeck, construction supervisor
31  FREDERICK ROAD PARK - Baltimore, Maryland - John A. Miller, designer — Destroyed by fire
32  Bay Shore, Virginia - John A. Miller, designer - Herbert P. Schmeck, construction supervisor — dismantled
33  ROCKY GLEN PARK - Scranton, Pennsylvania - John A. Miller, designer - Herbert P. Schmeck, construction supervisor — dismantled

**1921**

34  SARATOGA PARK, Pottstown, Pennsylvania - John A. Miller, designer - Herbert P. Schmeck, construction supervisor — dismantled
35  LAKESIDE PARK, Auburn, New York - John A. Miller, designer - Herbert P. Schmeck, construction supervisor — dismantled
36  MERRIMACK PARK, Lawrence, Massachusetts - John A. Miller, designer - Herbert P. Schmeck, construction supervisor — dismantled

**1922**

37  WOODLAWN PARK, Trenton, New Jersey - John A. Miller, designer - Herbert P. Schmeck and C.S. Ellis, construction supervisors — dismantled
38  SCHUYLKILL PARK, Pottsville, Pennsylvania - John A. Miller, designer - Herbert P. Schmeck and L.J. Mueller, construction supervisors — dismantled

**1923**

39  HERSHEY PARK, Hershey, Pennsylvania - Herbert P. Schmeck, designer - Herbert P. Schmeck, construction supervisor - 76 feet — dismantled in 1945

**1924**

40  BROAD RIPPLE PARK, Indianapolis, Indiana - Herbert P. Schmeck, designer - dismantled
41  DORNEY PARK, Allentown, Pennsylvania - Herbert P. Schmeck, designer
42  EUCLID BEACH PARK, Cleveland, Ohio - Herbert P. Schmeck, designer — dismantled
43  MEMORIAL PARK, Williamsport, Pennsylvania - Herbert P. Schmeck, designer - 66 feet 2 inches — dismantled
44  BELMONT PARK, Montreal, P.Q. Canada - Herbert P. Schmeck, designer - H.F. Allen, construction supervisor — dismantled
45  ISLAND PARK, Sunbury, Pennsylvania - Herbert P. Schmeck, designer - dismantled

**1925**

46  BERTRAND ISLAND PARK, Hopatcong, New Jersey - Herbert P. Schmeck, designer - George J. Baker, construction supervisor
47  SHADY GROVE PARK, Connellsville, Pennsylvania - Herbert P. Schmeck, designer - George J. Baker and James L. Martz, construction

supervisors - 62 feet 11 inches — dismantled

48  LAKESIDE PARK, E. Mahanoy Junction, Pennsylvania - Herbert P. Schmeck, designer — dismantled

49  SHELLPOT PARK, Wilmington, Delaware - Herbert P. Schmeck, designer - 65 feet 1 inch — dismantled

50  WOODLAWN PARK (Junior Coaster), Trenton, New Jersey - Herbert P. Schmeck, designer — dismantled

**1926**

51  LONG BRANCH PARK, Syracuse, New York - Herbert P. Schmeck, designer - 70 feet 1 inch — dismantled

52  ELITCH GARDENS, Denver, Colorado - Herbert P. Schmeck, designer - 65 feet 1 inch

53  CONEY ISLAND, Cincinnati, Ohio - (Wildcat) - Herbert P. Schmeck, designer — dismantled

54  CONEY ISLAND, Cincinnati, Ohio - (Twister) - Herbert P. Sch;meck, designer — dismantled

55  ZOO GARDENS, Cincinnati, Ohio - (Junior Coaster) - Herbert P. Schmeck, designer — dismantled

56  ROCKY POINT, Providence, Rhode Island - Herbert P. Schmeck, designer - 77 feet — dismantled

57  LENAPE PARK, West Chester, Pennsylvania - Herbert P. Schmeck, designer

58  SEA BREEZE PARK, Rochester, New York - Herbert P. Schmeck, designer - Frank H. Hoover, construction supervisor — Destroyed by fire

59  FERNBROOK PARK, Dallas, Pennsylvania - Herbert P. Schmeck, designer - 75 feet — dismantled

60  KAUFFMAN'S PARK, Mt. Gretna, Pennsylvania - Herbert P. Schmeck, designer - 69 feet 11 inches — dismantled

**1927**

61  LAKE COMPOUNCE, Bristol, Connecticut - Herbert P. Schmeck, designer - 73 feet 7 inches

62  CROOPS GLEN, Hunlock Creek, Pennsylvania - Herbert P. Schmeck, designer - 58 feet — dismantled

63  EDGEWOOD PARK, Shamokin, Pennsylvania - Herbert P. Schmeck, designer — dismantled

64  WOODSIDE PARK, Philadelphia, Pennsylvania - (Wildcat) - Herbert P. Schmeck, designer — dismantled in 1956

65  WOODSIDE PARK, Philadelphia, Pennsylvania - (Twister) - Herbert P. Schmeck, designer - 52 feet 10 inches — dismantled in 1954

66  Salisbury Beach, Massachusetts - Rebuilt Dodgem Corporation, Exeter, New Hampshire - Herbert P. Schmeck, designer - 74 feet 1/2 inch — dismantled

67  CHILHOWEE PARK, Knoxville, Tennessee - Herbert P. Schmeck, designer — dismantled in 1937

68  LAKEMONT PARK, Altoona, Pennsylvania - Herbert P. Schmeck, designer - 57 feet 11 inches — dismantled in 1938

69  Keansburg, New Jersey - Herbert P. Schmeck, designer — dismantled

**1928**

70  SAN SOUCI PARK, Wilkes Barre, Pennsylvania - Herbert P. Schmeck, designer - 77 feet 9 inches — dismantled

71  WARNER PARK, Chattanooga, Tennessee - Herbert P. Schmeck, designer — dismantled

72  BRADY LAKE PARK, Brady Lake, Ohio - Herbert P. Schmeck, designer — dismantled

73  ROCKY SPRINGS PARK, Lancaster, Pennsylvania - Herbert P. Schmeck, designer - James L. Martz, construction supervisor

74  MCCULLOUGH LAKE PARK, Lima, Ohio - Herbert P. Schmeck, designer - George J. Baker, construction supervisor - 64 feet 11 inches — dismantled

75  WHITE CITY PARK, Worcester, Massachusetts - Herbert P. Schmeck, designer - 82 feet 11 inches — dismantled

76  ERIE BEACH PARK, Erie Beach, Ontario - Herbert P. Schmeck, designer — dismantled

77  HASTINGS PARK, Vancouver, B.C. - Herbert P. Schmeck, designer — dismantled

**1929**

78  OCEAN VIEW PARK, Norfolk, Virginia (Alterations) - Herbert P. Schmeck, designer — dismantled

79  OLYMPIC PARK, Newark, New Jersey (Alteration) - Herbert P. Schmeck, designer — dismantled

80  PINE ISLAND, Manchester, New Hampshire - Herbert P. Schmeck, designer - William Marquet, construction supervisor — dismantled

81  MOUNTAIN PARK, Holyoke, Massachusetts - Herbert P. Schmeck, designer - 76 feet 6 inches

82  JOYLAND PARK, Lexington, Kentucky - Herbert P. Schmeck, designer - Frank H. Hoover, construction supervisor — dismantled

**1930**

83  IDORA PARK, Youngstown, Ohio - Herbert P. Schmeck, designer - George J. Baker, construction supervisor

84  Old Orchard Beach, Maine - Herbert P. Schmeck, designer - James L. Martz, construction supervisor - 57 feet 3 inches — destroyed by fire

85  LAKESIDE PARK, Dayton, Ohio - Herbert P. Schmeck, designer - Frank F. Hoover and James L. Martz, construction supervisors - 84 feet 2 inches — dismantled

86  LAKEWOOD PARK, Waterbury, Connecticut - Herbert P. Schmeck, designer - Frank F. Hoover, construction supervisor - 50 feet 6 inches — dismantled and rebuilt at Canobie Lake

87  DORNEY PARK, Allentown, Pennsylvania (Alteration) - Herbert P. Schmeck, designer

88  ENNA JETTICK PARK, Auburn, New York (Alteration) - Herbert P. Schmeck, designer - Frank F. Hoover, construction supervisor — dismantled

**1931**

89  MID CITY PARK, Albany, New York - Herbert P. Schmeck, designer — dismantled

90  ROCKY POINT PARK, Providence, Rhode Island (Flying Turns) - Herbert P. Schmeck, designer - Herbert P. Schmeck, construction supervisor — dismantled

**1932**

91  PARAGON PARK, Nantasket Beach, Massachusetts (Alterations) - Herbert P. Schmeck, designer - Herbert P. Schmeck, construction supervisor — coaster partially rebuilt in 1963

**1933**

92  CANOBIE LAKE PARK, Canobie Lake, New Hampshire from LAKEWOOD PARK, Waterbury, Connecticut - Herbert P. Schmeck, designer

**1934**

93  BERTRAND ISLAND, Lake Hopatcong, New Jersey (Alteration) - Herbert P. Schmeck, designer

**1935**

94  CONEY ISLAND, Cincinnati, Ohio (Junior Coaster) - Herbert P. Schmeck, designer — dismantled

95  KENNYWOOD PARK, Pittsburgh, Pennsylvania (Junior Coaster) - Herbert P. Schmeck, designer - Erwin Vettel, construction supervisor — dismantled in 1948

96  HUNT'S PIER, Wildwood, New Jersey (Junior Coaster) - Herbert P. Schmeck, designer — Destroyed by fire in 1943

97  HERSHEY PARK, Hershey, Pennsylvania (Alteration) - Herbert P. Schmeck, designer - Frank F. Hoover, construction supervisor — dismantled in 1945

**1936**

98  ELITCH GARDENS, Denver, Colorado (Alterations) (Wildcat) - Herbert P. Schmeck, designer

99  ELITCH GARDENS, Denver, Colorado (Junior Coaster) - Herbert P.

Schmeck, designer — dismantled

**1937**

100 CONEY ISLAND, Cincinnati, Ohio - Herbert P. Schmeck, designer — dismantled

**1938**

101 IDLEWILD PARK, Ligonier, Pennsylvania (Junior Coaster) - Herbert P. Schmeck, designer

**1939**

102 WILLOW GROVE PARK, Philadelphia, Pennsylvania (Alterations) (The Alps) - Herbert P. Schmeck, designer — dismantled

**1940**

103 BAYSIDE AMUSEMENT PARK, Clear Lake, Iowa - Herbert P. Schmeck, designer — dismantled

104 PORT ARTHUR PLEASURE PIER, Port Arthur, Texas - Herbert P. Schmeck, designer — dismantled

**1941**

105 FOREST PARK HIGHLANDS, St. Louis, Missouri - Herbert P. Schmeck, designer — destroyed by fire in 1963

106 SALISBURY BEACH, Salisbury Beach, Massachusetts (Alterations) - Herbert P. Schmeck, designer — dismantled

**1942**

**1943**

**1944**

**1945**

107 GEAUGA LAKE, Aurora, Ohio (Alterations) - Herbert P. Schmeck, designer - Frank F. Hoover, construction supervisor

108 PALISADES AMUSEMENT PARK, Palisades, New Jersey (Alterations) - Herbert P. Schmeck, designer - Joe A. McKee, construction supervisor — dismantled

**1946**

109 HERSHEY PARK, Hershey, Pennsylvania - Herbert P. Schmeck, designer - Frank F. Hoover, construction supervisor

**1947**

110 MEYERS LAKE PARK, Canton, Ohio - Herbert P. Schmeck, designer - William Marquet, construction supervisor — dismantled

111 PLAYLAND, San Antonio, Texas - Herbert P. Schmeck, designer

**1948**

112 CRYSTAL BEACH PARK, Crystal Beach, Ontario, Canada - Herbert P. Schmeck, designer - 89 feet 9 inches

**1949**

113 JOYLAND PARK, Wichita, Kansas - Herbert P. Schmeck, designer - Frank F. Hoover, construction supervisor

114 John Lorman, Venice, California (Junior Coaster) - Herbert P. Schmeck, designer - Rudy Illions, construction supervisor - dismantled

**1950**

115 KIDDIELAND (Arthur E. Fritz), Melrose Park, Illinois (Junior Coaster) - Herbert P. Schmeck, designer - Frank F. Hoover, construction supervisor

**1951**

116 FONTAINE FERRY PARK, Louisville, Kentucky - Herbert P. Schmeck, designer - dismantled in 1970

117 WALDAMEER BEACH, Erie, Pennsylvania (F.W.A. Moeller) (Junior Coaster) - Herbert P. Schmeck, designer - James L. Martz, construction supervisor

118 OLYMPIC PARK, Irvington, New Jersey (Alterations) - Herbert P. Schmeck, designer

119 CONEY ISLAND PARK, Havana, Cuba - Herbert P. Schmeck, designer - Frank F. Hoover, construction supervisor — dismantled

**1952**

120 KIDDYTOWN, Chicago, Illinois (Junior Coaster) - Herbert P. Schmeck, designer — dismantled

**1953**

**1954**

121 Las Vegas, Nevada (Junior Coaster) - Herbert P. Schmeck, designer — dismantled

**1955**

122 LINCOLN PARK, New Orleans, Louisiana (Junior Coaster) - Herbert P. Schmeck, designer — dismantled in 1968

**1956**

123 HUNTS OCEAN PIER, Wildwood, New Jersey (Junior Coaster) - John C. Allen, designer - James L. Martz, construction supervisor - 36 feet

124 ANGELA PARK, Hazelton, Pennsylvania (Junior Coaster) - John C. Allen, designer - 36 feet

125 GOODING ZOO PARK, Columbus, Ohio (Junior Coaster) - John C. Allen, designer - Frank F. Hoover, construction supervisor - 36 feet

**1957**

**1958**

126 ROCKY GLEN PARK, Moosic, Pennsylvania - John C. Allen, designer - Frank F. Hoover, construction supervisor - 55 feet

**1959**

**1960**

127 ROSELAND PARK, Canadaigua, New York - John C. Allen, designer - 68 feet

**1961**

128 WEDGEWOOD VILLAGE, Oklahoma City, Oklahoma - John C. Allen, designer - Frank F. Hoover, construction supervisor - 72 feet

**1962**

**1963**

129 MIRACLE STRIP AMUSEMENT PARK, Panama City, Florida -John C. Allen, designer - Frank F. Hoover, construction supervisor - 70 feet

130 PARAGON PARK, Nantasket Beach, Massachusetts (Alterations) - John C. Allen, designer

**1964**

131 CEDAR POINT, Sandusky, Ohio - Frank F. Hoover and John C. Allen, designers - Frank F. Hoover, construction supervisor

132 ELITCH GARDENS, Denver, Colorado - John C. Allen, designer - Frank F. Hoover, construction supervisor

**1965**

133 RIVERVIEW PARK, Chicago, Illinois - John C. Allen, designer - 55 feet

134 ELITCH GARDENS, Denver, Colorado - John C. Allen, designer — Raised to 91 feet

135 FAIR PARK, Nashville, Tennessee - John C. Allen, designer - Frank F. Hoover, construction supervisor - 65 feet

**1966**

136 GRAND STRAND PARK, Myrtle Beach, South Carolina - John C. Allen, designer - James L. Martz, construction supervisor - 72 feet

**1967**

137 LAKE WINNEPESAUKAH, Rossville, Georgia - John C. Allen, designer - James L. Martz, construction supervisor - 68 feet

**1968**

138 LAKESIDE PARK, Salem, Virginia - John C. Allen, designer - 85 feet

139 BELL'S AMUSEMENT PARK, Fair Grounds, Tulsa, Oklahoma

-John C. Allen, designer - James L. Martz, construction supervisor - 75 feet

**1969**

**1970**

**1971**

140  KINGS ISLAND, Kings Mills, Ohio - (Racer) - John C. Allen, designer - James R. Figley and James L. Martz, construction supervisors - 85 feet

141  KINGS ISLAND, Kings Mills, Ohio (Junior Coaster) - John C. Allen, designer - James R. Figley and James L. Martz, construction supervisors - 40 feet

**1972**

**1973**

142  SIX FLAGS OVER GEORGIA, Atlanta, Georgia - John C. Allen, designer - Bill Cobb collaborated in the structural design and Don Rosser designed the que building and the platform - Robert Cowan and James L. Martz, construction supervisors - 100 feet

**1974**

**1975**

143  KINGS DOMINION, Doswell, Virginia (Junior Coaster) - John C. Allen, designer - James R. Figley, construction supervisor - 40 feet

144  KINGS DOMINION, Doswell, Virginia - (Rebel Yell) - John C. Allen, designer - James R. Figley, construction supervisor - 85 feet

145  SIX FLAGS OVER MID-AMERICA, Eureka, Missouri - John C. Allen, designer - Bill Cobb collaborated in the structural design and Don Rosser designed the que building and the platform - 110 feet

# *Appendix III*

The following descriptions are taken from the brochure and poster accompanying the Smithsonian Institution's *Coast-to-Coast Coasters* exhibition. The show was assembled by Robert Cartmell and toured the U.S. 1975-80 sponsored by Congressional Bicentennial funds.

## Roller Coaster Etiquette

A roller coaster can be frightening (it has been used in attempts to cure smoking, stuttering, hiccups, and even blindness) but if you follow the next five rules, it can be an enjoyable experience.

WAIT YOUR TURN AND DON'T SHOVE. Most coasters are built to handle crowds quickly. You'll get there in a surprisingly short time. Don't shove people into the cars.

CHECK THE AGE OR HEIGHT RESTRICTIONS. Many parks will not allow children on the coasters, either for insurance reasons or because their particular cars are not suitable for small children.

HANG ON TO YOUR POSSESSIONS. Everything imaginable has been lost on roller coasters: Loose change, keys, wallets, wigs, clothes (including a complete paper dress), even false teeth. Many parks provide facilities for your possessions at the loading platform.

DON'T SMOKE. No one wants ashes in their eyes on a steep decline.

DON'T STAND. "No hands" may be okay — but standing is not. Almost all accidents are caused by passengers standing, changing seats, and not understanding the fury of a roller coaster. This is the most important rule: *Stay in your seat and you'll get home every time.*

## The Best Ride

Which seat is best? The front seat heightens the floating sensation because there's nothing in front or — so it seems — below. It gives the smoothest ride. It also adds the feeling of having the coaster to yourself. The rear seats are great for spectators because they can watch the other passengers, including the screamers and the "Look-Ma-no hands"-ers. Riders at the rear receive the roughest trip; it's the tail end of a giant whip, which becomes evident when you top a hill and the car seems to lift off the tracks.

Don't close your eyes unless you want the ride to be more frightening.

The fastest ride is at night in summer heat after a rainstorm. The heat loosens the heavy grease on the wheels, the night hours prevent any friction caused by the sun, and the rain on the tracks makes for easy gliding.

# Appendix IV

The following is the original December 17, 1972, article from the *Albany-Times-Union* describing the author's meeting with Orville Wright and their discussions of circuses, toys, and roller coasters.

## Kitty Hawk Anniversary Recalls Childhood Chats With Orville Wright

*EDITOR'S NOTE: Times Union art critic Robert Cartmell didn't stand at Kitty Hawk to watch the Wright brothers open the field of aviation. But as a child in Ohio, he was a constant visitor to an aged Orville Wright from whom he gained a unique insight not only into flight but circuses, toys and roller coasters. Cartmell's reminiscences follow.*

### By Robert Cartmell
### Art Critic

The first powered heavier-than-air machine to achieve sustained flight rose from its starting track and soared 120 feet 69 years ago today at Kitty Hawk, N.C.

Short as this flight was, it marked the beginning of man's conquest of the air. Orville Wright was at the controls; Wilbur Wright balanced the machine at take-off.

THIS EPOCHAL event was witnessed by just seven men: the Wright brothers and five others who, more than they knew, stood that day on the threshold of history.

It is one of the great thrills of my life and a landmark in my childhood when I knew Orville Wright. Actually, it's a case of a child knowing no fear since I simply knocked on the door of his Hawthorn Hill estate and introduced myself. An adult probably would have been turned away but a child was treated with great kindness and gentleness.

THIS WAS in 1946-47, in Oakwood, Ohio, a suburb of Dayton. My grammar school, on Harman Avenue, was almost across the street from the Wright estate.

That was sheer magic. The early Wright planes fascinated me because they looked like kites with their struts and fabric and the propellers gave them a toy-like appearance. In comparison, the later planes looked bulky and seemed to belong on the ground.

MY PLANS to visit the Wright estate were never taken seriously since very few people entered their door (and apparently few people had the courage to test them). But with a child's audacity, I entered.

What did we talk about? What did a child and a 76-year-old earth-shaker have in common? Circuses, toys, and roller-coasters!

My lengthy and flamboyant introduction covered thoughts on why his 1903 airplane was my favorite and why, with it struts and all, it looked like a roller-coaster. Further explanations were given on the sense of flying that a coaster gives on its first drop.

WRIGHT SEEMED delighted with all this and in turn mentioned that he and Wilbur built circuses when they were children. He seemed particularly interested in talking about toys and explained that he had designed many for manufacture. The similarties between his planes and kites pleased him since he and Wilbur were master kite builders.

Many of these toys and other Wright inventions were stored throughout the house. I was able to see many of them on subsequent trips. Hawthorn Hills became a great treasure-trove.

OF COURSE, it all came to an end. My father, stationed at Wright Field, was transferred to Texas. I wanted to correspond with Wright but it would have been too late. He passed away January 30, 1948.

Now, 25 years later, after spending many days looking through books and miles of microfilm (including the earliest mention in the "New York Times" of the 1903 flight), a few things have become clearer about the Wright brothers.

TOYS DID figure prominently in the lives of both brothers.

For instance, one day their father came home from a short trip, bringing the children a present. He held something in his hands and then tossed it toward them. It was a toy helicopter.

Instead of flopping to the floor, it ascended to the ceiling where it fluttered before it fell. That helicopter set up a milestone in the lives of the Wright boys. The idea of their future conquest of the air might well have been born then and there.

THE WRIGHT brothers were by no means the first who sought the secret of flight. Particularly in Europe, able men had delved deep and risked much in the effort to fly like a bird. Certain theories of aerodynamics had been developed and were generally accepted as accurate.

One of the major setbacks to the hopes of the Wrights was the discovery, through their own experiments, that these previously accepted theories were incorrect. This meant that they had to start from the beginning and develop their own tables of air pressures.

TWO DEVELOPMENTS of the Wrights made it possible to build an airplane that would fly. One was a crude wind tunnel and the other was an ingenious set of balances made out of old hack saw blades and bicycle spokes. With these comparatively crude instruments, they compiled data which made flight possible.

The wind-tunnel experiments in their bicycle shop were carried on for two months. In those few weeks, however, they accomplished something of almost incalculable importance. They had not only made the first wind-tunnel in which miniature wings were accurately tested but were the first men to compile tables of figures from which one might design an airplane that could fly.

EVEN TODAY, in wind-tunnels used in various aeronautical laboratories equipped with the most elaborate and delicate instruments modern science can provide, the refinements obtained over the Wright's figures are surprisingly small.

THE BROTHERS now began to study wing structure, but hit upon many difficulties. A simple incident set them on the right track. In selling a customer an inner tube for a tire, Wilbur had taken the tube from the pastboard box and was idly twisting the box back and forth as he talked to the customer.

In doing so, he noticed that although the vertical sides remained rigid at the ends, the top and bottom sides could be twisted so that they made various angles at the opposite ends. He immediately wondered why the wings of a gliding machine could not be warped from one end to the other in the same way.

In this way, the wings could be put at a greater angle at one side than the other and there would be no structural weakness.

Although the plane was assembled in Kitty Hawk by September 23, 1903, weather and various mechanical mishaps postponed the day of trial until December 14.

ON THE TOSS of a coin, Wilbur won the right to make the first trial. The machine climbed a few feet,

stalled and fell. Several parts were broken, requiring two days for repairs. There were other minor delays and then came the fateful day of December 17.

This time Orville was the pilot. The few spectators stood silently by, little realizing that they were participating in an event that would be "forever known."

Orville lay flat in the pilot's place with Wilbur running alongside, a hand on the wing, until the machine left the rail. This, in the words of one of the historians of the flight, is what happened:

"SIGNALS that all was in readiness were exchanged. The motor turned, the propellers whirled, a restraining wire was released; the machine rolled along a crude runway, then took off under its own power and flew for twelve unbelievable seconds for 120 incredible feet."

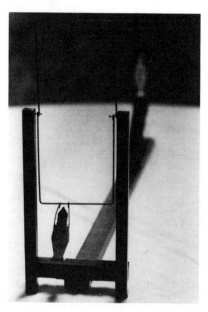

(App.: 18). *Flips-and-Flops*. The Wright Brother's interest in roller coasters, toys, and related mechanical objects is not well documented and would make a fine book. The *Flips-and-Flops* was manufactured and designed by Orville and older brother Lorin (there were five children). A 2″ figure is propelled from a springboard seat, does a somersault, catches the top of a wire apparatus, and revolves around like an acrobat. Another airplane toy called the *Wright Flyer* sold over a million copies before the Depression. It also appeared in cereal boxes. Courtesy Ivonette Wright Miller.

# Notes

—*Preface*—

[1]Mark James, *Roller Coaster* (New York: Screen Gems-Columbia Music, Inc., 1973).

[2]See "The Roller Coaster" in Albert Einstein and Leopold Infeld, *The Evolution of Physics: The Growth of Ideas from Early Concepts to Relativity and Quanta* (New York: Simon and Schuster, 1961), pp. 47-51.

[3]A fine example of this recognition can be found in Ed Cowley, "The Roller Coaster as Very High Art," *Coaster World* 4 (Spring, 1983): 16.

[4]The first carousel club met 20-22 October 1973 at Heritage Plantation, Sandwich, Massachusetts. The club's name at the time was "National Carousel Roundtable." Its present name is "National Carousel Association."

[5]John Allen, interview by the author at the Philadelphia Toboggan Company at its old location in Germantown, Pennsylvania, 17 May 1973.

—*Chapter I*—

[1]*Letters From a Lady who Resided Some Years in Russia* quoted in Audrey Kennett, *The Palaces of Leningrad* (New York: G.P. Putnam's Sons, 1973), p. 252.

[2]*Travelling Sketches in Russia and Sweden* quoted in Suzanne Massie, *Land of the Firebird: The Beauty of Old Russia* (New York: Simon and Schuster, 1980), p. 365.

[3]*Letters from the Continent* quoted in Kennett, *Palaces of Leningrad,* p. 252.

[4]Reports quoted from "Importation to France of the Game of Russian Mountains" in D'Allemagne, *Récreations et Passe-Temps,* pp. 345-56.

[5]Ibid., p. 348.

[6]From an original engraving (n.d.) in the collection of Robert H. Blundred, Executive Vice-President of International Association of Amusement Parks and Attractions, North Riverside, Illinois.

[7]*Journal Du Havre* quoted in William F. Mangels, *The Outdoor Amusement Industry* (New York: Vantage Press, Inc., 1952), pp. 99-100. Mangels incorrectly dates the article 1848.

—*Chapter II*—

[1]*Appleton's Illustrated Handbook of American Summer Resorts: Including Tours and Excursions with Maps* (New York: D. Appleton and Company, 1877), p. 133.

[2]John B. Bachelder, *POPULAR RESORTS and How to Reach Them: Combining a Brief Description of the Principal Summer Resorts in the United States and the Routes of Travel Leading to Them* (Boston: John H. Bachelder, 1874), p. 44.

[3]Quote found in the Lansford, Pennsylvania *Valley Gazette* (n.d.) collected in the scrapbooks of Ric Choley, Assistant Park Director and Architect, Mauch Chunk Lake Park (Carbon County Recreation Authority), Jim Thorpe, Pennsylvania.

—*Chapter III*—

[1]*Frank Leslie's Weekly* quoted in Mangels, *Outdoor Amusement Industry,* p. 89.

[2]Hermann Bormann of Philadelphia, Pennsylvania, "Sinuous Pleasure Railway," *United States Patent Office* (Application filed 14 August 1890; patented 21 April 1891), Patent #450,660: p. 1 of 3 written pages with 2 additional illustrated pages.

[3]From the biography of La Marcus Thompson prepared for William F. Mangels's American Museum of Public Recreation, now part of the Frederick Fried Archives, New York.

[4]From the 1910 La Marcus Thompson Scenic Railway Company catalogue in the Frederick Fried Archives, New York.

[5]James A. Griffiths, personal letter to John Miller, n.d. (c.1936), now part of the Frederick Fried Archives, New York. This is by no means a complete list of Thompson roller coasters. By 1888, he had built at least 20 in the United States and 24 more abroad including Glasgow, London, Manchester, Blackpool, Brighton, Liverpool, Paris, Boulogne, and Barcelona.

[6]Allen interview, 17 May 1973.

—*Chapter IV*—

[1]From Dr. Russell Nye's lecture, "Ten Ways of Looking at an Amusement Park," at the *Coastermania* conference, Sandusky, Ohio, June 30 - July 2, 1978, sponsored by Bowling Green State University and Cedar Point Amusement Park.

[2]*Final Report of the Director of Works of the World's Columbian Exposition,* Volume 3, 1892, p. 39, found in the Ryerson Library, the Art Institute of Chicago.

[3]Maxim Gorky, *Articles and Pamphlets* (Moscow: Foreign Languages Publishing House, 1950), p. 26.

—*Chapter V*—

[1]"Excellent Public Opening and Everybody Delighted," *Haverhill* (Massachusetts) *Gazette,* 16 September 1887, p. 3, col. 3.

[2]Ibid., "Narrow Escape," 26 December 1888, p. 3, col. 4.

—*Chapter VI*—

[1]Einstein, *Evolution of Physics,* pp. 47-51.

[2]W. Earl Austen, interview by the author at Conneaut Lake Park, Conneaut Lake Park, Pennsylvania, 13 June 1973.

[3]Andy Brown, interview by the author in South Zanesville, Ohio, 14 & 15 June 1973.

[4]Allen interview, 17 May 1973.

[5]Mangels, *Outdoor Amusement Industry,* p. 101.

—*Chapter VII*—

[1]"Park Industry Owes Much to Late Frederick Ingersoll," *Billboard* 41 (20 April 1929): 2.

[2]Ibid.

[3]From the *Pittsburgh Luna Park* catalogue, 7 May 1906, p. 3, found in the Carnegie Library of Pittsburgh: Pennsylvania Division.

[4]Ibid., pp. 14-15.

[5]"Toboggan: A Laughter-Provoking Method of Enjoyment," *The White City (Chicago) Magazine and Souvenir Program* 1 (August 1905): 20-21.

—*Chapter VIII*—

[1]Brown interview, 14 & 15 June 1973.

[2]From the *1923 Miller and Baker Catalogue,* 5th edition (Miller & Baker, Inc., Suite 3041, Grand Central Terminal, New York City), p. 7 from the collection of Barbara Charles, Washington D.C.

[3]Allen interview, 17 May 1973.

[4]Brown interview, 14 & 15 June 1973.

[5]*Miller & Baker* catalogue (1923), p. 1.

[6]Ibid., p. 44.

[7]From the 1923 Miller and Baker *Dip-Lo-Docus* catalogue, pp. 5-6 in the collection of the author.

[8]A recent book, *Smile: A Picture History of Olympic Park 1887-1965,* is helping correct this neglect. Still, the park remains virtually unknown.

[9]Brown interview, 14 & 15 June 1973.

[10]Ibid.

[11]From a list given to the author by Andy Brown, 15 June 1973.

[12]Aurel Vaszin, interview by the author at International Amusement Devices's offices at their old location in Dayton, Ohio, 24 May 1974.

*—Chapter IX—*

¹This comment was published in *Vanity Fair's* recent republication: Jeanne Ballot Winham, "Flashback: Very Innocent Bystander," *Vanity Fair* 46 (December 1983): 140. Jeanne Ballot Winham, Secretary to the Editor in the 1920's, notes on p. 143: "every French, Italian, German, or Hungarian artist wanted to see Coney Island. ...Benito, Bret-Koch, Garetto—they all wanted to ride the Scenic Railways (roller coasters nowadays), so I always found myself at the top of the first incline with a terrified foreigner who without fail gasped in English, 'Oh my God!' " For an encyclopedic look at the magazine, see Cleveland Amory and Frederic Bradlee, eds., *VANITY FAIR: Selections from America's Most Memorable Magazine. A Cavalcade of the 1920s and 1930s* (New York: Viking Press, 1960).

²Garry Cooper, "The World that was at Belmont and Western," *Chicago Tribune Magazine,* 16 May 1976, p. 24.

³Gorky, *Articles and Pamphlets,* p. 26.

⁴"Coney's Latest Ride, the Cyclone, Opens," *Billboard* (9 July 1927): 74.

⁵Oliver Pilat and Jo Ranson, *Sodom by the Sea: An Affectionate History of Coney Island* (Garden City, New York: Doubleday, Doran & Co., 1941), p. 225.

⁶Vernon Keenan II, personal letter to the author, 9 June 1974.

⁷The best source of information on these coasters can be found in the Volume 6, No. 1 (1984) *Amusement Park Journal,* an issue devoted entirely to roller coasters of the Philadelphia Toboggan Company.

⁸The Rocky Springs *Wildcat* stood for years unused with occasional promises of reopening the ride. In summer 1984, the coaster was destroyed and Rocky Springs's properties auctioned.

⁹Andy Vettel, interview by the author at Kennywood Park, West Mifflin, Pennsylvania, 12 June 1973.

¹⁰Poster text for the Smithsonian Institution's *Coast to Coast Coasters* exhibition (Washington, D.C.: Smithsonian Institution, 1976).

¹¹Robert Cartmell, "Killer Roller Coasters: Ten Mean Mothers Want to Take You for a Ride," *Oui* 6 (November 1977): 78.

*—Chapter X—*

¹"73 rides costing $600,000 Built by Traver last Year," *Billboard* (5 January 1924): 86.

²*Billboard* (23 August 1924): 78.

³"Good Rides Pay," *Billboard* (31 December 1927): 73.

⁴Harry Davis, interview by the author in Bartow, Florida, March 5, 1978.

⁵Harry G. Traver of Beaver Falls, Pennsylvania, "Amusement Ride," *United States Patent Office* (Application filed 19 March 1925; Patented 21 May 1929), Patent #1, 713, 793: p. 1 of 8 written pages with 8 additional illustrated pages.

⁶Jean Scott, "Master of Many Trades is Harry G. Traver Whose Know-How aids Navy and Carnivals," *Standard Star* (New Rochelle, New York), 13 September 1952. Traver's final move was to New Rochelle, New York where he died 26 September 1961 at the age of 84.

⁷Louis Botto, "Playland: Where it All Began," *New York Daily News Sunday Magazine,* 21 May 1978, p. 30.

*—Chapter XI—*

¹Chuck Barris, *Palisades Park,* Claridge Music, Inc. (ASCAP) as recorded by Freddie Cannon and Frank Slay and his Orchestra (Swan: S-4106-P).

²Mario Puzo, "Meet me Tonight in Dreamland," *New York,* 3 September 1979, p. 28, col. 1.

³National Amusement Device has officially changed its name to International Amusement Devices, Inc. and, as of this writing, is located in Sandusky, Ohio.

⁴The *Island Queen* was a white and green floating palace that carried 4000 passengers, boasted 7000 electric lights and a mammoth dance floor. You could hear her calliope a mile from the docks. It was the return trip under moonlight, though, that many remember. The *Island Queen* burned September 9, 1947.

⁵Lou DuFour, "Maddox Lit up his Cigar and the Schencks's Funpark went up in Flames," *Amusement Business.* This undated article with the further caption, "Glorious Years - XXXIII," by amusement park historian DuFour, was found in the Frederick Fried Archives.

⁶"Designer Joe McKee Built Box that Helped Win Wife," *Billboard,* 25 November 1950, p. 66.

⁷Richard D. McFadden, "Palisades Park will be Revived: To be Resur-

rected on Site in Morris County," *New York Times,* 27 August 1972, sec. 1, p. 25, col. 1.

*—Chapter XII—*

¹Allen interview, 17 May 1973.

²Ibid.

³Ibid.

⁴Ibid.

⁵Richard Schickel, *The Disney Version* (New York: Simon and Schuster, 1968), p. 310.

⁶From *A Brief History* supplied by Arrow Huss, Inc., Clearfield, Utah (n.d.).

⁷It is known that in the early 1940's, National Amusement Device, Dayton, Ohio, drew elaborate plans for a *Loop-the-Loop.* Proof of its construction has yet to appear.

*—Chapter XIII—*

¹"Coast to Coast on a Coaster," *Actionews* (a monthly publication of the International Association of Amusement Parks and Attractions, North Riverside, Illinois), February 1983, p. 1.

²Robert Cartmell, "The Quest for the Ultimate Roller Coaster," *New York Times,* 9 June 1974, sec. 10, p. 1+.

³Robert Cartmell, "Amusement Parks in the United States," *Albany-Times-Union,* 7 March 1971, sec. F1, p. 1+.

⁴John T. McQuiston, "Aquarium is Getting a Piece of Long Island," *New York Times,* 5 March 1972, sec. 1A (Brooklyn, Queens, Long Island), p. 4.

⁵Tom Smith, "William L. Cobb: Ace Interview by Tom Smith," *Coaster World,* 3 (Spring, 1982): 28.

⁶For a particularly pungent view of the proceedings, see John H. Baskin, "High Rollers," *Ohio Magazine,* July, 1978, pp. 56-64.

⁷Paul Goldberger, "Mickey Mouse Teaches the Architects," *New York Times Magazine,* 22 October 1972, p. 41, col. 2.

⁸Eric Oatman, "RCA Space Mountain: Sure Cure for Boredom," *Senior Scholastic,* 27 February 1975, p. 26, col. 2.

⁹Michael Demarest, "Pop Xanadus of Fun and Fantasy," *Time,* 4 July 1977, p. 32, col. 2.

¹⁰Bro Utall, "The Ride is Getting Scarier for 'Theme Park' Owners," *Fortune,* December 1977, pp. 167-172+.

¹¹"Free Floaters" (B. Cooper, M. Abbate, L. Peyser), personal letter to the author, 14 June 1974.

¹²Isaac Asimov, "My Amusement Park of the Future," *Seventeen,* July 1973, p. 65+.

*—Appendix I—*

¹The interviewer worked his fear to great advantage. The broadcast, "The All-American Pleasure Railway," was so successful that it won the prestigious *National Headliners Award* for 1974.

²Sara Davidson, "Cousteau Searches for his Whale," *New York Times Magazine,* 10 September 1972, p. 83.

³Kenneth Burke, *The Rhetoric of Religioin* (Boston: Beacon Press, 1961), p. 42.

⁴Charles Lindbergh quoted by Charles S. Houston in "Stress-Seekers in Everyday Life" in *Why Man Takes Chances: Studies in Stress-Seeking,* Foreword and ed. by Samuel Z. Klausner (Garden City, New York: Anchor Books / Doubleday & Company, 1968), p. 56.

⁵Einstein, *Evolution of Physics,* pp. 47-51.

⁶Allen interview, 17 May 1973.

⁷As John Allen explained during his 1973 interview, if you weigh 150 pounds, 3 g's would increase your weight three times or, at this point on the roller coaster, you would weigh 450 pounds.

⁸Vettel interview, 12 June 1973.

⁹Allen interview, 17 May 1973.

¹⁰The enthusiastic and humorous maintenance crew at LeSourdsville Lake, Middletown, Ohio (David, Bill, Tom, and others) was most cooperative and instrumental in the completion of this section on how a coaster works. It is a shame the complete 16 June 1973 interview could not be used. Their assistance is acknowledged and very much appreciated. Hereafter, they will be referred to as "The LeSourdsville Crew."

¹¹From a January 1982 Press Release supplied by Great America, Gurnee, Illinois.

[12]Allen interview, 17 May 1973.

[13]Vettel interview, 12 June 1973.

[14]LeSourdsville Crew interview, 16 June 1973.

[15]Name withheld, personal letter to the author (n.d.).

[16]Jeff Millar, "Astroworld's 'Cyclone' blows in," *Houston Chronicle,* 12 June 1976, sec. 2, p. 1, col. 4.

[17]LeSourdsville Crew interview, 16 June 1973.

[18]Neil Sedaka, *Laughter in the Rain: My own Story* (New York: G.P. Putnam's Sons, 1982), p. 16.

[19]Keats quoted by Marvin Zuckerman in *Sensation Seeking: Beyond the Optimal Level of Arousal* (Hillsdale, New Jersey: Lawrence Erlbaum Associates, Publishers, 1979), p. 218.

[20]George Mallory quoted by Charles Houston in *Why Man Takes Chances,* ed. Klausner, p. 58.

[21]William James, *Collected Essays and Reviews* (New York: Longmans, Green and Co., 1920), p. 384.

[22]Dr. Lawrence Balter quoted in Michael Iachetta, "Getting High on Downs and Ups," *Los Angeles Times,* 16 May 1976, Sunday Calendar.

[23]Richard Stander, Sr. during a phone-in conversation with the author on *Contact,* WGY Radio, Schenectady, New York, 5 June 1984.

[24]Erik H. Erikson, *Toys and Reasons* (New York: W.W. Norton & Company, Inc., 1977), p. 17.

[25]Andy Brown interview, 14 & 15 June 1973.

[26]Vee K. Wertime, personal letter to the author, 1974.

[27]Dr. Marvin Zuckerman quoted in Dr. S.V. Didato, "Am I a Thrill-Seeker?," *Parade Magazine,* 15 May 1983, p. 13, col. 2.

[28]Ibid.

[29]Ben Colli quoted in John Skow, "Risking it All," *Time,* 29 August 1983, p. 58.

[30]W.H. Stevenson, ed. with text by David V. Erdman, *The Poems of William Blake* (London: Longman Group Limited, 1971), p. 587.

[31]Peter Bird quoted in John Skow, "Risking it All," *Time,* 29 August 1983, p. 55.

[32]Samuel Z. Klausner, "Fear and Enthusiasm in Sport Parachuting," in *Motivations in Play, Games and Sports,* James A. Knight and Ralph Slovenko, eds. (Springfield, Illinois: Charles C. Thomas, Publishers, 1967).

[33]Samuel Z. Klausner, "Empirical Analysis of Stress-Seekers" in *Why Man Takes Chances,* Klausner, ed., p. 136.

[34]Ibid., pp. 151-52.

# Bibliography

—*Books and Selected Catalogues*—

Adorno, Theodore and Herkheimer, Max. "The Culture Industry: Enlightenment as Mass Deception" in *Dialectic of Enlightenment*. Translated by John Cumming. New York: Herder and Herder, 1972.

Amory, Cleveland and Bradlee, Frederic, eds. *Vanity Fair: Selections from America's Most Memorable Magazine. A Cavalcade of the 1920s and 1930s*. New York: Viking Press, 1960.

*Amusement Business' 75th Anniversary Souvenir Issue: Billboard Publications 1894-1969*. New York: Communications Center of the Fun Industry, 1969.

Amusement Park Books, Inc. (Bush, Lee; Chukayne, Edward C.; Hehr, Russell Allon; Hershey, Richard F.). *Euclid Beach is Closed for the Season*. Cleveland: Dillon / Liederback, Inc., 1977.

_____. *Euclid Beach Park: A Second Look*. Mentor, Ohio: Amusement Park Books, Inc., 1979.

Badger, Reid R. *The Great American Fair*. Chicago: Nelson-Hall, Inc., Publishers, 1979.

Bobrick, Benson. *Labyrinths of Iron: A History of the World's Subways*. New York: Newsweek Books, 1981.

Braithwaite, David. *Fairground Architecture*. London: Hugh Evelyn, 1968.

Brown, Stephen. *The Pike (Past its Peak)*. Seal Beach, California: SCB Photographics, 1984.

Burg, David F. *Chicago's White City of 1893*. Lexington: University of Kentucky Press, 1976.

Butler, Frank M. *The Book of the Boardwalk*. Atlantic City: 1954 Association, 1952.

Caillois, Roger. *Man, Play and Games*. Translation by Meyer Barash. New York: Free Press, 1961.

*The Coaster Enthusiast's Guide to Cedar Point*. Sandusky, Ohio: Cedar Point Marketing Department, 1978.

Conant, James B. *Science and Common Sense*. New Haven: Yale University Press, 1951.

Cooke, Rupert Croft and Cotes, Peter. *Circus, A World History*. London: Paul Ecek Ltd., 1976.

D'Allemagne, Henry Rene. *Recreation et Passe-Temps*. Paris: Hachette, 1905.

Edwards, Richard Henry. *Popular Amusement*. New York: Association Press, 1915.

Erikson, Erik H. *Toys and Reasons: Stages in the Ritualization of Experience*. New York: W.W. Norton & Company, 1977.

Evans, Sondra, ed. *Looff Family Photo Memoirs*. Garden Grove, California: Cameo Productions and Marge Swenson, 1982.

Finch, Christopher. *The Art of Walt Disney*. New York: Harry N. Abrams, Inc., 1973.

Fox, Charles Phillip. *Circus Parades*. Watkins Glen, New York: Century House, 1953.

Fried, Frederick, and Fried, Mary. *America's Forgotten Folk Arts*. New York: Pantheon Books, Random House, Inc., 1978.

Fried, Frederick. *A Pictorial History of the Carousel*. New York: A.S. Barnes and Company, Inc., 1964.

Funnell, Charles E. *By the Beautiful Sea: The Rise and High Times of that Great American Resort, Atlantic City*. New York: Knopf, 1975.

Griffen, Al. *Step Right Up, Folks*. Chicago: Henry Regency Company, 1974.

Harris, Neil. *Humbug: The Art of P.T. Barnum*. Boston: Little, Brown, 1973.

Hemphill, Herbert W. Jr. and Weissman, Julia. *Twentieth-Century American Folk Art and Artists*. New York: E.P. Dutton & Company, Inc., 1974.

*A History of Coney Island*. New York: Burroughs and Company, 1904.

*History of Coney Island: List and Photographs of Main Attractions*. New York: Burroughs and Company, 1904.

Hulten, K.G. Pontus. *The Machine: As Seen at the End of the Mechanical Age*. New York: The Museum of Modern Art, 1968.

Ilyinsky, Paul. *Good-Bye Coney Island, Good-Bye....* Englewood Cliffs, New Jersey: Prentice-Hall, Inc., 1972.

Jacques, Charles J. Jr. *Kennywood: ...Roller Coaster Capital of the World*. Vestal, New York: The Vestal Press Ltd., 1982.

Johnson, Rossiter, ed. *A History of the World's Columbian Exposition*. 4 vols. New York. Appleton.

Kasson, John F. *Amusing the Millions*. New York: Hill and Wang Publishing Co., 1978.

Kennett, Audrey. *The Palaces of Leningrad*. New York: G.P. Putnam's Sons, 1973.

Klausner, Samuel Z., ed. *Why Man Takes Chances: Studies in Stress-Seeking*. Garden City, New York: Anchor Books, Doubleday & Company, Inc., 1968.

Kyriazi, Gary. *The Great American Amusement Parks*. New Jersey: Citadel Press, 1976.

McCullough, Edo. *Good Old Coney Island*. New York: Charles Scribner's Sons, 1957.

_____. *World's Fair Midways*. New York: Exposition Press, 1966.

Mangels, William F. *The Outdoor Amusement Industry*. New York: Vantage Press, Inc., 1952.

Massie, Suzanne. *Land of the Firebird: The Beauty of Old Russia*. New York: Simon and Schuster, 1980.

*Miller and Baker Inc. 1923 Catalogue*. Reprints of this catalogue are now available from Amusement Park Journal / P.O. Box 157 / Natrona Heights, Pennsylvania 15065.

Munch, Richard, *Harry G. Traver: Legends of Terror*. Mentor, Ohio: Amusement Park Books, 1982.

Munch Richard; Reed, Jon-Michael; and Waldrop, John. *Roller Coaster Fever*. New York: Starlog Press, 1979.

Mundy, Peter. *The Travels of Peter Mundy in Europe and Asia, 1608-1667*. Printed for the Hakluyt Society, 1907-36.

Nathan, Robert. *Amusement Park*. New York: Dial Press, 1977.

Nye, Russel B. *Society and Culture in America*. New York: Harper and Row / New American Nation Series, 1974.

Onosko, Tim. *Funland USA*. New York: Ballantine Books, 1978.

Ostrander, Gilman. *American Civilization in the First Machine Age, 1890-1940*. New York: Harpers, 1970.

*Philadelphia Toboggan Company Catalogue*. Reprints of this 1929 catalogue are now available from Amusement Park Journal / P.O. Box 157 / Natrona Heights, Pennsylvania 15065.

Pilat, Oliver and Ranson, Jo. *Sodom by the Sea*. New York: Garden City Publishing Co., 1941.

Pougin, Arthur. *Dictionaire Historique et Pittoresque du Theatre et des Arts QuiS'y Rattachent.* Paris: Librarie de Firmin Didot et Cie., 1885.

Reed, James. *The Top 100 Amusement Parks of the United States.* Quarryville, Pennsylvania, 1978.

Schickel, Richard. *The Disney Version: The Life, Times, Art and Commerce of Walt Disney,* New York: Simon and Schuster, 1968.

*See Coney Island of Today.* New York: Cupples and Leon, 1904.

Siegel, Alan A. *Smile, A Picture History of Olympic Park, 1887-1965.* Irvington, New Jersey: Irvington Historical Society, 1983.

Silver, Nathan. *Lost New York.* New York: Schocken Books, 1972.

*Step Right Up!: Amusements for All / Show Business at the Turn of the Century.* Rochester, New York: Margaret Woodbury Strong Museum, 1977. (Catalogue for the exhibition at the Memorial Art Gallery, Rochester, 3 June - 25 September 1977.)

Walford, Cornelius. *Fairs, Past and Present: A Chapter in the history of Commerce.* 1883. Reprint, New York: A.M. Kelley, 1968.

Weedon, Geoff and Ward, Richard. *Fairground Art Forms of Traveling Fairs, Carousels, and Carnival Midways.* London: White Mouse Editions, 1981.

Wilmeth, Don B. *Variety Entertainment and Outdoor Amusements: A Reference Guide.* Westport, Connecticut: Greenwood Press, 1982.

Wlodarczyk, Chuck. *Riverview: Gone but not Forgotten 1904-1967.* Chicago: Riverview Publications, 1977.

Zuckerman, Marvin. *Sensation Seeking: Beyond the Optimal Level of Arousal.* Hillsdale, New Jersey: Lawrence Erlbaum Associates, Publishers, 1979.

—*Magazines and Newspapers*—

*ACE News.* 1979 to present. (American Coaster Enthusiasts / P.O. Box 8226 / Chicago, Illinois 60680.)

"America's 28 Most Exciting Amusement Parks." *Seventeen,* July 1973.

*Amusement Park Journal.* Charles J. Jacques, Jr. ed. 1979 to present. (P.O. Box 157 / Natrona Heights, Pennsylvania 15065.)

Aronson, Arnold. "The Total Theatrical Environment." *Theatre Crafts,* September 1977.

Auger, Helen. "From the Crystal Palace to the World Tomorrow." *Travel,* April 1939.

Ayres, Drummond B. "New Amusement Parks, Riding the American Boom in Leisure." *The New York Times,* 30 May 1976.

Baskin, John H. "High Rollers." *Ohio Magazine,* July 1978.

Batt, Harry J., Sr. "Thrills Termed the Source of Ride Successes." *Amusement Business (Section II—1974/75 Guide to Amusement Rides),* 19 October 1974.

"Behind the Scenes of *Rollercoaster.*" *American Cinematographer,* June 1977.

Bennett, K.W. "Amusement Parks on Dizzying Expansion Whirl." *Iron Age,* 16 August 1973.

*The Billboard.* November 1894 to December 1949 (*Amusement Business* thereafter to present). Billboard Publishing Company, Cincinnati, Ohio.

Botto, Louis. "Playland: Where it all began." *New York Daily News Sunday Magazine,* 21 May 1978.

Bright, H. "Disney's Fantasy Empire." *Nation,* 6 March 1967.

*Brooklyn Eagle.* 1841 to 1955. Before 1849 under titles *Brooklyn Eagle and King's County Democrat* and *Brooklyn Daily.*

Bunner, H.C. "Making of the White City." *Scribner's Monthly,* 12 (October 1892): 398-418.

Carryl, Guy Wetmore. "Marvelous Coney Island." *Munsey's Magazine,* 25 (September 1901): 84.

Cartmell, Robert. "Killer Roller Coasters: Ten Mean Mothers Want to Take you for a Ride." *Oui,* November 1977.

——————. "The Quest for the Ultimate Roller Coaster." *The New York Times,* 9 June 1974.

——————. "Roller Coaster: King of the Park." *Smithsonian,* August 1977.

——————. "The Terrifying Machine that Americans Love." *Search,* Spring 1976.

*Coaster World.* 1979 to 1983. Continued as *RollerCoaster.* (American Coaster Enthusiasts / P.O. Box 8226 / Chicago, Illinois 60680.)

Coates, Robert M. "It's the Illusion that Counts." *New Yorker,* 8 May 1954.

Cohen, M. "Fantasy World in Amusement Parks." *Redbook,* April 1973.

Cooper, Garry. "The World that was at Belmont and Western." *Chicago Tribune Magazine,* 16 May 1976.

Cowley, Susan C. and Proffitt, Nicholas. "Coastermania." *Newsweek,* 19 June 1978.

Cox, Richard. "Coney Island, Urban Symbol in American Art." *New York Historical Society Quarterly* 60 (January - April 1976): 35-52.

Cuber, John F. "Patrons of Amusement Parks." *Sociology Social Science Research* XXIV (September 1936): 63-68.

Davidson, Randall. "Buckle Up." *Theatre Crafts,* September 1977.

Demarest, Michael. "Pop Xanadus of Fun and Fantasy." *Time,* 4 July 1977.

"Dips a Wrenching Release from Earthly Cares: Cult of Coaster Riders Pursue Ultimate Thrill." *Los Angeles Times,* 13 March 1977.

"Disneyland: Building for Fun is Serious Work." *Engineering News - Record,* 7 May 1959.

Francis, Devon. "How You are Thrilled...But not Killed." *Popular Science Monthly,* July 1949.

Fried, Frederick. "Doorway to the Future: History of Fun Rides shows Numerous Ideas being Updated for Today's Market—With More to Come!" *Amusement Business* (Section II—*1975/76 Guide to Amusement Rides*), 27 September 1975.

Gillman, Lucy P. "Coney Island." *New York History* 36 (July 1955): 255-90.

Goldman, Leslie. "Along for the Ride." *American Cinematographer,* June 1977.

Gyory, Andrew. "Playing 'Tricks' on Gravity." *Scholastic Science World,* 13 May 1983.

Hatt, Rollin Lynde. "The Amusement Park." *Atlantic Monthly* 99 (May 1907): 668.

Hellman, Hal. "Those Incredible New Amusement Parks: A Taste of Thrills to Come." *Futurist,* August 1980.

Hillinger, Charles. "Scary Rides Knock Their Fans for a Loop: Roller Coaster Buffs Hold Convention." *Los Angeles Times,* 10 June 1978.

Huxtable, Ada Louise. "The Fun and Seriousness of Resort Design." *New York Times,* 17 July 1971.

——————. "Photographs Recall the Glories of Chicago's Columbian Exposition." *New York Times.*

——————. "You can't Go Home to Those Fairs Again." *New York Times,* 28 October 1973.

Jones, Iris Sanderson. "The Wish to Whoosh: A clinical Closeup of 'Coastermania'." *The Detroit News Magazine,* 13 August 1978.

Joseph, R. "Travel Notes." *Esquire,* December 1971.

"Just for Fun." *Compressed Air Magazine,* April 1968.

Karlen, A. "Capsule History of World's Fairs." *Holiday,* July

1964.

Kneeland, Douglas E. "Coaster Nuts Talk Old Thrills and Test a New One." *New York Times*, 5 July 1978.

Lasch, Christopher. "The Narcissistic Personality of Our Times." *Partisan Review* 44 (1977): 9-19.

Leighton, G.R. "World's Fairs: From Little Egypt to Robert Moses." *Harper's Monthly*, August 1960.

Lemoke, Daryl. "The King of Rides Returns." *Los Angeles Times*, 28 December 1975.

Lines, Harry. "From Cyclone to Scream Machine." *Theatre Crafts*, September 1977.

Lutz, Michael A. "Cyclone Leaves Texans Screaming." *Chicago Tribune*, 13 March 1977.

McHugh, T. "Walt Disney's Mechanical Wonderworld." *Popular Mechanics*, November 1957.

"Marriott's Great America." *Theatre Crafts*, September 1977.

Markoutsas, Elaine. "Thrills and Chills are Part of the Topsy-Turvy World of Rollercoasters." *Chicago Tribune Tempo*, 7 July 1977.

"The Mechanical Joys of Coney Island." *Scientific American* 99 (15 August 1908): 109.

Meier, Hugo A. "American Technology and the Nineteenth Century World." *American Culture*, Fall 1968.

Miller, Jeff. "Astroworld's Cyclone Blows in." *Houston Chronicle*, 12 June 1976.

Morgenstern, J. "What Hath Disney Wrought!" *Newsweek*, 18 October 1971.

Murphy, Thomas. "The Evolution of Amusement Machines." *Journal of the Royal Society of Arts* XCIX (7 September 1951).

"New Thrillers Defy Gravity." *Popular Science Monthly*, August 1927.

"Old Country Imports Loch Ness Monster." *The Times Herald* (Newport News, Virginia), 7 March 1978.

Phillips, B.J. "Those Roller Rides in the Sky." *Time*, 4 July 1977.

Puzo, Mario. "Meet me Tonight in Dreamland." *New York*, 3 September 1979.

"Ride 'em and Weep." *Saturday Evening Post*, 9 June 1945.

*RollerCoaster*. 1984 to present. Continues *Coaster World*. (American Coaster Enthusiasts / P.O. Box 8226 / Chicago, Illinois 60680.)

"Roller Coaster Ride." *National Geographic World*, May 1978.

Sedulus. "Mickey Mouse Slouches Towards Bethlehem." *New Republic*, 14 April 1973.

Simpson, Janice C. "Manufacturers of Amusement Park Rides Try to Dream up New Thrills for Surging Market." *The Wall Street Journal*, 13 October 1976.

Skow, John. "Risking it All." *Time*, 29 August 1983.

"Sleuth among the Roller Coasters." *Saturday Evening Post*, 20 July 1957.

"Some New Mechanical Amusement Devices." *Scientific American*, 15 October 1921.

*Street Railway Journal*. October 1884 to December 1903. After 1903 (to present) under various titles including *Transit Journal* and *American Street Railway Investors*.

Swetnam, George. "It drops Like a Thunderbolt." *Pittsburgh Press*, 19 May 1968.

"Tail Spinning: Evaluation of California Roller Coasters." *Sunset*, July 1976.

Thompson, Frederic. "Amusing the Million." *Everybody's Magazine*, 19 (September 1908): 378-86.

Tilyou, Edward F. "Human Nature with the Brakes Off - Or: Why the Schoolma'am Walked into the Sea." *American Magazine*, 94 (July 1922): 19+.

"Ups and Downs." *Holiday*, July 1949.

Utall, Bro. "The Ride is Getting Scarier for 'Theme Park' Owners." *Fortune*, December 1977.

Wandres, J. "Coastermania: It's Spreading like Fear." *Friends*, April 1979.

Willatt, N. "Roller-Coaster Industry: U.S. Amusement Parks Have Had their Ups and Downs." *Barrons*, 25 May 1959.

Wright, Amos W. "World's Fairs of 1889-1892." *Harper's Weekly* 33 (10 August 1889): 652.

—Taped Interviews (selected)—

Allen, John. Philadelphia Toboggan Company, Germantown, Pennsylvania. Interview, 17 May 1973.

Austen, W. Earl (and others). Conneaut Lake Park, Pennsylvania. Interview, 13 June 1973.

Brown, Andy. South Zanesville, Ohio. Interview, 14 & 15 June 1973.

Davis, Harry. Bartow, Florida. Interview, 5 March 1978.

Hall, George C., Jr. Crystal Beach Amusement Park, Ontario, Canada. Interview, September 5, 1973.

The LeSourdsville maintenance crew (David, Bill, Tom, and others). LeSourdsville Lake, Middletown, Ohio. Interview, 16 June 1973.

Schetterer, June. New Rochelle, New York. Interview, 30 September 1974.

Vaszin, Aurel. International Amusement Devices, Dayton, Ohio. Interview, 24 May 1974.

Vettel, Andy (and others). Kennywood Park, West Mifflin, Pennsylvania. Interview, 12 June 1973.

—Other—

Correspondence: Over 10,000 roller coaster and amusement park letters to the author, 1971 to present.

Frederick Fried Archives which includes the William F. Mangels collection.

Notes on Russell Nye's "10 Ways of Looking at an Amusement Park," *COASTERMANIA*, Cedar Point Amusement Park, Sandusky, Ohio, 2 July 1978.

Notes on Marcello Truzzi's "Sociological Ruminations on the Roller Coaster and its Raiders," *COASTERMANIA*, Cedar Point Amusement Park, Sandusky, Ohio, 1 July 1978.

Robert Cartmell collection (around 20,000 roller coaster items).

Smithsonian Institution's 1975 travelling exhibition, *Coast-to-Coast Coasters*.

United States Patent Office. Patents, Reports, and Gazettes, 1797 to present.

# Index